Grave Robbers and Gold Diggers

The Definitive Defense and Deterrent Playbook for the Affluent

THE BLOODLINE ALLIANCE

ISBN – Softcover: 978-1-0694253-0-0
ISBN – Hardcover: 978-1-0694253-1-7
ISBN – EPUB: 978-1-0694253-2-4

Published by TBA Verlag

Printed in the United States of America | 2025

Disclaimer
The information presented in this book reflects insights drawn from leading experts, practitioners, and lived experiences across multiple disciplines. It is intended for general educational and informational purposes only.

This book does not constitute legal, tax, financial, or psychological advice and should not be relied upon as a substitute for independent, professional guidance. Readers are encouraged to seek qualified counsel regarding their own unique circumstances, including but not limited to the laws and regulations applicable in their specific jurisdiction.

This book has been reproduced under license and authority of The Bloodline Alliance, Switzerland, a Swiss society organized under Section 60 of the Swiss Civil Code. All rights reserved. For more information, visit www.thebloodlinealliance.org.

All intellectual property, proprietary frameworks, and trade secrets referenced herein are the exclusive property of The Bloodline Alliance and are protected under international copyright and intellectual property law. Unauthorized reproduction, distribution, or adaptation of any part of this work without prior written consent is strictly prohibited.

To those who walked this path before us—
who bore the weight, the wounds, and the silence—
so others might see the truth more clearly.

May your pain not be in vain.
May your story light the way for those still finding their own.

Choose Your Own Adventure

(Avoid Your Own Misadventure)

This isn't a novel. It's a survival manual.

You don't need to read *Grave Robbers and Gold Diggers* cover to cover—or in any particular order—to get exactly what you need out of it. In fact, we *encourage* you to flip to the chapter list that follows and jump straight to whatever grabs you.

Some chapters might not apply to your life right now. Others will feel like they were ripped directly from your private nightmares.

Start wherever you like. Skip freely. Bounce around. Come back later. Share a chapter with a friend who's in the danger zone. Highlight a paragraph that explains the thing you couldn't quite put into words. This book is designed to meet you wherever you are in your journey—and to equip you with real tools that no one warned you you'd need.

Once you've seen enough to convince you just how real—and how *dangerous*—the gold digger threat is to your emotional, legal, and financial future, skip ahead to Chapter 53 to learn about the *ultimate old money defense system*. It's called the Family First Trust, and it's engineered to stop even the most cunning gold diggers cold.

And if you're ready to take action, don't miss Chapter 66, where you'll find a QR code to set up your own Family First Trust in minutes—with a special offer just for readers of this book.

Read it your way, and remember:

✓ **It's essential to lock down your wealth *before* you get engaged.**

✓ **When you're dealing with a calculating economic predator, a prenup alone is like bringing a knife to a gunfight.**

Contents

Someone is sitting in the shade today because someone planted a tree a long time ago.

Warren Buffett

Preface

Before we begin, a word about prejudice and unconscious bias. Gold digging knows no gender, no sexual orientation, no color, no race, and no religion. It is a profound societal sickness that inflicts extraordinary emotional and economic harm on its victims. The damage gold diggers cause often spans generations, leaving scars that are both personal and systemic.

Anyone who interprets this book as misogynistic is missing the point entirely. Heterosexual couples are statistically more prevalent in society, and men historically have earned more than women. The outsized prevalence of heterosexual couples results in an outsized share of births and adoptions, which in turn results in an outsized share of the $30B in annual child support payments made in the US. This is further exacerbated by the epidemic of reproductive coercion (aka "baby trapping"), with a small but incredibly dangerous subset of the female predators targeting affluent males. Thus, the statistical odds tilt toward heterosexual women as the primary perpetrators and heterosexual men as the primary victims of gold digging. But make no mistake: Gold digging transcends all demographics and exploits anyone who is economically vulnerable.

These predators hunt us and our loved ones like prey, for the sole purpose of exploitation. They leave destruction in their wake, siphoning billions of dollars of wealth every year into the hands of morally bankrupt individuals who have mastered the art of the con.

Should we have empathy for those who suffer from mental illness—who demonstrate signs of narcissism or psychopathy? Absolutely. Does that mean we shouldn't educate ourselves and proactively defend our families and assets against such predators? Absolutely not. That would be naïve—a mistake society has been making for far too long.

It is impossible to have an honest dialogue about what gold diggers do without exposing their actions for what they are—despicable, predatory, and devoid of moral grounding. These are predators living among us, hunting us and those we care about. And it's not just OK to say that what they do is wrong—it's necessary.

This book is about awareness, self-preservation, and self-defense. It aims to teach gold diggers' intended victims how to recognize and deflect these predators before they can cause harm.

We acknowledge that the gold diggers of the world—and their enablers—will be horrified, angered and embarrassed to see their playbook and severe personality defects laid bare for all to see. That is the point. This is not just a book—it's a movement that will continue to cast an unflinching spotlight on gold digging in all its forms. The days of scheming in the shadows and getting away with it are coming to an end. Let the reckoning begin.

ACKNOWLEDGEMENTS

The Bloodline Alliance extends its deepest gratitude to the esteemed experts, brave advocates, and tireless warriors who have contributed not only to the creation of this book, but also to the greater movement of financial and emotional self-defense for victims of financial predators worldwide. Your wisdom, courage, and expertise have laid the foundation for a new era—one where individuals are no longer passive victims of a system designed to exploit them, but informed and empowered protectors of their own legacies.

To the legal minds who dissected the systematic flaws of a broken legal system that encourages and rewards economic exploitation instead of punishing it, we recognize your bravery. You have exposed the insidious tactics employed by those who manipulate the courts to their financial advantage, and your insights have armed victims with the legal knowledge they need to fight back. Your work in unraveling these injustices and crafting ironclad defenses will be a shield for countless individuals who would otherwise fall prey to the same predatory schemes.

To the psychologists and psychiatrist who offered invaluable insights into the darkness of Dark Triad predators, we thank you—not only for exposing the depths of their manipulation, but also for showing people how to identify and avoid them before they strike. Understanding the psychological playbook of those who hunt and exploit is one of the most powerful defenses we have, and your research and analysis have made that knowledge accessible to those who will benefit from it most.

To the families who entrusted us with the responsibility of sharing the core principles and legal mechanics of dynastic wealth preservation with those who need it most, we extend our deepest gratitude. Your willingness to allow these powerful strategies to be adapted and woven into the Family First Trust ensures that generational wealth remains safeguarded from economic opportunists. Through your insights and commitment to legacy preservation, you have empowered others to fortify their own financial futures with the same strategies and peace of mind. You have helped ensure that hard-earned wealth stays where it belongs—within the bloodline of each family, protected from opportunistic predators.

To the masters of multi-jurisdictional marriage and divorce-focused asset and income protection—your highly specialized expertise and the incredibly nuanced precision of your strategies and legal architecture were essential to this book. Those who wish to safeguard their financial futures will find no greater shield and no stronger deterrent than what you have built.

To the accountants, tax lawyers, and corporate trustees, your expertise in asset protection, income shielding, and tax efficiency has been of incalculable value. Your contributions have made it possible for individuals to structure their wealth in a way that makes economic exploitation impossible, neutralizing one of the most devastating weapons used against them. Because of your work, financial security is no longer a fragile illusion—it is an impenetrable reality.

To the survivors—the men and women who have endured the unthinkable, who have been deceived, exploited, and drained by those who saw them as nothing more than financial targets—we thank you for your courage in sharing your war stories. Your pain will not be in vain. You have illuminated the battlefield so that others may navigate it without falling into the same traps. The wisdom you have shared is a lifeline to those who still have time to protect themselves, and your voices will echo as a warning to future generations.

And to our incredibly talented editor and ghostwriter, who merged the contributions and perspectives of a diverse collection of contributing authors into the cohesive narrative that became the first edition of this book—this book would not have been possible without you.

While The Bloodline Alliance remains steadfast in our commitment to respecting the privacy of those who contributed their insights and expertise, let this acknowledgment serve as an everlasting testament to your impact. The world will be a better place because of your generosity of spirit and your contributions to our cause. Those who will be protected because of your wisdom and counsel will live in eternal gratitude.

You have made an extraordinary difference. Because of you, countless individuals will be spared economic ruin, emotional devastation, and generational trauma. Because of you, the perverse financial incentive to bring children into the world as pawns for economic extraction is being dismantled. And because of you, those who might have otherwise fallen prey to exploitation will instead be empowered to protect themselves—choosing relationships built on authenticity, mutual respect, and genuine love.

Evermore thanks.

Reader Advisory:

To the Inevitable Critics and Naysayers:

We welcome and encourage open dialogue about the uncomfortable topics raised in this book, but it is important that dialogue be based on facts, not distortions or moral grandstanding. Victims of economic exploitation—whether through reproductive coercion or marriage fraud—have the right to voice their concerns and defend themselves without being silenced, shamed, or gaslit by those who benefit from the status quo.

Attempting to suppress these discussions through cancel-culture tactics is itself a form of abuse. If your response to these hard truths is to try to silence victims rather than engage in reasoned debate, then let's be clear: That makes you an enabler of exploitation.

An Uncomfortable Truth

Like it or not, the uncomfortable truth—backed up by irrefutable data—is this that heterosexual women are by far the greatest perpetrators of these forms of fraud.

This is not speculation or conjecture. This is statistical reality. And yet, acknowledging this fact is often treated as taboo—as though pointing out a real and demonstrable trend is somehow an attack on all women. This book is an attack on *predators*, whether they be women *or* men.

Calling out economic predators is not misogyny. This is not a "feminist issue." This is a crisis that society in general—and women in particular—need to have an honest conversation about. These crimes are reaching epidemic levels, and yet no one is talking about them openly because it's an uncomfortable topic. Every day, the predators among us continue to thrive by leveraging that societal discomfort to their economic advantage.

Yes, it is a small subset of the population committing these crimes, but the damage they inflict is extraordinary—and it's not just financial.

- The emotional and psychological devastation inflicted on victims is immeasurable.
- The children born into the world as economic pawns suffer consequences no one wants to acknowledge.
- The legal system itself is manipulated and corrupted, reinforcing perverse financial incentives that allow these crimes to flourish unchecked.

And yet, instead of addressing the predators, there are those who would rather villainize the victims for speaking up—or even for taking the most basic self-preservation steps to protect themselves from an obviously broken system.

Don't Conflate the Laws' Intended Purpose with Those Who Abuse Them

The vast majority of people are good and decent. This book is not an attack on genuine victims who rely on laws designed to protect the vulnerable. But let's not pretend that those same laws aren't weaponized by a small but dangerous subset of financial predators who abuse them to extract wealth under false pretenses.

- Reproductive coercion is not a "parenting decision"—it is economic entrapment, and, in many jurisdictions, a crime punishable under fraud, coercion, and extortion laws.
- Marrying under false pretenses with the intent to extract financial gain is not a "relationship goal"—it is premeditated theft.
- Gold digging—deceiving a partner about intentions to gain financial benefits—is not just immoral. In many cases, it constitutes fraudulent misrepresentation, unjust enrichment, and, when linked to marriage, financial fraud.

- Scheming for unjust enrichment through fraudulent misrepresentation and marriage fraud is not "securing stability" or "protecting a future"—it is financial exploitation.

If you are offended by this book, ask yourself why. If you truly believe that economic exploitation is fair, then own that position and what it says about your moral compass—but don't expect the victims to accept the abuse in silence.

"But It's Fair!" – No, That's Rationalization

Some may argue that the current laws are fair, but let's be honest—what many really mean is that they like the status quo because it disproportionately benefits those perceived as underdogs at the expense of those "who can afford it."

That's not about fairness. That's rationalization.

- Fair means no one should be able to bring a child into the world as an economic pawn to secure a financial annuity for themselves.
- Fair means any adults capable of working to support themselves, do.
- Fair means no one should be able to attach themselves to a former spouse's income for years to fund a luxury lifestyle, while leaving the hardworking payor unable to save for retirement.

Victims of economic exploitation did not sign up to be human ATMs—and they have every right to speak out, protect themselves, and push for reforms.

A Challenge to the Naysayers, DTGD Enablers, and Abusers

If you are philosophically opposed to the content of this book, the substance of this movement designed to protect men *and* women from economic exploitation, or the very idea that victims have the right to defend themselves against financial predators, we invite you to make an intelligent, fact-based argument that:

a. Does not villainize the victims in any way
b. Does not conflate the authentic suffering of those whom family law legislation was designed to protect with the predators who hide behind it and abuse those laws to perpetrate fraud
c. Does not criticize victims for taking proactive legal steps to protect themselves and their families from these predators

So far, we haven't heard a single argument that meets that very simple standard.

Focus Criticisms on the Predators, not the Victims

Criticizing the core concepts of this book and attacking those who use legal tools to protect themselves is nothing more than an attempt to villainize the victims while defending those who exploit the system.

Some have suggested this book and the legal defense systems it endorses are aggressive, but they pale by comparison to the economic and emotional assault these predators wage upon us and our loved ones every day. That is why The Bloodline Alliance will continue to relentlessly pursue expansions to the protections we offer.

No romantic partner or child deserves to be made a victim of these predators.

INTRODUCTION: THE WORLD OF DARK TRIAD GOLD DIGGERS

In every generation, there are those who prey on the goodwill, trust, and resources of others by. These individuals—often charming, attractive, and seemingly ideal partners—are wolves in sheep's clothing, carefully crafting a façade to conceal their true motives. Some of them are gold diggers. While this term has been popularized and even romanticized in films, songs, and stories, the truth is far more sinister.

Gold diggers are not merely opportunists or materialists. Every gold digger possesses at least one of the traits of narcissism, Machiavellianism, or psychopathy—a dark triad that defines a predator intent on exploiting others for personal gain.

Unlike the caricatures often seen in pop culture, gold diggers are calculated and insidious, operating with a strategic mindset that makes them far more dangerous than most realize. Their goals extend beyond targeting wealth: They dismantle families, destabilize legacies, and leave emotional and financial devastation in their wake. This book is a response to their strategies—a guide to identifying, thwarting, and ultimately defeating DTGDs.

What Is a DTGD?

A Dark Triad Gold Digger (DTGD) is an individual whose actions, motivations, and manipulative tactics align with at least one of the three defining traits of the Dark Triad:

- Narcissism: A belief that they are entitled to the resources of others.

- Psychopathy: A lack of empathy and remorse, enabling them to exploit without hesitation.
- Machiavellianism: A cunning ability to scheme and manipulate to achieve their goals.

DTGDs view their targets not as partners, but as resources to be mined and discarded. Their methods are as much psychological warfare as they are economic exploitation, creating a complex web of manipulation that disarms their victims.

It is essential to clarify: Not all romantic partners are DTGDs. This book is not intended to foster paranoia, but to empower readers to differentiate between relationships filled with authenticity and love and those that are covertly exploitative and toxic. By equipping you with these tools, we hope we can help you focus your energy on building relationships that show authentic promise for a life of mutual respect, love, and happiness.

What is a Grave Robber?

A Grave Robber is a variant of the DTGD who still seeks to extract wealth through marriage, but, rather than cashing out through divorce settlements, does so by securing their payday through inheritance. Instead of orchestrating a rapid financial extraction via family courts, Grave Robbers play the long game—marrying significantly older partners with the intent of outliving them and inheriting the maximum possible estate. The predatory intent remains the same—only the execution differs. Where traditional DTGDs weaponize family law to siphon wealth, Grave Robbers entrench themselves within estate planning, isolating their partners from heirs, influencing wills, bearing children to expand their economic entitlements (while strategically displacing heirs), and positioning themselves as the inevitable primary beneficiaries.

The Threat to You and Your Family

If you are wealthy, come from a family with intergenerational assets, or are on a career trajectory likely to result in significant future earnings, you are a prime target. DTGDs excel at recognizing subtle signs of affluence—even when efforts are made to downplay them. They exploit emotional vulnerabilities, such as loneliness, a desire for connection, or misplaced trust, inserting themselves into their victims' lives with surgical precision.

The consequences of such relationships can be devastating. Financial losses may include drained accounts, predatory divorce settlements, and inheritance disputes. Beyond finances, DTGDs sow discord within families, destroy reputations, and derail legacies meant to endure for generations.

A Book About Psychological Warfare and Economic Exploitation

The DTGD playbook operates on two fronts: psychological warfare and economic exploitation. This book carefully dissects these tactics through both lenses, arming you with countermeasures designed to thwart their advances and to proactively defend against their ability to entrench themselves in your life and finances.

You will learn how DTGDs think and act, the subtle ways they infiltrate lives, and how to recognize their manipulative strategies. You will also gain practical tools to protect your assets, your income, your family, and your emotional well-being, ensuring that you can move through the world with confidence and clarity.

Why This Book Matters

Grave Robbers and Gold Diggers is not just a guide—it is a roadmap for reclaiming control, safeguarding your legacy, and empowering your family against an insidious threat. Through its pages, you will discover:

- The traits and tactics that define DTGDs
- How to spot red flags and protect yourself proactively
- Legal, financial, and emotional strategies to counteract their influence
- The role of The Bloodline Alliance in creating a DTGD-free future for you and your loved ones

By the end, you will have the tools to ensure that your life story is one of empowerment, not exploitation.

A Future Without DTGDs

As you begin this journey, remember that not all romantic partners are DTGDs, but all DTGDs are predators. This book will give you the clarity to spot the difference and the tools to defend yourself and your family. Together, we can build a world where DTGDs no longer thrive—a world where wealth and legacies are preserved and relationships are rooted in love and authenticity.

Let's begin.

THE THREAT

1

The Unseen War on Wealth

The Silent Battlefield You Didn't Know You Were On

Most wars begin with a declaration—a defining moment where battle lines are drawn and everyone involved knows the stakes. But this war—the one targeting your wealth, your financial autonomy, and your future—begins in silence with a Trojan Horse of malice disguised as love. There are no sirens, no warnings, no grand pronouncements of intent. By the time you realize you're under attack, the enemy is already inside your walls, preparing to burn your empire to the ground.

This is not an exaggeration. DTGDs are *all* financial predators. If you have wealth, status, or even just the potential for either, you are likely already in their crosshairs. They are hunting you *and your children*—not for love, not for companionship, not for shared dreams, but for what you have and what they can take.

You may not want to believe it. You may tell yourself that you're too smart, too careful, too well-advised to be ensnared. But DTGDs don't attack where you're strong—they attack where you're vulnerable. And the place where you are most vulnerable is your heart.

Gold Digging: A Billion-Dollar Industry of Exploitation

Gold digging is not just an unfortunate byproduct of modern relationships—it is a multi-billion-dollar *industry* that causes economic, emotional, and generational devastation on a staggering scale. DTGDs prey on the successful, the driven, and the fortunate, leveraging emotional manipulation, legal loopholes, and societal blind spots to extract wealth, leaving behind a wake of destruction that can take decades to repair.

Why You Are the Perfect Target

You might believe that your intelligence, your business acumen, or your experience in high-stakes negotiations makes you immune. But your success is exactly what makes you vulnerable. DTGDs don't go after failures—they go after winners. They seek out individuals who are driven, accomplished, and, most importantly, unprotected.

They know that people like you—builders, visionaries, wealth creators—have been conditioned to believe in fairness, partnership, and the meritocracy of effort. And that is what they exploit.

By the time you start questioning whether their intentions are genuine, they will have already rewritten the narrative. "You're paranoid." "You're controlling." "You're being unfair." They will convince you that protecting your assets is a betrayal of their love, that asking for a prenup is an admission of doubt, and that putting up boundaries means you don't trust them.

If you fall for that, you've already lost.

The Family Court System: A Rigged Game You Can't Win

Here's what no one tells you until it's too late: Once a DTGD gets you into the legal system, you have already lost.

Family courts are not built to protect the wealth you earned. They are not interested in fairness or economic logic. They are designed for redistribution. The law favors the spouse who has less, and is weaponized by those who enter marriage fully intending to cash out at the highest possible rate.

If a DTGD marries you and sticks around for a few years, they have a guaranteed financial exit package—whether they have contributed anything or not.

- Division of assets? They're getting half—maybe more.
- Spousal support? You're paying it.
- Child support? If they have a child with you, they have locked in 18+ years of financial extraction, often at rates far beyond what is needed to actually raise a child.

And that's assuming they don't launch false allegations, custody battles, or deliberate legal delays to drain your finances further through litigation fees.

The Best Defense Is a Strong Offense

If you think simply asking for a prenuptial agreement is enough to protect you, you're dangerously mistaken. The prenup conversation comes way too late in the game when you're dealing with a DTGD. To truly protect yourself, you need a full-scale economic defense system that is operational before they ever enter your life.

Above all else, this book is about defense and empowerment. It is designed to inform you about:

- Detection mastery: Learning to spot red flags and subtle manipulation tactics—and learning to run non-verbal tests to spot them—so you can avoid and disrupt potential entanglements before they begin.
- Bulletproof defensive systems: A prenup is important, but it is not nearly enough. DTGDs use a multi-pronged assault on your financial well-being, and your defenses must be just as sophisticated.
- The ultimate deterrent: A strategy that has been used discreetly by the ultra-wealthy for generations, and that will save you money, anguish, and time wasted—one that makes a prenup compulsory, without negotiation. (Chapter 53)

The Only Way to Win Is not to Play

There is no negotiating with DTGDs. There is no "I'll protect myself later" strategy that will work. If you do not set your defenses up before they enter your life, you are already at a severe disadvantage.

This is where The Bloodline Alliance's Family First Trust (FFT) comes in. It is not just an asset protection tool—it is your financial fortress and the ultimate DTGD deterrent.

- It locks down your wealth before a DTGD even has access to it.
- It ensures that no marriage, divorce, or custody battle can result in economic destruction.
- It stands as a stalwart beacon of deterrence that sends a clear message that you are untouchable—long before a predator ever makes their move.

DTGDs don't target victims who are financially protected. They don't waste time on individuals who have clear, unbreakable safeguards in place. They move on to easier prey.

That is the ultimate goal—to make you an impossible target.

The Bloodline Alliance: Elite Wealth Preservation

To combat the growing threat of economic exploitation, The Bloodline Alliance—a Swiss society organized under Section 60 of the Swiss Civil Code—was established as a global institution dedicated to gathering, refining, and disseminating best-in-class defense systems for wealth protection, legacy preservation, and defensive legal architecture for the affluent. TBA is not merely a financial think tank—it is a private alliance of legal minds, estate architects, and financial strategists who serve as the silent custodians of dynastic wealth. Through its certified trustee network and proprietary legal frameworks, TBA exists to ensure that family wealth remains protected, generation after generation. For more information, please visit www.thebloodlinealliance.org.

TBA's Family First Trust: The Ultimate Fortress

In the chapters that follow, you will see references to Family First Trusts or FFTs—a term that will become critical as you understand the mechanics of true financial defense. The following is a brief overview of how The Bloodline Alliance's FFT works. We will cover it in detail in Chapters 53 to 62 but it is important to understand the core concepts now, as context for how enacting this strategy serves as the ultimate defense and deterrent. Ideally, this structure helps you avoid gold diggers altogether—or, at the very least, fully protects you if one breaches your defenses. Feel free to skip ahead if you want a full breakdown of how it works and why the FFT is essential. In the meantime, here's what you need to know:

✓ The trust itself is a private family wealth fortress designed to provide education, entrepreneurship, and housing funding for you and future generations of your family. In doing so, it also ensures that your assets and future income are legally inaccessible in a divorce. At the same time, it serves a dual purpose as the ultimate deterrent for any party focused on economic extraction. It's existence signals an economic dead end for those who would seek to exploit you.

✓ The trust mandates a qualifying prenuptial agreement (QPA). If your significant other (SO) isn't willing to participate in good faith negotiations on a prenup (red flag), the trust automatically activates, adeptly protecting assets and future income on multiple fronts to prevent any potential financial encroachment. Importantly, this automatic springing mechanism occurs *before* marriage, proactively blocking a predator focused on economic exploitation from any opportunity to extract wealth through marriage.

✓ The trust protects the settlor during their lifetime and ultimately converts into a multi-generational "family first" fund designed to support education, entrepreneurship, and housing for the settlor's blood relatives (typically the settlor's children, or alternatively their nieces and nephews). Any attempt by an economic assailant to circumvent the settlor's "family first" fund is not only futile, it also fully exposes the aggressor as a bona fide gold digger seeking to cause economic harm to the interests of the trust's beneficiaries so they can instead extract wealth for themselves. The gold digger is exposed by their own hand.

By design, the FFT is the ultimate DTGD deterrent—a financial fortress designed to preemptively block the common attack vectors of asset hijacking, divorce exploitation, child support entrapment, and inheritance manipulation. Unlike a simple prenuptial agreement, which can be challenged, diluted, or outright bypassed by a calculating DTGD, the FFT ensures that your premarital assets (including post-marital appreciation), income (both during and after marriage), intellectual property, business holdings, and retirement savings are legally shielded from DTGDs. This is not just an asset and income protection strategy—it is a psychological deterrent that signals to financial predators that you are untouchable before they even attempt their multifaceted economic extraction schemes.

Without the FFT, your wealth, businesses, and future earnings are prime targets for DTGDs looking for lifetime entitlements through legal loopholes, coercive pregnancies, and court-facilitated financial extractions. The FFT removes the incentive before they ever make a move, ensuring that your financial security remains in your hands—not in the grasp of someone who never earned it.

Why A Prenup Alone Isn't Nearly Enough Protection from a DTGD

A prenup alone isn't nearly enough protection in a world where DTGDs have mastered the art of circumventing them. Courts are more than willing to invalidate prenuptial agreements under the flimsiest of excuses—claiming they were signed under duress, lacked full disclosure, or are simply "unfair" in hindsight. A prenup, no matter how well-written, is still subject to the whims of biased judges and manipulative legal challenges that can turn even the strongest contract into a meaningless piece of paper.

> **Disturbing but true:** *One of the most common legal challenges to a prenup is "coercion"—and courts have ruled that simply discussing a prenup too close to the wedding date can be grounds to void it.*

Even if prenups do hold up, DTGDs can bypass them entirely with one well-timed "accidental" pregnancy—a financial weapon that locks in 18+ years of state-enforced financial servitude. High earners are especially at risk of reproductive coercion, with child support awards reaching into the tens of thousands *per child, per month*. The FFT eliminates these loopholes entirely, ensuring that your wealth is off-limits, no matter how aggressively DTGDs try to entrench themselves in your bank accounts. The only way to truly protect your assets and financial future is to remove the economic incentive before DTGDs ever attempt to exploit you—to make yourself an economically unviable target—and that is exactly what the FFT was designed to do.

The Other Problem With Prenups

If you've studied the art of negotiation, you already know one of its most essential rules: never start by asking for what you think is fair. Instead, you begin by anchoring high—asking for considerably more than your actual bottom line—and include a few deliberate throwaways. These are the items you're perfectly happy to concede later, so the other party feels like they've "won" something. This strategic give-and-take allows you to land where you wanted all along. But if you make the rookie mistake of starting with your idea of fairness, any attempt to "meet in the middle" almost guarantees you'll walk away with less than fair.

Prenup negotiations follow the same dangerous dynamic. There's an unspoken cultural expectation that both parties must compromise—even if one side enters the conversation anchoring with terms that are absurdly one-sided or omit critical protections. In these cases, agreeing to "split the difference" often introduces unacceptable economic risks. That's where your FFT becomes your strongest ally. It doesn't negotiate. It doesn't compromise. But it *does* hold prior claims over nearly everything at stake. Your FFT shifts the balance by enforcing baseline protections that cannot be ignored or watered down during prenup negotiations.

If your partner—or their legal team—pushes for a prenup that inadequately protects your premarital assets or future income, the FFT kicks in. You may have a prenup, but if it's not a *qualifying* prenup according to your FFT, the trust deed obligates you to deploy additional asset and income protection mechanisms by design. In other words, any attempt to dilute prenup protections doesn't just fail—it *triggers* a more aggressive fallback strategy. The DTGD may think they've maneuvered you into a weaker prenup, but instead they've activated a preordained sequence that reroutes your wealth to safer ground. And since you've already disclosed the FFT's existence and its rules, they can see it coming. They just can't stop it. Checkmate.

The FFT: Preemptively Nullifying Economic Attachment Schemes

If you want to distill the DTGD agenda down to its foundational objective, it's actually quite simple: DTGDs seek to create legally enforceable economic attachment rights to your assets, income, and legacy. Every scheme they deploy, every manipulation they orchestrate, and every legal loophole they exploit serves one primary function—securing a financial stranglehold on your wealth, both during your lifetime and after your death.

Their financial attack vectors include:

- Your property: Real estate, businesses, investments
- Your future creations: Businesses, intellectual property, royalties, licensing fees
- Your inheritance(s): Wealth passed down to you
- Your retirement funds: Pensions, 401(k)s, and long-term savings
- Your future income: Through spousal support and child support
- Your estate when you pass: Claiming inheritance rights, disputing wills, and displacing rightful heirs

Grave Robber DTGDs take this strategy even further. Not content with temporary financial extraction, they play the long game—attaching themselves to your estate and displacing your heirs to the greatest extent possible. Their goal is to rewrite your financial legacy in their favor and erase your intended beneficiaries entirely.

Once you fully grasp that economic attachment rights are the core motivator behind these predators, you begin to appreciate just how powerful the FFT truly is. It doesn't just protect assets—it preemptively nullifies every single financial attack vector DTGDs seek to exploit. It sends a signal that as simple as it is profound:

- You understand that economic predators exist, and that their primary strategy is securing attachment rights to your wealth.

- You have preassigned all economic attachment rights, eliminating their ability to stake a legal claim.
- There is nothing to attach to.
- There is nothing to negotiate.
- The trust is already structured, the protections are preestablished, and the door is closed.

If someone truly loves you for you, they will recognize and respect the wisdom of this structure. But DTGDs won't admit to your face how horrified they are when they realize you had the foresight to mitigate every angle of attack before they could deploy it. It infuriates them even more because it's not a direct accusation—it's just a quiet, airtight legal structure that renders them powerless.

That's the ultimate checkmate. You beat DTGDs at their own game before they've even had the chance to make their first move. As soon as they realize your wealth is protected by a bulletproof fortress purpose-built to neutralize every DTGD trick in the book, they will be clamoring to press the ejection seat button themselves so they can move on to easier prey—and that's exactly the point.

By the time you finish this book, you will understand why the FFT is not just a legal tool, but also a financial fortress that renders every angle of a gold digger's attack ineffective.

Disturbing but true: *Kanye West was ordered to pay $200,000 per month in child support following his divorce from Kim Kardashian—a total of $43.2 million over 18 years. This staggering sum is paid despite the fact that both parents are billionaires and share equal custody of their four children.*

Let that sink in. A man with joint custody, whose ex-wife has a higher net worth than him, is still required to fork over nearly a quarter of a million dollars each month for children who already live in ultra-luxury. Child support in high-income cases has nothing to do with the actual cost of raising a child—it's about wealth redistribution.

Post-Engagement but *Pre*-Wedding. Still Eligible to Establish Your FFT? Yes.

Even if you're already engaged, The Bloodline Alliance can still protect you, provided two simple conditions are met. First, you must be willing to move quickly and follow the guidance of your trustee. Second, you agree to a self-directed "grace period," meaning you won't set a wedding date that is less than one year from the date your FFT is established. If your wedding date is already at least a year away, you're good to go. If it's scheduled sooner, you can postpone it to qualify. To begin, simply indicate your engagement status in the comments field of the enrollment form and let your trustee know the intended wedding date (if one has been set). As long as that date falls outside the one-year window, your trustee will prioritize your enrollment and fast-track the next steps.

Is the FFT an Appropriate Engagement Gift?

There's never a wrong time to give the gift of protection against one of life's biggest financial unknowns. If the idea of presenting a trust fund as an engagement gift feels awkward, consider offering it as The Anonymous Gift (TAG - see Resources). But please — don't withhold it from someone you care about simply because the timing feels unconventional. For at least half of all marriages, the consequences of going unprotected are life-altering. Gift recipients will follow the same simple steps as self-directed enrollment outlined above.

The USA: A Financial Warzone for High-Value Men

American men, things not as bad as you think—they're way worse. You *are* being systematically exploited by a legal system designed to strip you of your wealth and autonomy, all while ensuring that your predators face no accountability for their crimes. Reproductive coercion is a crime that occurs every day, but it's virtually impossible to prove, which is why predators keep getting away with it—and getting very rich because of it.

In response to this systematic abuse of American men, TBA developed a USA-specific version of the FFT—the USA-Fortified Family First Trust variant (USAF-FFT). This version of the trust is custom-engineered to neutralize the American legal system's most egregious financial loopholes, ensuring that outlandish percentage-based child support awards are capped, spousal support is minimized or neutralized entirely for able-bodied DTGDs who are perfectly capable of working to support themselves, and wealth extraction is no longer a viable strategy for targeting USAF-FFT-protected men.

You hold in your hands a gold-plated invitation to protect yourself with a digital signing session that will immediately protect you *for life*. If you are already convinced that you need this protection, skip ahead to Chapter 5 and then Chapters 53 to 62, where we outline exactly how the USAF-FFT works and how to implement it immediately.

2

What Is a Dark Triad Gold Digger (DTGD)?

The Apex Predator of Relationships

Gold diggers are not just materialistic opportunists looking for an easy ride. They are predators, and every single one of them operates within the Dark Triad framework. While some gold diggers manifest all three Dark Triad traits—narcissism, Machiavellianism, and psychopathy—others lean more heavily toward one trait, while still exhibiting elements of the others. Every gold digger is driven by at least one of these traits and uses it as their primary means of economic and emotional extraction.

Understanding what makes a gold digger so dangerous is not just an intellectual exercise—it is a necessity. The damage they inflict is catastrophic, and by the time their victims realize what has happened, they are often financially gutted, emotionally hollowed out, and legally entrapped in an ongoing cycle of exploitation.

This chapter breaks down exactly how gold diggers think, operate, and embed themselves into the lives of their targets. Their tactics are not random—they are methodically executed with cold, ruthless efficiency. The only way to avoid falling prey is to recognize who they are, what they want, and how they weaponize relationships for personal gain.

The Dark Triad: The DNA of DTGDs

The Dark Triad is a psychological framework consisting of three distinct but overlapping personality traits—narcissism, Machiavellianism, and psychopathy. These traits are associated with manipulation, lack of empathy, and a relentless pursuit of self-interest at the expense of others. When applied to financial predators like gold diggers, they form the blueprint for economic and emotional exploitation. While every gold digger operates within this framework, they typically exhibit one dominant trait that defines their primary strategy for infiltration and extraction, while leveraging the others when necessary.

The Narcissistic-Leaning DTGD: Entitlement on Overdrive

A narcissistic-leaning DTGD is not just self-absorbed—they are pathologically convinced that they deserve everything you have simply because they exist. Their grandiose self-image allows them to justify extreme financial parasitism with a straight face.

- Unwavering superiority: They believe they are inherently more special than others, making them entitled to luxury, status, and financial support without contribution.
- Manipulative charm: Their charisma is a finely tuned weapon, designed to mirror their target's desires and reflect them back to create the illusion of a perfect match.
- Blame shifting and gaslighting: When their actions are questioned, they will never accept responsibility. Every failure, conflict, or

setback will be rewritten so that they are the victim and their target is the aggressor.
- Lavish spending, no contribution: They see their partner's wealth as an extension of their own, and often drain resources without ever providing anything of equal value in return.

A narcissistic DTGD does not merely crave attention—they crave financial dependency. Their goal is not just to be admired, but to be financially sustained indefinitely.

The Machiavellian-Leaning DTGD: The Master Strategist

DTGDs with high Machiavellian traits are chess players in a game where their victim doesn't even realize they're a piece on the board. They approach relationships with cold calculation, long-term planning, and a ruthless willingness to exploit.

- Strategic deception: They carefully curate a persona that aligns with their target's dreams, desires, and expectations, ensuring rapid trust and deep emotional entanglement.
- Emotional exploitation: They feign shared struggles, vulnerabilities, or traumatic pasts to lower their victim's defenses and accelerate commitment.
- Incremental entrapment: They do not demand large sums immediately. Instead, they build control incrementally—small financial favors, merging finances, creating a narrative of dependence—until their victim is completely ensnared.
- Legal and social manipulation: These DTGDs will position themselves as the victim in every scenario, ensuring that even friends, family, and legal professionals see them as the one deserving of protection and sympathy.

A Machiavellian DTGD will manipulate not just their victim, but an entire ecosystem—their target's friends, family, and even legal professionals—to reinforce their deception and tighten their grip.

The Psychopathic-Leaning DTGD: Exploitation Without Remorse

Psychopathic DTGDs introduce the most dangerous element into the equation: a total absence of empathy, guilt, or conscience.

- Cold-blooded calculation: They see relationships as financial heists, carefully planned down to the smallest detail.
- Extreme risk-taking: Unlike other DTGDs, psychopathic ones engage in bold, reckless financial deception—forging documents, draining accounts, or orchestrating false allegations to gain financial leverage.
- Callous discarding: When their victims no longer serve a purpose, they vanish—often leaving their targets in emotional and financial ruin.
- Litigation as a weapon: They will drag their victims through false claims, endless legal battles, and reputational destruction to extract the highest possible payout.

Not every DTGD exhibits overt psychopathy, but those who do are particularly dangerous. They escalate their schemes without hesitation, leaving victims not just broken, but systematically annihilated.

Recognizing the Predator Before It's Too Late

Every DTGD is a predator. Whether they lean heavily on narcissism, Machiavellianism, psychopathy, or a combination of all three, their goal is the same: total economic, psychological, and social control over their victims.

By the time most targets realize they are being hunted, it is too late. That is why early detection is critical. Recognizing their methods and motivations is not just self-defense—it is survival.

Some of the most notable red flags include:

- Over-the-top charm that feels too rehearsed, too perfect, and too rapid.
- An unrelenting fixation on financial discussions, either by exaggerating their financial struggles or subtly probing yours.
- A victim narrative that is deployed at strategic moments to guilt-trip their target into financial entanglement.
- A pattern of financial dependency, past lawsuits, or failed relationships—signs that their entire history has been built on extraction, not contribution.

DTGDs do not change. They do not suddenly develop love, empathy, or integrity. The only things that stop them are the realization that their target is financially untouchable or the threat of exposure (the DTGD's greatest fear).

This is why financial fortifications must be in place before these people enter your life. Because once they're in, extracting them is an entirely different war—one that most victims are too broken to fight.

Recognizing their methods and motivations is the first line of defense against their insidious tactics. Forewarned is forearmed.

3

Are All Gold Diggers Dark Triads? Yes.

The Myth of the "Harmless Gold Digger"

Popular culture has long romanticized the gold digger archetype—painting them as charming opportunists who simply exchange affection for financial security. Music, films, and social media have reinforced the image of the gold digger as playful, ambitious, and typically harmless. They are often portrayed as savvy individuals leveraging their desirability to obtain material comfort, as if it were just another form of hustle.

This myth is dangerously misleading.

Gold diggers are not harmless opportunists. They are, by definition, predators who manipulate, extract, and destroy. Every gold digger operates within the Dark Triad framework, utilizing at least one of the traits of narcissism, Machiavellianism, and psychopathy—often in carefully curated combinations—to achieve their financial objectives.

This chapter dismantles the fiction that some gold diggers are "harmless." It demonstrates how all gold diggers exhibit Dark Triad tendencies, making them fundamentally dangerous. Whether they rely on charm, calculated deception, or ruthless exploitation, every gold digger follows the same playbook of psychological and financial destruction.

The Predator's Toolbox: Dark Triad Traits in Action

Gold diggers don't just "get lucky" in securing financial resources—they execute deliberate strategies grounded in narcissism, Machiavellianism, and psychopathy. These traits do not exist in isolation. They blend into an exceptionally effective strategy for manipulation and long-term financial entrapment.

Narcissism: The Entitled Exploiter

At the heart of narcissistic DTGDs is a deep-seated sense of entitlement—an unshakable belief that they deserve wealth, luxury, and comfort without having to earn it.

- Exploiting admirers: DTGDs use charm, sexuality, and perceived exclusivity to lure financially stable targets into relationships where they gradually escalate demands.
- Demanding excess: To a narcissistic gold digger, extravagant spending, gifts, and financial support are not luxuries—they are entitlements. Any resistance from their targets are framed as selfishness.
- Projecting superiority: They weaponize belittlement, making their victims feel lucky to have their attention. The goal is to instill doubt and dependence, ensuring the targets remain compliant.

Dr. Craig Malkin, author of *Rethinking Narcissism*, states:

"Narcissists excel at painting a flattering picture of themselves that makes others want to give them what they desire."

For a DTGD, this is not just a personality quirk—it is a predatory strategy designed to extract resources.

Machiavellianism: The Puppet Master

Machiavellian-leaning DTGDs do not rely on impulse—they are patient, strategic, and methodical in their approach. Relationships are financial conquests, carefully orchestrated to maximize gain while minimizing risk.

- Strategic patience: A Machiavellian DTGD is willing to invest months or even years cultivating a victim's trust before fully exploiting them.
- Manufacturing vulnerability: They fabricate sob stories designed to elicit sympathy and financial generosity from their targets.
- Leveraging social networks: By embedding themselves within targets' social circles, they make it harder for their victims to cut ties without severe personal or reputational consequences.

As highlighted in *Psychology Today*:

"Machiavellian individuals excel at creating strategic alliances, often at the expense of their targets."

Their manipulations are not impulsive—they are meticulously planned, ensuring that, once their victims are entrapped, financial extraction becomes inevitable.

Psychopathy: Exploitation Without Conscience

Psychopathy removes the emotional barriers that prevent most people from engaging in deception and exploitation. A psychopathic-leaning DTGD is the most dangerous of all, operating without guilt, remorse, or fear of consequences.

- Cold emotional detachment: A psychopathic DTGD does not develop genuine emotional bonds. Their charm is a performance, fine-tuned to their targets' insecurities.
- High-risk financial gambits: They are willing to forge documents, take out hidden loans, or siphon funds into their own ventures, regardless of legal or moral consequences.

- Callous abandonment: When their victims no longer serve a financial purpose, they are discarded without hesitation—often leaving them financially and emotionally shattered.

Dr. Robert Hare, the leading expert on psychopathy, warns: "Psychopaths are emotionally shallow and lack remorse, making them highly effective manipulators."

A psychopathic DTGD pushes boundaries most people wouldn't ever consider crossing, making them a relentless and exceptionally destructive force.

Mental Illness vs. Deliberate Strategy

Are DTGDs driven by mental illness, or are they highly self-aware manipulators? While some DTGDs may operate from a place of psychological dysfunction, many are entirely conscious of their manipulative tactics.

The Role of Mental Illness

Certain mental health disorders can contribute to DTGD behavior, but they do not excuse or justify their exploitation.

- Narcissistic personality disorder (NPD): Pathological narcissists exhibit chronic entitlement, lack of empathy, and exploitative behavior.
- Antisocial personality disorder (ASPD): This includes individuals with psychopathic traits who exploit with no moral restraint.
- Borderline personality disorder (BPD): Some DTGDs may exhibit unstable emotions and impulsive financial behaviors, leading to erratic exploitation.

While these disorders explain certain behaviors, they do not account for the conscious, strategic deception exhibited by DTGDs.

Deliberate Exploitation: A Calculated Game

For many DTGDs, their actions are not impulsive symptoms of mental illness—they are carefully engineered manipulations designed for maximum gain.

- They know exactly what they're doing.
- They choose their targets strategically.
- They adapt their methods based on what works.
- They exploit legal loopholes to maximize extraction.

Understanding the difference between mental dysfunction and deliberate predation allows victims to approach countermeasures effectively—shifting from compassion and excuses to action and defense.

Awareness Is Your Best Defense

By recognizing that all gold diggers operate within the Dark Triad spectrum, we strip away the illusion that some are harmless. Whether they lean on narcissism, Machiavellianism, psychopathy, or a blend of all three, every gold digger is a DTGD—and every DTGD is a financial and psychological threat.

The best defense is awareness and preparation. Educate yourself, establish financial safeguards, and recognize the warning signs before becoming entangled. DTGDs do not change, and they do not stop. The only way to protect yourself is to remain vigilant, informed, and uncompromising in your financial security.

4

DTGD Economic Incentives: A Multi-Billion-Dollar Reward System for Fraud

The Greed Factor: How A Broken System Invites DTGD Exploitation

The modern family law system is a goldmine for DTGDs—a legally sanctioned reward system for fraudsters who manipulate, exploit, and financially annihilate their victims under the guise of love. The system is not just broken—it actively incentivizes predatory behavior. With no meaningful consequences and virtually guaranteed payouts, aspiring DTGDs don't just stumble upon their grifts—they learn from those who have come before them and refine their craft to maximize their haul.

The DTGD Training Ground: Watching and Learning from the Masters

Aspiring DTGDs don't enter the world blind. They watch, learn, and take notes. They see how other DTGDs entrench themselves, how they manipulate their victims into financial submission, and how they use the family law system as a weapon. The most successful DTGDs operate like career criminals, passing down tactics to friends (and their own children) like trade secrets, ensuring the next generation of economic predators are even more ruthless and efficient.

They see:

- How courts favor the "weaker" party, and they learn how to weaponize victimhood.
- How spousal support is calculated, and they learn to intentionally limit their own earning potential to maximize payouts.
- How child support is structured, and they learn that having children with high-earning targets locks in decades of guaranteed income.
- How "sacrificing a career" plays into alimony awards, and they strategically avoid career advancement so they can claim financial dependency.
- How asset division rules work, and they orchestrate post-marital acquisitions to dramatically increase their haul in a divorce.
- How inheritances that are *protected* from redistribution by legal statutes can be accessed by cunningly laid traps that commingle funds in joint accounts or real estate purchases.

They don't just happen to win these financial wars—they train for them. And the system doesn't just allow this exploitation—it enables it.

Marriage Fraud: The Legally Sanctioned Heist

In virtually any other financial transaction, fraudulent misrepresentation is illegal. You can't lie about an investment opportunity, fake your credentials to get a job, or forge a contract to seize someone else's property. But when it comes to marriage and divorce, fraud is disturbingly rampant and virtually impossible to prove.

DTGDs deliberately deceive their victims, feigning love and commitment while secretly scheming to extract the maximum possible financial benefit. This is premeditated fraud, plain and simple. Yet when the mask finally slips—when they file for divorce at the most financially opportune moment after securing legal entrenchment—the courts don't care about intent. The only thing that matters is how much the victim has to pay.

The most calculated DTGDs give award-worthy performances to ensure their victims believe the love is real—and equally impressive performances in divorce court to frame their scheming as victimhood. They plan ahead, pretending to be low-maintenance, hardworking, and loyal—but doing so just long enough to solidify their economic position. Once the legal system ensures their financial windfall, they drop the act. And the courts? They play along. They enforce settlements, order alimony, and grant child support without question. The system incentivizes, rewards, and protects the fraudsters while punishing the *real* victims for decades.

The Billion-Dollar Industry: A System Built for Exploitation

The financial incentive for DTGDs is astronomical. Consider the numbers:

- The U.S. divorce industry is valued at $50 billion annually (and that only includes divorce industry service providers, not the actual settlements).
- Child support payments total $30 billion per year.
- Spousal support payments are believed to be even higher.
- High-asset divorce settlements reach into the tens of billions annually, shifting wealth from producers to predators.

If this were any other industry, we'd be calling for reform—but because it's cloaked in the language of "family law" and "fairness," society turns a blind eye. This is not fairness. This is financial predation disguised as justice.

What's At Stake for You?

If you are a high earner or hold significant assets (or are on a career trajectory pointed in that direction), the system is already stacked against you. You need to understand exactly how much you stand to lose if you walk into marriage unprotected.

Without safeguards in place, you are exposing:

- Your premarital assets.
- Post-marital appreciation on those assets (if you own real estate or investments, expect to split the appreciation).
- Assets acquired during the marriage (including everything you buy and build together).
- Businesses, creative works, and intellectual property you conceive during the marriage. (Even if they originate exclusively from your premarital skills and credentials, they are automatically marital property in many jurisdictions.)
- Your post-marital income, potentially indefinitely (spousal support and child support ensures that DTGDs continue to profit off your labor even after they leave).
- Your retirement savings and pension income (long-term alimony can see gold diggers cashing in on money meant to sustain you in your old age).
- Your inheritance. (If funds are co-mingled, DTGDs can stake a claim—and they are masters at forcing co-mingling through real estate and "family" purchases.)

And what do these DTGDs risk? Nothing.

How to Fight Back

The system is built for exploitation, but that doesn't mean you have to play along.

In Chapters 50 to 52, you will be given the tools to calculate your aggregate lifetime financial exposure—the staggering sum of money you could lose if you don't take preemptive action.

Marriage is just as much a financial contract as it is an emotional commitment—and in a system designed to reward fraud, marrying without adequate financial protections is gross financial negligence. It's a reckless game of Russian Roulette where the odds are not in your favor.

Will you be a DTGD victim, or will you enter marriage with an economic forcefield protecting you?

5

AMERICAN MEN: THE SYSTEM *IS* RIGGED AGAINST YOU

Nowhere on earth is the DTGD baby-trapping epidemic more acute than in the United States. Why? Because nowhere else are the financial incentives for reproductive coercion so absurdly high. The American family court system is not merely broken—it is an economic extortion engine that rewards deception, punishes financial success, and bleeds men dry for decades, all under the guise of "fairness."

With one well-timed "accidental" pregnancy, an economic predator can lock in a six-figure salary for the next 18+ years—no effort, no accountability, just pure financial extortion. For high earners, this can easily equate to millions of dollars in lifetime obligations. The fact that this crime is not only overlooked but actively encouraged by the system should outrage anyone who values personal and financial autonomy.

This is why TBA took decisive action.

The USA is hands down the most dangerous jurisdiction on earth for men when it comes to baby trapping. However, it also offers the best legal protection available in the form of domestic asset protection trusts (DAPTs). When paired with the USAF-FFT, this creates the ultimate deterrent for DTGDs. It doesn't just protect you from financial exploitation—it erases the incentive for a DTGD to target you in the first place.

Why the US Variant Is Essential: A Legal System Rigged for Exploitation

Unlike the standard FFT, which triggers the establishment of a qualifying prenup *or* a qualifying foreign asset protection trust (FAPT) after an engagement event, the US variant mandates any male who hasn't had a vasectomy establish a DAPT *regardless* of whether or not their SO agrees to a prenup. For your own protection, you want *both*—and it is strongly advised you back away from any romantic partner who resists the prenup. Your DAPT is not an optional safeguard. For US residents, it is a legal requirement for your own protection. Why? Because a prenup alone is meaningless in a system where a DTGD can completely bypass it with one so-called "accident"—a premeditated pregnancy that locks in a lifetime financial windfall chiseled out of your future earnings.

American family courts do not care about intent or fraud. They do not care that you were deceived, manipulated, or coerced. The only thing that matters is how much money can be siphoned from you to support the DTGD's newly-minted luxury lifestyle.

This is not a worst-case scenario—this is the default outcome for unprotected men in the US.

The USAF-FFT works in perfect harmony with its DAPT counterpart, ensuring that the formula for calculating child support maxes out a DTGD's entitlements at between $2500 and $4000/mo. That's certainly enough to take care of your child, but nowhere near the multi-million-dollar payout DTGDs are seeking to extract by baby trapping you. Compare this to the $10,000 to $50,000 *per month, per child* that high earners are routinely forced to pay and the difference is staggering.

The US variant of the FFT is not just a legal tool—it is a proactive economic counterstrike against those who would seek to exploit the system—and *you*—for personal gain.

Why the Double-Layered Defense?

One layer isn't enough in a country where the system is designed to strip men of their financial security the moment DTGDs engage in reproductive coercion.

The USAF-FFT ensures that:

1. Your prenup is reinforced by the structural firewall of your DAPT.
   - Courts frequently disregard prenups, particularly in states with anti-male bias.
   - A DAPT places assets beyond court reach, ensuring that wealth remains secure.

2. Your income never becomes an open target.
   - Your DAPT directs all income to you, just as before.
   - However, if divorce is initiated, trustee intervention caps your income distribution at $8,000 per month—ensuring that child and spousal support calculations remain in the $2,500 to $4,000 per month range.

3. Spousal and child support exposure is minimized.
   - The income cap limits the basis for support obligations.
   - This removes the incentive for DTGDs to target high-earning men for strategic pregnancies or financial extraction.

4. Your trust remains active for your children—but not your ex.
   - The trust deed explicitly excludes your ex from receiving any direct benefits.
   - However, trustees retain full discretion to ensure children's quality of life remains well-supported without funneling

money to fund an extravagant lifestyle for an ex or an opportunistic one night stand.

- The US male version also includes language specifically encouraging trustees to pay childcare expenses directly rather than handing money to the ex, preventing misuse of funds intended to benefit your children.

Mandatory DAPT for US Resident Males

- US resident males who have not had a vasectomy must request a qualifying prenuptial agreement and are required to establish a qualifying DAPT whether their SO agrees to a prenup or not.
- The only exception? Your trust protector—who you personally appoint—can modify the DAPT rules if adjustments are warranted for legitimate reasons.
- The trust protector has full discretion to increase, decrease, or even terminate the agreement—but only if doing so poses no risk of economic harm to the trust's beneficiaries (you, your children, and your blood relatives).

Does Defending Against Baby Trapping Only Work for Men Who Get Married?

No. In fact, if you plan on living your best single life indefinitely, you are an ultra-high risk target for baby trapping and should set up your USAF-FFT + DAPT immediately. Unlike marriage, where you actively sign up for a lifetime of financial entanglements, one opportunistic pregnancy is all it takes to lock you into 18+ years of forced financial servitude—with zero legal recourse once the child is conceived.

Your income shield will only work if it is in place *before* a pregnancy occurs. If you don't want children yet (or ever), it is essential to get ahead of the threat now. Then, make it clear to any potential partners before intimacy begins that your financial future is protected and inaccessible. A one-night stand is all a DTGD needs to turn your bank account into her personal annuity—no marriage required. Think of the USAF-FFT as a condom for your finances—without it, you're rolling the dice with your entire future. Get covered, or get comfortable with the reality that, sooner or later, the system will extract its pound of flesh, one child support order at a time.

If You Find Our Candor Too Harsh, Give Your Head a Shake

If reproductive coercion could be legally proven, the women who engage in it would be sent to prison, because it is a very serious crime. Instead, what do they get when they target affluent males? Multimillion dollar state-sponsored economic rewards for committing fraud and bringing children into the world without the consent of the target.

The USAF-FFT is designed to cap child support entitlements at an absolute maximum of $4000/mo. Over 18 years, that works out to $864,000. Close to a million dollars is still a grotesque economic reward for brazen fraud, but $864,000 isn't enough for most DTGDs. Those who practice reproductive coercion against affluent men aren't after survival—they are after *millions.*

The DTGD's Real Calculation: The Stigma of Single Motherhood

DTGDs do not see children as human beings. Instead, they see them as assets or liabilities. If you have visible signs of wealth, a reproductive coercion-focused DTGD will automatically classify you as a high-value target. But if you communicate to a DTGD that you are protected with a USAF-FFT, they will immediately reclassify you as a low- to zero-value target.

- A child is only a net positive when they help DTGDs secure considerably more child support than is needed to support them.
- A single mother with a hefty child support check from a high-status man can use that income as social proof, presenting herself as economically self-sustaining (with someone else's money)

rather than an economic predator. This enables them to move with ease from one victim to the next.

- On the other hand, a child is a net negative when they drain resources and limit the DTGD's ability to attach to their next target.

Why This Matters: Target Neutralization

The ultimate goal of this structure is to remove the economic incentive to trap you in a fraudulent pregnancy.

No DTGD wants to live on $2,500 to $4000 per month, especially when they are expected to spend the money on someone other than themselves. These predators are in it for high-dollar payouts, not basic subsistence income. When they realize the potential payout is negligible, they move on.

Take the Target Off Your Back—or Prepare to Pay the Price

American men, it's time to wake up. You have been targeted, exploited, and drained for far too long. It's time to stop being reactive and start proactively defending your future, your freedom, and your economic autonomy against exploitation.

Take action. Lock down your wealth. Protect yourself. Implement the USAF-FFT and shut down the economic assault.

No more games. No more extortion. No more weaponized pregnancies.

Lock it down—or be prepared to pay for a lifetime.

6

Why DTGDs Target You: The Financial and Emotional Profile of a Victim

The Anatomy of a Target

DTGDs do not strike randomly. They are calculated, strategic, and relentless in identifying individuals who are both financially lucrative and emotionally exploitable. Understanding why DTGDs target certain people is not just about recognizing external wealth—it's about uncovering the specific traits, circumstances, and blind spots that can make someone vulnerable to their tactics.

For the affluent reader, this chapter is meant to unsettle you. You have worked hard to build wealth, and you may believe that intelligence and business acumen make you immune to financial predators. But DTGDs don't attack where you are strong. They infiltrate where you are unguarded, leveraging not only your assets, but your values, your ambitions, and your emotions against you.

Financial Criteria: DTGDs' Goldmine

DTGDs are expert assessors of wealth potential. They study patterns of affluence and can identify high-value targets with frightening efficiency. If you fall into any of the following financial categories, understand that you are already on their radar:

- Publicly visible wealth – If you showcase luxury assets (real estate, cars, jewelry, high-end travel), DTGDs take notice. Wealth visibility makes you an easy mark.
- Intergenerational wealth – Those from old-money families or who stand to inherit significant estates are especially attractive.
- Highly liquid assets – Business owners, stock traders, or anyone with significant cash flow are prime targets because their money moves frequently and is easier to access.
- Self-made individuals with limited generational safeguards – Unlike those raised with structured financial defenses, self-made individuals are often overly trusting in relationships, believing that their work ethic and intelligence make them immune to being exploited.
- Privacy-focused wealth – Ironically, those who keep their wealth quiet may still be targeted. DTGDs frequently infiltrate social circles, charities, networking events, and industry groups to identify hidden affluence.

Emotional Profile: DTGDs' Key to Access

While financial status determines whether you are a viable payday, your emotional makeup determines whether you could be a willing participant in their long con. DTGDs don't just seek wealth—they seek targets who are susceptible to manipulation.

Here's what makes you vulnerable:

1. Being Overly Generous and Guilt-Prone

If you pride yourself on being a provider, a protector, or a fixer, you are a DTGD's dream. They will mirror your values, presenting themselves as people who just need "a little help" or "support during a tough time." Your kindness becomes a financial pipeline they can manipulate.

How they exploit you:

- They craft hardship stories that tug at your conscience.
- They introduce subtle financial dependencies early on.
- They invoke guilt if you suggest financial boundaries.

2. Seeking Validation

Affluent individuals often derive a sense of self-worth from their success. DTGDs know this and use constant admiration, sexual chemistry, and idealization to create an addiction to their approval. They make you feel like a god—until they don't.

How they exploit you:

- They rush intimacy and commitment, reinforcing the idea that they "see the real you."
- They create an emotional rollercoaster, withholding affection to make you work harder.
- They love-bomb, then subtly test whether they can make you doubt yourself.

3. Being a Workaholic or Distracted Partner

If you're always closing deals, building your empire, or managing investments, you might assume your partner values the lifestyle you provide and will not risk losing it.

But DTGDs don't just want wealth—they want control over it. They thrive in relationships where the affluent partner is too distracted to notice financial shifts until it's too late.

How they exploit you:

- They slowly integrate into your financial world while you're preoccupied.
- They engineer dependency—handling more and more "small financial tasks" until they control key aspects of your money and asset base.
- They isolate you from objective financial oversight (e.g., advisors, accountants, or family).

4. Being in Late Stages of Life

Older, divorced, or widowed individuals—especially those who have already experienced love and loss—are high-value marks. DTGDs exploit the desire for companionship, blending caregiver dynamics with financial dependence.

How they exploit you:

- They accelerate commitment, knowing that you feel the pressure of time.
- They isolate you from adult children and long-time advisors.
- They manipulate estate planning, ensuring they inherit over family members.

The Ultimate Trap: Thinking "This Could Never Happen to Me"

Perhaps the most dangerous trait of all is overconfidence. The belief that "I'm too smart to be conned" is exactly what allows DTGDs to succeed. They rely on:

- Your belief that you'd "spot the red flags" (they are experts at concealing them).
- Your assumption that they'd never risk losing your financial support (they don't care—they know exactly how much they

can extract before they leave).

- Your faith that financial manipulation only happens to "other people" (DTGDs target the best and brightest, precisely because they expect it the least).

If You Have What They Want, You Are at Risk

Being wealthy, successful, and powerful does not protect you from DTGDs—it attracts them. The only true protection is awareness and preemptive legal, financial, and emotional safeguards.

7

Love as a Weapon: How DTGDs Exploit Romantic Vulnerability

Blinded by Love (and Limerence)

Love is a force that binds, blinds, and reshapes perception. For DTGDs, this profound emotion becomes a weapon—one of the most effective tools for manipulation. By leveraging the emotional intensity of love and its more obsessive counterpart, limerence, DTGDs dismantle rational defenses and establish control.

This chapter explores how DTGDs manipulate romantic vulnerability, focusing on the psychological mechanisms they exploit. By understanding these tactics, readers can recognize the signs and regain control before becoming entangled in these emotionally destructive relationships.

The Neurochemistry of Love and Limerence

Falling in love triggers significant neurochemical changes in the brain. Dopamine, the "feel-good" neurotransmitter, creates euphoria and a sense of reward, much like the effects of stimulant drugs such as cocaine. This dopamine surge fosters a sense of addiction to the partner, impairing judgment and fostering emotional dependency.

Simultaneously, hormones like oxytocin and vasopressin, which promote bonding and trust, flood the brain. While these chemicals strengthen emotional connections, they also suppress the prefrontal cortex—the brain's decision-making center. This suppression results in idealization of the partner, hyper-focus on their positive traits, and a diminished ability to evaluate risks.

Limerence: Obsessive Infatuation

Limerence is an intensified state of romantic attachment characterized by intrusive thoughts and obsessive focus on the object of affection. In this heightened state, victims are more likely to overlook red flags and rationalize problematic behaviors. A 2010 study published in *The Journal of Neurophysiology* confirmed that romantic love activates the same neural pathways as addictive substances, leaving individuals vulnerable to exploitation by manipulative partners like DTGDs.

Key Differences Between Healthy Love and Limerence:

- Healthy love: Balanced, supportive, and allows for mutual growth. Both partners maintain individuality and respect boundaries.
- Limerence: Overwhelming, all-consuming, and marked by dependency. The partner becomes an obsession, impairing judgment and rationality.

How DTGDs Engineer Emotional Dependency

DTGDs excel at inducing and sustaining the neurochemical haze of love and limerence. Their deliberate strategies create deep emotional attachment, ensuring their victims become reliant on their presence and validation.

1. Love Bombing
From the outset, DTGDs overwhelm their victims with attention, compliments, and grand gestures. This tactic creates a dopamine rush, making the victims crave their validation and presence.

- Example: Lavish gifts, excessive compliments, and declarations of "you're the only one who understands me" within weeks of meeting.

2. Manipulating Love Languages
DTGDs identify and exploit their victims' primary love languages—whether it's words of affirmation, acts of service, physical touch, quality time, or gifts. By tailoring their behavior to meet these needs, DTGDs create the illusion of deep compatibility and emotional connection.

3. Intermittent Reinforcement
This psychological tactic mirrors the reward patterns behind gambling addiction. DTGDs alternate between affection and withdrawal, keeping victims in a state of seeking approval and validation. The unpredictability strengthens the emotional bond, as victims cling to moments of affection while ignoring the periods of neglect or manipulation.

4. Isolation
DTGDs sow seeds of distrust toward the victim's friends and family, monopolizing their time and eroding external support networks. By isolating their victims, DTGDs ensure their narratives remain unchallenged.

- Key warning sign: Phrases like "Your friends don't really understand us" or "Your family is just jealous of what we have."

Impairment in Decision-Making

Once emotionally dependent, victims often experience a significant decline in their ability to make rational decisions. DTGDs exploit this vulnerability to further their manipulation and control.

Common Examples of Impaired Decision-Making:

- Overlooking red flags: Victims rationalize inconsistencies in the DTGD's stories, dismiss controlling behaviors, or ignore a lack of genuine interest beyond material possessions.
- Financial risk-taking: Under the DTGD's influence, victims make uncharacteristically risky financial decisions, such as co-signing loans, merging bank accounts, or funding extravagant purchases.
- Erosion of boundaries: Victims compromise their values or personal boundaries to maintain relationships, leaving them more vulnerable to manipulation.

Exploitation of Wealth

Once a victim's defenses are dismantled, DTGDs pivot to extracting wealth and resources, often framing financial support as proof of devotion or necessary for the relationship's success.

1. Emotional Blackmail
DTGDs leverage their victims' feelings of love to elicit financial support. They frame monetary sacrifices as demonstrations of commitment or "necessary investments" in their shared future.

2. Fabricated Emergencies
By creating false crises, such as urgent medical needs or impending financial ruin, DTGDs manipulate their victims into providing monetary aid under the guise of altruism.

3. Leveraging Long-Term Commitments
Shared living arrangements, joint debts (e.g., a car purchase or real estate), co-mingled finances, "accidental" pregnancies, and marriage become tools for sustained financial control. These emotional and legal entanglements make it increasingly difficult for victims to extricate themselves from the relationships.

Recognizing the Pattern
Understanding the dynamics of love and limerence is the first step in breaking free from DTGD manipulation. Victims often struggle to recognize exploitation while under the influence of these powerful emotions, but key indicators include:

- A persistent sense of walking on eggshells or feeling anxious about pleasing the partner.
- Financial decisions that feel coerced or out of character.
- Estrangement from friends, family, or support networks due to the partner's influence.

Love as a Source of Strength, not Manipulation

While love and limerence are deeply human experiences, they can be weaponized by DTGDs to impair judgment and exploit wealth. By recognizing the tactics used to engineer emotional dependency, individuals can regain clarity and take proactive steps to protect themselves.

Proactive Measures to Counter Emotional Manipulation

1. Journal red flags: Keep a written record of concerning behaviors and emotional reactions. Reviewing these entries can provide clarity when the relationship feels overwhelming.
2. Consult trusted advisors: Share observations with friends, family, or therapists who can offer objective perspectives.
3. Set boundaries early: Establish financial and emotional boundaries at the outset of any relationship, and be wary of those who

challenge them.

4. Educate yourself: Learn about the neurochemical effects of love and limerence to recognize when emotions are impairing judgment.

Love should empower and enrich lives, not serve as a tool for manipulation. Knowledge is the antidote to exploitation, enabling victims to reclaim their autonomy and build relationships rooted in trust and authenticity.

8

THE DAMAGE DTGDs INFLICT

The High Stakes of Ignoring the Signs

Entering a relationship without safeguards—whether a prenuptial agreement or trust structures—is like placing your entire life's fortune on a single spin of the roulette wheel. The risk is enormous, the odds aren't in your favor, and when a DTGD is sitting across from you at the table, you're not just playing against chance—you're playing against a master manipulator who knows how to rig the game.

For those who fall prey to DTGDs, the losses extend far beyond finances. These calculated predators don't just take your money. They extract emotional security, sever relationships, and leave a lasting impact that reverberates through your family for generations. The damage is systemic, seeping into every corner of life—and rebuilding from that kind of devastation is no easy feat.

This chapter will walk you through the wreckage left behind by DTGDs—the financial destruction, the emotional fallout, the impact on family and reputation, and, ultimately, the long-term cost of failing to recognize the warning signs. The goal here isn't to stoke fear, but to inspire vigilance. Understanding the consequences makes it clear why you must protect yourself before you ever say, *"I do."*

Economic Devastation: The Long Road to Recovery

The financial toll of a DTGD doesn't happen overnight—it builds like a slow, calculated heist. Victims often don't recognize they're being drained until it's too late. The legal system, unfortunately, isn't built to protect the financially responsible. Instead, it's built to redistribute wealth under the guise of "fairness." By the time a DTGD is finished, you may find yourself financially ruined and forced to rebuild for years—if not decades.

Asset Depletion: When Everything You've Built Disappears

A DTGD is a financial black hole, capable of stripping away everything you've worked for. They do this in multiple ways:

- Liquidated properties: If you own properties, you may be forced to sell them to satisfy financial obligations. Jointly owned homes become battlegrounds, and, in many cases, the DTGD walks away with the majority of the profits.
- Lost investments: Business assets, intellectual property, and stock portfolios often aren't spared. You may be forced to cash out early or give up a significant share of what you've built.
- Savings and retirement funds: Many victims watch as their hard-earned savings and retirement accounts are siphoned away through settlements, legal fees, and ongoing financial obligations. The dream of retiring comfortably turns into a nightmare of delayed retirement—or worse, never retiring at all.

Long-Term Financial Burdens: A Life Sentence of Payments

The devastation doesn't stop at asset division. The state has mechanisms in place to ensure DTGDs continue to profit long after the ink on divorce decrees dries. These include:

- Spousal support: Depending on where you live, alimony payments can last for years, and sometimes indefinitely. The idea of supporting someone who actively sought to exploit you—and who is perfectly capable of working to support themselves—is enough to induce rage, but under the law, it's often perfectly legal.
- Child support manipulation: Many victims of DTGDs find themselves paying inflated child support far beyond what is necessary to care for the children. DTGDs weaponize the system, using children as financial pawns to extract more wealth.
- Endless legal fees: Even after divorce, disputes over payments, modifications, and financial obligations can keep you bouncing in and out of court, further depleting your resources.

Rebuilding after a DTGD is an uphill battle. You're not just dealing with the emotional wreckage of betrayal—you're starting over financially, often in your 40s, 50s, or beyond. It's a setback that few ever fully recover from, and that will typically push their retirement age out by years while dramatically reducing their standard of living in both their working years and retirement.

Emotional Fallout: The Silent Casualty

The financial loss of DGTDs can be staggering, but the emotional destruction they leave in their wake is just as crippling. The mind games they play can leave even the most confident, successful individuals questioning their own worth, intelligence, and ability to trust others.

Self-Esteem Erosion: The Damage Runs Deep

DTGDs are masters of psychological manipulation. They don't just exploit your finances—they exploit your emotions. Through a combination of love bombing, gaslighting, and calculated withdrawal, they create a state of dependency that makes their victims feel unworthy, inadequate, and utterly lost when the relationship ends. Rebuilding self-esteem after that kind of psychological warfare isn't easy.

Post-Traumatic Stress: The Lingering Effects of Betrayal

Many victims of DTGDs experience symptoms that mirror PTSD:

- Flashbacks to moments of manipulation and betrayal
- Anxiety and hypervigilance, making it difficult to trust future partners
- Depression and emotional numbness that lingers for years

The sense of loss extends beyond financial stability. It can include the loss of confidence, identity, and the ability to believe in one's own judgment. Healing requires therapy, self-reflection, and time, but even with all of these, the scars still remain.

Collateral Damage: The Ripple Effect on Families

DTGDs rarely operate in isolation. Their impact extends far beyond their primary victims. Families are torn apart, children are used as leverage, and intergenerational wealth that was meant to support future generations is drained to support DTGDs' greed.

The Children: Unwilling Participants in the Scheme

When children are involved, the devastation can be even greater. DTGDs manipulate custody arrangements, fabricate abuse allegations, and alienate children from the non-custodial parent to ensure maximum financial gain. The long-term damage is incalculable—children of these relationships often struggle with trust issues, emotional instability, and broken relationships with the parents who were erased from their lives.

Generational Consequences: The Legacy of Loss

- Drained inheritance: Money that was meant to benefit children and grandchildren is often lost in the financial warfare of divorce.
- Educational sacrifices: Funds earmarked for private schooling or college tuition may be redirected to satisfy financial settlements.

The financial toll of a DTGD relationship isn't just measured in lost income—it's measured in lost futures.

Reputation and Social Standing: The Calculated Attack

DTGDs are rarely satisfied with financial destruction. They will work to obliterate your reputation, using smear campaigns, false allegations, and character assassinations to ensure you're not just financially crippled, but socially and professionally ruined, as well.

When this happens, fighting back becomes a costly endeavor. Legal battles to counter defamation, attempts to rebuild professional credibility, and damage control within personal and social circles can take years. Many victims never recover their standing, even when the truth is revealed.

Awareness as the First Line of Defense

The damage inflicted by DTGDs is far-reaching. It's not just about money—it's about emotional health, family integrity, and future stability. Recognizing the red flags early, protecting yourself with the right legal structures, and having the courage to walk away before entanglement is critical.

No one wants to believe they could fall victim to a DTGD. But the truth is, even the smartest, most successful people have been taken down by these predators. Awareness isn't paranoia—it's power.

9

DARK TRIADS IN AFFLUENT CIRCLES

Predators in High Society

Affluent communities represent prime hunting grounds for DTGDs. Unlike opportunists who prey on accessible or unsuspecting targets, DTGDs operating in these circles employ sophisticated strategies designed to exploit the unique vulnerabilities of high-net-worth individuals. By blending charm, manipulation, and strategic deception, DTGDs embed themselves in wealthy environments, extracting financial and emotional gains while evading detection.

This chapter explores how DTGDs exploit affluent environments, the vulnerabilities that make these communities susceptible, and the strategies individuals and families can use to protect themselves from manipulation and financial harm.

Why Affluence Attracts DTGDs

Wealthy communities provide an ideal ecosystem for DTGDs. Financial privilege often obscures red flags, while societal perceptions of wealth and success make it easier for predators to gain trust and avoid scrutiny.

The "Follow the Money" Principle
DTGDs naturally gravitate toward environments where the potential for substantial financial gain is highest. Their preferred spaces include:

- Exclusive clubs and events: Charity galas, private fundraisers, and elite gatherings offer direct access to affluent individuals in a setting conducive to networking and trust-building.
- High-end networking venues: Country clubs, private gyms, and luxury lounges provide a casual yet exclusive environment for initial introductions.
- Digital platforms: Niche dating apps and professional networks like LinkedIn or Raya reveal lifestyle details and income levels that aid in targeting.

Wealth as a Magnet

Visible displays of wealth in affluent circles act as beacons for DTGDs. Subtle indicators such as designer clothing, luxury vehicles, or discussions about high-value investments signal opportunity. These predators are adept at picking up on clues during even casual interactions, using them to position themselves for exploitation.

The Tactics of DTGDs in Affluent Circles

Operating in high-net-worth environments requires DTGDs to employ refined strategies tailored to the cultural norms and dynamics of wealth. These tactics enable them to infiltrate social spaces and build influence without raising suspicion.

Blending in as Equals

DTGDs adopt personas that align with the expectations of affluent communities in order to gain credibility and trust:

- Fabricating backgrounds: Claiming prestigious education, high-status careers, or influential family connections.
- Mimicking lifestyles: Renting luxury items or curating social media profiles to project an image of affluence.
- Leveraging connections: Using mutual acquaintances or weak social ties to gain entry into exclusive circles and enhance credibility.

Exploiting Social Norms

Affluent individuals often adhere to strict codes of decorum, which DTGDs manipulate to avoid confrontation or scrutiny:

- Evasion tactics: Deflecting inquiries about their finances or backgrounds with charm and vague explanations.
- Rapid trust-building: Mirroring the targets' values, interests, and aspirations to accelerate emotional connections.
- Emotional intelligence: Navigating complex family dynamics to position themselves as indispensable confidants.

The Long Con

DTGDs in affluent circles are characterized by patience. They are willing to invest significant time—months or even years—building trust and embedding themselves in their targets' lives. This gradual approach reduces suspicion and maximizes their influence over financial decisions.

Unique Vulnerabilities of Affluent Communities

While wealth provides many advantages, it also introduces vulnerabilities that DTGDs are uniquely equipped to exploit. Understanding these weak points is essential for prevention.

Privacy and Isolation
Affluent individuals often value privacy, which can inadvertently create conditions that are conducive for manipulation:

- Insular social circles: Smaller networks limit access to external perspectives, making it harder for others to recognize or address red flags.
- Limited transparency: DTGDs will often mimic the "quiet wealth" values accepted in affluent circles to conceal personal details, reducing the likelihood of scrutiny from acquaintances or advisors.

Emotional Susceptibility
Despite financial security, emotional vulnerabilities persist among the affluent, creating opportunities for exploitation:

- Loneliness: Wealthy individuals may feel isolated by their success, making them more susceptible to manipulative attention.
- Trust-related challenges: Long-standing reliance on advisors or partners can lead to blind trust in new relationships.

Strategies for Defense in Affluent Circles

Mitigating one's vulnerability to DTGDs requires proactive measures that emphasize awareness, legal protections, and strong support networks. The following strategies are tailored to the unique challenges of high-net-worth environments.

1. Trust, but Verify
    - Conduct thorough background checks on new acquaintances, especially those seeking financial involvement.
    - Cross-check claims about education, career, and connections for inconsistencies.
    - Use digital tools to verify public records and social media profiles.

2. Establish Legal Safeguards
   - Trust structures first: Implement tools like FFTs, DAPTs, and FAPTs to shield assets from exploitation.
   - Prenuptial agreements: Clearly define asset division and financial expectations before entering marriage.
   - Cohabitation agreements: Protect premarital assets in long-term relationships that don't involve marriage.

3. Strengthen Support Networks
   - Maintain strong connections with trusted friends, family, and advisors who can offer objective perspectives.
   - Encourage open discussions about new relationships to identify potential red flags early.

A New Approach to Vigilance

DTGDs are calculated predators who exploit the unique vulnerabilities of affluent circles by blending in and manipulating trust. By recognizing their tactics and adopting proactive measures, individuals can safeguard their wealth, emotional well-being, and family legacies from predation. Affluence is not just a target for DTGDs—it is a proving ground where their methods become increasingly sophisticated. Remaining vigilant, informed, and prepared ensures that wealth remains a legacy, not a liability.

10

The DTGD's Goal: Redistribution of Your Wealth and Your Indentured Servitude

The Silent Contract You Never Signed

There's something profoundly unsettling about the idea that the moment you say, *"I do,"* you're also saying, *"I agree to whatever the state decides is fair if this doesn't work out."*

But that's the reality. Without a prenuptial agreement, you're not entering a marriage on your own terms—you're signing up for the state's default contract. And make no mistake, that contract was *not* designed to protect you. It was designed to redistribute your wealth in the event of a divorce.

DTGDs know this. They depend on it.

They don't just see marriage as a union of love and partnership.

They see it as a state-enforced financial entrapment—one where they can extract resources without consequence. The state's one-size-fits-all approach to asset division, spousal support, and entitlement ensures that, once they gain legal entrenchment, the system does the rest of the work for them.

Fortunately, you don't have to play by those rules.

You can *opt out.* You can reclaim your agency. But first, you have to wake up to what's really at stake.

The Price of Ignorance: What Happens When You Don't Have a Prenup

If you are foolish enough to forego the opportunity to set your own terms, you are making a decision that could haunt you for decades—potentially for the rest of your life. If you are affluent, the risks are even worse. No one is immune to the reality that half of all marriages end in divorce. Without a prenup, you're not just risking assets—you're risking your financial autonomy and freedom.

Let's break down exactly what's at stake:

1. Marital Asset Redistribution
   - Everything acquired during the marriage, regardless of who earned it, is divided in divorce.
   - Even the *appreciation* of assets you owned before marriage may be split.

2. Spousal Support
   - If your partner earns significantly less than you, you may be legally obligated to fund their lifestyle for years (if not decades).
   - Payments severely limit your ability to enjoy your life and the fruits of your labor post-divorce.

3. Retirement Savings and Future Earnings
   - Spousal support is often calculated to ensure the lower-earning spouse maintains the marital standard of living.

- Your future income, bonuses, and even pension payouts may be included in settlement calculations.

4. Child Support & Custody Manipulation
   - DTGDs exploit family law to maximize child support payments, using children as financial leverage.
   - Payments often far exceed actual costs, effectively funneling wealth into the DTGD's hands under the guise of "maintaining the child's standard of living."

Spousal Support: Modern-Day Indentured Servitude

For many people, divorce doesn't mean freedom. It means years—sometimes decades—of legally mandated financial servitude.

Critics of the system argue that long-term spousal support has become a relic of a time when marriage was an economic necessity for women. Today, with both partners usually capable of financial independence, why are we still enforcing lifetime financial obligations?

Why Spousal Support Feels So Unjust

1. It's an extended financial burden.
   - Payments often continue for years, sometimes indefinitely depending on the length of the marriage and the recipient's circumstances.

2. It disrupts your retirement savings.
   - Many payors struggle to build retirement savings while fulfilling alimony obligations.

3. It creates a disincentive to work.
   - The guaranteed financial support often discourages recipients from seeking employment or financial independence.

A Growing Movement for Reform

Financial experts and legal scholars are calling for changes to the system. Specifically, they are advocating for:

- Time-limited support: Phasing out lifetime alimony in favor of short-term, rehabilitative support.
- Income thresholds: Limiting payments for recipients with sufficient earning capacity.
- Default opt-outs: Encouraging couples to address spousal support *before* marriage through prenuptial agreements rather than relying on state-imposed rules.

The Cost of Spousal Support vs. the Cost of Freedom

If you need a wake-up call, let's talk numbers.

Imagine being required to pay $5,000 per month in spousal support for 10 years. That's $600,000 in total payments, not including adjustments for inflation or legal fees.

Now, imagine you invested that same $5,000 per month in a diversified portfolio with a 6% annual return. In the same 10 years, your portfolio would grow to over $820,000. After 20 years, you would have accumulated over $2.2 million in retirement savings—instead, your ex would have turned the idea of retirement into a distant fantasy.

The opportunity cost is staggering. And the real tragedy? Most people don't realize this until it's too late.

Using a Prenup to Opt-Out of Spousal Support

A prenuptial agreement is the most powerful way to avoid state-imposed financial obligations. By explicitly addressing spousal support, you can override the default system with a clear and unequivocal waiver of spousal support.

The FFT: The Ultimate Safeguard

If a prenup is your contract, the FFT is your enforcement mechanism. Here's why it's essential:

- It mandates a prenup. Without one, the trust automatically locks down your assets and future income, protecting them from the possibility of future spousal claims.
- It prevents legal loopholes. The structure ensures your wealth remains shielded.
- It deters DTGDs. Knowing there's no financial payday, most DTGDs who get wind of your protection system will abandon their scheme before it starts.

Control Your Financial Future

Wealth isn't just about money. It's also about freedom to make choices, build the life you want, and live on your own terms.

Marrying without a prenup is not an act of love—it's an act of financial negligence. The state's contract isn't written for you, it's written for redistribution. The only way to reclaim your autonomy is to opt out of the system before it traps you.

A prenup, backed by the FFT, isn't just about financial security—it's about self-respect.

11

Every DTGD's Nemesis: The Prenuptial Agreement

Why DTGDs Recoil at the Very Mention of a Prenup

The prenuptial agreement is one of the greatest weapons in your arsenal against DTGD exploitation. A well-crafted prenup is a financial firewall, eliminating the ambiguity and legal loopholes that a DTGD will attempt to exploit. That's why, in order of preference, a DTGD wants:

- No prenuptial agreement at all
- A "thin" prenup that leaves openings for legal attacks later
- A "shaky" prenup that they can strategically invalidate in divorce proceedings

Common DTGD tactics to invalidate or undermine prenups include:

- Claims of coercion: "I was pressured by my partner or their family."
- Last-minute signing arguments: "I signed too close to the wedding. I felt pressured and wasn't given time to review it."
- Lack of independent legal advice: "I didn't have my own lawyer, so it's unfair."
- Unconscionability claims: "The agreement is too one-sided to be enforceable."

This is why your approach to a prenup must be airtight, aggressive, and legally bulletproof from day one.

Did You Know That You Already Have a Prenup?

Most people assume prenups are optional. They are not. If you marry without a custom prenuptial agreement, you are automatically bound by the state's default prenup—a legal framework that prioritizes wealth redistribution. This is exactly what a DTGD *wants.*

The State's Default Prenup: What You're Agreeing to by Default

- Redistribution of assets: Everything acquired during the marriage—regardless of who earned it—becomes joint property.
- Spousal support (alimony): The higher-earning spouse may be required to pay alimony for years or even decades.
- Child support and custody leverage: DTGDs use child support laws to extract wealth well beyond actual child-rearing costs.

Without a custom prenup, the legal system is pre-built to favor the lower-earning spouse in divorce proceedings—making DTGDs virtually guaranteed to walk away richer than they entered.

Why DTGDs Fear a Custom Prenup

A properly drafted prenup disrupts the DTGD's entire financial playbook. It ensures:

- Outcome customization: Defines asset division, inheritance protection, and financial fairness on your terms.
- Full transparency: Forces both parties to disclose all financial details before marriage, preventing later claims of ignorance.
- Family wealth safeguards: Shields premarital assets, business holdings, and inherited wealth from being siphoned away.

However, a prenup alone is not enough. DTGDs are experts at circumventing prenups through legal loopholes, or having them invalidated altogether. That's where the FFT comes into play.

How the FFT Enhances Prenup Protections

A prenup protects you in divorce, but the FFT protects you by proactively securing your wealth and preventing economic entrenchment before the marriage has even started.

- Compulsory prenup requirement with built-in failsafe: Requires both parties to have independent legal advice to negotiate a prenup, but allows a DTGD to refuse.
- And if the DTGD refuses a prenup? No problem. Your assets and future income are locked down in other ways before they can lay claim to them through marriage.
- Automatic deterrence: The existence of the FFT signals to DTGDs that exploitation will be impossible, causing most to move on to easier prey.

The Preemptive Approach: How to Introduce the Prenup

If you casually mention a prenup without establishing its necessity, you risk triggering a manipulation storm filled with guilt-tripping and emotional coercion:

- "Why don't you trust me?"
- "A prenup is unromantic!"
- "You're already planning for a divorce!"
- "This means you don't believe in us."

To avoid this, it is important to shift the framing. Instead of presenting the prenup as optional, make it a non-negotiable financial policy.

1. Frame it as a requirement beyond your control.

- "This isn't about trust. I am legally required to have a prenup or an alternate mechanism because I set up an education, entrepreneurship, and housing fund for my nieces and nephews that requires me to protect the fund from third-party claims that include the possibility of divorce." (see Chapter 63) Or…
- "This isn't about you and me. It's a family policy that applies to all of us to protect future generations. For me, there's no way around it."

2. Pre-disclose FFT terms before negotiation.

- If you have an FFT, disclosure is a requirement. Make your partner aware that your trust is in place and share the trust deed with them before sitting down to discuss anything further. A quick read of your trust deed signals there is nothing left to debate.
- If they refuse to participate in negotiating a prenup, assets and future income will automatically be protected in alternative ways prior to a marriage event. The DTGD has no leverage.

Choosing the Right Prenup: The State's Version or Yours?

When you get married, you will have a prenup—the only question is whether it's yours or the state's default version.

A DTGD fears a custom, airtight prenup because it strips them of financial leverage. But a prenup alone is not enough. By pairing it with an FFT, you create an impenetrable financial fortress, ensuring that your wealth remains protected no matter what.

The key to preventing DTGD exploitation is not just defending against attacks—it's ensuring they never see you as a viable target to begin with.

12

Psychological Warfare: Breaking Down Prenup Objections

The Telltale Language of a Predator

For a DTGD, a prenup isn't just a legal contract—it's an existential threat. Their entire long-term financial strategy hinges on securing unrestricted access to your assets and future income. A well-structured prenuptial agreement slams that door shut. When faced with this obstacle, DTGDs don't necessarily just walk away—they adapt, manipulate, and escalate.

Understanding how DTGDs react before, during, and after prenup discussions is crucial. This chapter is about how they object and what they do next when their initial strategies fail.

Stage 1: The First Line of Resistance—Emotional Manipulation

The moment a prenup is introduced, the DTGD's first instinct is to provoke emotional conflict rather than rational debate. The goal is to shift the focus away from financial security and onto your commitment, trust, and love.

Common emotional objections include:

- *"A prenup is unromantic. You're already planning for us to fail."*
- *"If you really trusted me, this wouldn't even be a conversation."*
- *"This feels like you're treating me like some kind of gold digger."*

"• *If we're planning on forever, why does it matter?"*

DTGDs frame prenups as an attack on the relationship rather than a rational financial measure. The mistake most people make is trying to argue the logic of a prenup with someone who is determined to make it an emotional battleground.

Counter-strategy:

- Preempt the emotional manipulation. Before raising the topic, make it clear that this is non-negotiable and not personal.
- Shift the blame. Use external factors as reasoning. *"This isn't about you and me. It's a family policy that applies to everyone in my position."*
- Refuse to engage in guilt traps. When they say, *"You don't trust me,"* respond by saying, *"This isn't about trust—it's about ensuring fairness for both of us."*

If emotional tactics fail, the DTGD pivots to the next stage: delaying and undermining.

Stage 2: Passive Sabotage—Stalling, Delays, and Excuses

Once the emotional angle is exhausted, DTGDs will typically shift into a deliberate delay strategy. They hope that, by running out the clock, they can force you into a position where signing a prenup becomes impractical or legally questionable.

Common delay tactics include:

- Dragging out legal review: *"I haven't had time to meet with an attorney yet."*
- Claiming confusion: *"I don't understand all this legal stuff—I need more time."*
- Last-minute drama: *"I just don't feel good about this anymore. Can we talk after the wedding?"*
- Suggesting last-minute revisions: *"I'll sign, but I just want to tweak a few things."*

Counter-strategy:

- Set firm deadlines. Make it clear that the prenup must be signed well before the wedding—no exceptions. Be *unmistakably clear.* If the prenup isn't signed six months before the wedding date, the wedding date *will* be pushed out (or called off, as the case may be when a DTGD attempts to manipulate timelines to their advantage at your expense).
- Use independent legal review early on. Ensure they have their own attorney so they can't claim *"I didn't know what I was signing."*
- Maintain financial control. Until the prenup is signed, avoid any financial co-mingling or shared investments.

If delaying fails, the DTGD moves to their last-ditch effort: compliance with a hidden agenda.

Stage 3: The Trojan Horse—Agreeing to Sign While Harboring Future Sabotage Plans

A DTGD who realizes they can't avoid signing won't necessarily give up. Instead, they will plan their attack from inside the system. This is where they begin setting financial traps that circumvent the prenup entirely.

Post-prenup manipulation strategies include:

- Prenup invalidity claims: *"I felt pressured to sign"* (coercion/duress). *"I didn't fully understand what I signed"* (an attempt to challenge the prenup in court).
- Strategic parenthood: An "accidental" pregnancy to circumvent the prenup (child support operates independent of prenups and guarantees long-term entitlements).

Final Thought: The Prenup Is Just the First Battle

Signing a prenup does not mean the fight is over. DTGDs are long-term strategists who see financial extraction as an endurance game. If they can't win before the marriage, they'll try to win during it.

The key to real protection is not just having a prenup, but also anticipating and neutralizing post-nuptial financial sabotage before it happens. At the end of the day, the only people who fear a prenup are the ones who see a financial advantage in not having one. If someone genuinely loves you for you—not for your money—a prenup should be nothing more than a formality that reinforces mutual respect.

If someone fights you tooth and nail over it, that's your biggest red flag yet. Don't just walk away—run.

13

Hiding Fraud Behind Systemic Inequalities

The DTGD's Exploitation Narrative

Like it or not, statistical evidence illustrates an irrefutable truth: Heterosexual women are by far the greatest perpetrators of these forms of fraud and abuse. Meanwhile, heterosexual men are by far the most common victims.

But when dissecting the insidiousness of how DTGDs manipulate their victims and the legal system, there is another fundamental truth that must also be acknowledged: Systemic disadvantages do exist. Women, on average, continue to receive lower wages, face career stagnation due to caregiving responsibilities, and have fewer financial opportunities. These facts are well-documented and supported by economic data.

Having acknowledged this, it is important to note that this chapter is not about those inequalities and realities. This chapter is about how DTGDs weaponize these truths as a smokescreen for their own fraud, laziness, and greed—deliberately hiding behind legitimate struggles to justify premeditated financial extraction from their victims.

DTGDs do not suffer in the way that victims of real systemic disadvantages do. They are not languishing in low-wage jobs or locked out of financial mobility due to discriminatory hiring practices. No, DTGDs are schemers perfecting a well-oiled con that leverages the struggles of genuinely disadvantaged individuals to mask their opportunism. It is a cover-up of staggering effectiveness, allowing DTGDs to manipulate public sympathy, cancel critics, and extract wealth with impunity.

If you dare to call them out, they will shame you, gaslight you, and label you as heartless—as someone who just "doesn't get it." But we *do* get it. It's time to drag these con artists out from the shadows of authentic suffering and expose them for what they truly are.

The Well-Rehearsed Narrative: A Rinse-and-Repeat Economic Windfall

Why reinvent the wheel when the same fraudulent narrative works time and time again? The DTGD playbook is not innovative—it is a predictable, cynical manipulation of existing social narratives designed to extract maximum financial gain from divorce after divorce and settlement after settlement. It follows the same rinse-and-repeat formula because it is highly effective.

DTGDs do not present themselves as con artists—they present themselves as victims. They craft a sob story, a narrative so steeped in half-truths and selective framing that it deflects all scrutiny while painting them as a wronged party in need of justice. They weaponize legitimate gender-based inequities to frame their strategic financial extractions as justified compensation rather than outright theft.

- *"I gave up my career for this marriage—I deserve to be supported for life."*
- *"I was emotionally and financially controlled—I am entitled to half of everything."*
- *"I sacrificed so much for them—they need to pay for what they've done."*

Make no mistake: Real victims do exist. But DTGDs are not real victims. They are grifters abusing a system designed to protect the vulnerable so they can cash out with a personal payday.

Fraud Disguised as Advocacy

DTGDs do not advocate for social justice. They hide behind it, using real societal problems as a personal shield against accountability. When challenged, they aggressively conflate criticism of their actions with criticism of the broader movement they parasitize.

- If you call out their financial exploitation, they accuse you of not supporting gender equality.
- If you demand accountability, they claim you are victim-blaming.
- If you attempt to protect yourself, they argue that you are "planning for the end" and "don't believe in love."

This is why their fraud has been so successful and remained unchallenged for so long—they have wrapped themselves in the armor of an authentic cause, making any criticism of them feel like an attack on progress itself.

Time to Call It What It Is

For too long, people have been too polite, too afraid of backlash, and too hesitant to point out what is painfully obvious: There is a predatory class of individuals who systematically manipulate societal protections for their own financial gain.

Enough is enough. It is time to separate legitimate suffering from weaponized victimhood. DTGDs are not struggling against systemic oppression—they are weaponizing the suffering of others for personal enrichment.

This is not about punishing or blaming the economically disadvantaged. This is about dragging economic predators into the light and holding them accountable for the lives they destroy.

They ruin marriages. They bankrupt victims. They disinherit children. They gut legacies built over generations. And they do all of this while playing the victim, counting on society's discomfort in questioning their narrative.

The time for discomfort is over. The conversation has begun and the fraud must be exposed. The predators must be stopped.

14

Hypervigilance Among the Affluent Has Never Been More Important

Things Are About to Get a Lot Worse for the Affluent

A new era of scarcity is upon us, and for DTGDs, the survival game is about to get far more brutal. The economic and technological landscape is shifting in ways that threaten to reduce the number of eligible victims dramatically. As their primary sources of financial extraction dwindle, DTGDs will be forced to escalate their tactics—moving faster, becoming more covert, and deploying ever-more manipulative strategies to entrench themselves before their targets recognize the threat.

The convergence of three seismic changes is on the verge of triggering this perfect storm:

- AI's displacement of traditional high-income earners and the impending onset of universal basic income (UBI).
- The advent of male birth control, ending reproductive coercion as a DTGD strategy.
- The mainstreaming of affordable legal deterrents against DTGD exploitation.

These three factors will force DTGDs into a ruthless competition for fewer and fewer high-value targets, a scenario that will bring chaos to their game while making them more desperate than ever. Some will be forced to adapt, while others will be left with no choice but to support themselves—a fate they've spent their entire existence avoiding.

1. AI's Displacement of Wealth and the Imminent UBI Shift

For generations, gold diggers have thrived in social and professional settings where wealth was predictable and accessible—luxury bars, networking events, corporate workplaces, and high-end social circles. But AI is dismantling this entire economic order. Experts predict that 80% of today's jobs will be replaced by artificial intelligence *in the very near future,* forcing governments worldwide to implement UBI to prevent widespread economic collapse.

For DTGDs, this is a catastrophe that will result in:

- Fewer self-made millionaires: The traditional pipeline of ambitious professionals climbing the corporate ladder will shrink dramatically. New wealth creation will consolidate into the hands of AI entrepreneurs, data monopolists, and a handful of outlier industries, leaving far fewer accessible targets.
- Hypervigilance among already-affluent targets: Those with preexisting wealth will defend it with never-before-seen levels of legal protections and deterrents, knowing that wealth will be virtually impossible to replace in the post-AI era of humanity centered

around a UBI-based economy.
- AI-vetted social circles: High-net-worth individuals are increasingly relying on AI-driven partner vetting systems, using sophisticated tools to filter out financial opportunists before even meeting them.
- Economic Darwinism in full effect: With the general population living on government stipends, the dating market will polarize and DTGDs will be forced to compete with one another in ways they never have before.

For the first time, DTGDs will be fighting for a drastically smaller slice of financial opportunity—and the first to lose will be the ones who can't adapt.

2. The Advent of Male Birth Control: The End of "Baby Trapping"

For decades, reproductive coercion has been one of the most effective tools in a female DTGD's arsenal, with 9.7% of men reporting having been targeted in this way (the rate is even *higher* among the affluent). The ability to lock in child support entitlements for 18+ years through strategic pregnancies has been a failsafe mechanism for DTGDs to secure long-term financial extraction.

But this pillar of the DTGD strategy is about to collapse.

- Reversible male birth control pills and injectables: Pharmaceutical advances are bringing temporary but highly effective male contraceptives to market, giving men full control over their reproductive choices. This is an absolute game-changer for putting an end to reproductive coercion.
- Vasectomies are on the rise: More high-net-worth men are opting for vasectomies, eliminating the risk of coerced pregnancy altogether. A growing trend among the affluent is to freeze sperm before undergoing vasectomies, allowing them to have children

only on their own terms, rather than being trapped into parenthood via deception.

This development neutralizes one of the most devastating (and disturbingly common) DTGD strategies. Without the ability to leverage children for financial entrenchment, many female DTGDs will lose one of their most reliable methods of wealth extraction almost overnight. Equally devastating to their playbook, DTGDs will no longer be able to circumvent prenups by having "accidental" pregnancies that lock in decades of child support entitlements.

3. High-Caliber Legal Deterrents Becoming More Accessible

Historically, DTGDs thrived because their targets lacked knowledge and legal defense tools. The idea of setting up a high-end asset protection system or ironclad prenup alternative was once reserved for the ultra-wealthy, requiring specialized attorneys and tens of thousands of dollars in legal fees. That is no longer the case.

Today, for less than $1,000, an individual can set up a proactive financial defense system that legally blocks DTGDs from ever gaining access to their assets and future income. This includes the rise of services like:

- FFTs: Trust structures that automatically lock up assets and future income prior to a marriage event and DTGD financial entrenchment.
- Digital background checks: AI-powered tools that screen potential partners for financial opportunism before committing to a relationship.
- Comprehensive prenup packages: Fully customizable, ironclad prenups are now available at a fraction of their historical cost.

As these tools become mainstream among the affluent and soon-to-be-affluent, the potential victim pool will shrink even further. More people will enter relationships with financial protections already in place, making it exponentially harder for DTGDs to find unguarded prey.

What This Means for the Future

With fewer wealthy, accessible victims, expect to see a world where:

- DTGDs must compete viciously against one another for a dwindling number of exploitable targets.
- More DTGDs will be forced to hold actual jobs, as their ability to siphon wealth through marriage, child support, and manipulation erodes.
- Male victims will become significantly harder to trap, due to reproductive control and legal foresight.

This does not mean DTGDs will disappear. Instead, they will evolve into even more aggressive, strategic, and ruthless predators, using new deception tactics and pivoting to fresh opportunities for exploitation.

The War Is About to Escalate

The new era of DTGD scarcity will push these individuals to the brink, forcing them to resort to tactics we have yet to see fully play out. Expect:

- Shorter manipulation timelines: DTGDs will work faster, knowing their window to entrench is closing.
- More covert legal maneuvering: Expect more challenges to prenuptial agreements, more fabricated domestic abuse claims, and new legal loopholes weaponized for financial gain.
- Attempts to circumvent AI-driven screening: DTGDs will attempt to outmaneuver AI-driven vetting and infiltrate the lives of even those who are hypervigilant in their defenses.

For those who are informed and protected, the risks will mitigated.

But for those who remain ignorant and unprotected, the risks will be greater than ever before.

The age of easy wealth extraction is ending. What comes next will be even more ruthless, more calculated, and more dangerous.

The only defense? Be prepared before they find you.

15

ARE THEY A DTGD OR THE REAL DEAL?

The Question of Authenticity

Not every less-monied spouse is a DTGD. Recognizing this distinction is vital to avoid unnecessary paranoia while fostering relationships built on trust, mutual respect, and authenticity. DTGDs are cunning and manipulative, while authentic partners—the "Real Deal"—seek genuine connection over financial gain.

This chapter explores how to differentiate between a DTGD and a genuine partner. It provides actionable strategies to evaluate intent and behavioral cues that signal authenticity. As a guiding principle, remember that the Real Deal will have no hesitation discussing financial boundaries or signing a prenuptial agreement.

Defining the Real Deal

Authentic partners prioritize the health and happiness of their relationships over personal gain. They value connection, shared goals, and mutual support. Their behavior consistently reflects transparency, independence, compromise, and respect.

Key Traits of the Real Deal

- Transparency: Openly discusses finances, goals, and boundaries, without evasion.
- Independence: Maintains a career, personal goals, financial literacy, or a combination of the three, demonstrating self-sufficiency.
- Compromise: Actively works to resolve conflicts and meet mutual needs collaboratively.
- Respect: Honors values, boundaries, and concerns without resorting to manipulation.

In contrast, DTGDs are defined by entitlement, deceit, and exploitation. Understanding these differences enables you to effectively evaluate relationships.

Key Indicators of Authenticity

1. Comfort with a Prenup: A prenup is not a "trap," but a test of intent. Authentic partners ultimately understand the prenup's purpose: fostering clarity and fairness. To this end, they:
    - Respect your desire for financial transparency and security.
    - Engage in open discussions about the agreement's terms.
    - Seek independent legal advice without resistance.

On the other hand, DTGDs resist or manipulate the conversation, often using objections like "It's so unromantic" or "You don't trust me."

2. Consistency in Behavior: Authenticity is reflected in predictable, stable actions. Genuine partners:
    - Follow through on promises.
    - Exhibit stable emotional and financial behaviors over time.

- Avoid dramatic shifts in personality or values.

In contrast, DTGDs often exhibit erratic behavior, including sudden changes in generosity, affection, or financial habits.

3. History of Independence: The Real Deal demonstrates self-sufficiency through:
    - Sustained career pursuits or personal ambitions.
    - Financial responsibility without reliance on others.
    - Avoiding premature merging of finances or enmeshment.

DTGDs fabricate narratives of their own financial independence and encourage financial enmeshment to gain control.

4. Respect for Financial Boundaries: Authentic partners respect financial boundaries by:
    - Supporting your desire for clarity and security.
    - Avoiding undue pressure to make financial sacrifices.
    - Accepting "no" without resentment.

On the other hand, DTGDs push against boundaries, using guilt, coercion, or emotional appeals to bypass them.

5. Focus on Long-Term Goals: The Real Deal aligns with you on shared, future-focused goals, such as:
    - Building a stable future together.
    - Supporting each other's personal and professional growth.
    - Prioritizing long-term well-being over short-term gratification.

DTGDs prioritize immediate material benefits over building a meaningful connection.

Testing for Authenticity

Practical scenarios and discussions can reveal whether a partner's intentions are genuine or manipulative.

1. Observe Under Stress: True character is revealed during adversity. Assess how your partner handles:
    - Financial setbacks: Do they respond with support and collaboration or manipulate the situation?
    - Unexpected changes: Are they solution-oriented or dismissive?
    - Conflict: Do they compromise or resort to control and blame?
    - Genuine response: Authentic partners remain supportive, adaptable, and collaborative.

2. Discuss the Future: Conversations about the future reveal intentions. The Real Deal will:
    - Engage in honest discussions about shared goals.
    - Address challenges openly and realistically.
    - Prioritize mutual planning over unilateral benefits.

By contrast, DTGDs avoid specifics, exaggerate commitment, or focus disproportionately on material aspects.

3. Look for Reciprocity: Healthy relationships are built on give and take. Evaluate whether your partner:
    - Contributes emotionally and practically.
    - Shows appreciation and reciprocates acts of kindness.
    - Balances the relationship dynamics fairly.

DTGDs exploit imbalances, consistently taking without giving.

When in Doubt: The Prenup Test

A genuine partner views a prenuptial agreement as an opportunity for clarity and trust-building. The Real Deal will approach the discussion with:

- Maturity: Recognizing its fairness and purpose.
- Collaboration: Actively participating in creating balanced terms.
- Respect: Seeking independent advice to protect mutual interests.

DTGDs may deflect, delay, or manipulate the discussion, framing it as an insult to trust or love.

Authenticity: The Foundation of Lasting Relationships

Distinguishing between a DTGD and a genuine partner is essential for long-term happiness and security. By focusing on authenticity, transparency, and mutual respect, you can build a relationship that stands the test of time. The Real Deal embraces fairness, compromise, and shared goals, proving their intentions through consistent actions.

DTGD Attack Vectors

16

Archetype #1: The Classic Con—No Prenup, No Escape

DTGDs operate with one primary objective: financial extraction. However, their methods vary, depending on circumstances, legal positioning, and the target's level of financial protection. Each DTGD will follow a predictable pattern, but the specific tactics they employ will depend on how well-defended their target is against economic entrapment.

This section of the book will break down the most common DTGD archetypes, showing how they adapt their strategies based on the level of financial security in place. Some DTGDs prefer the "long game" of asset accumulation, while others use high-speed, high-reward cons that allow them to extract wealth and move on. The baseline strategy, however—the gold standard of DTGD success—is securing a no-prenup marriage.

If a DTGD can bypass legal safeguards completely, they maximize their financial windfall with minimal effort. Every DTGD archetype builds off this foundation, adding more elaborate tactics for cases where targets have partial protections in place. But if they can walk into a marriage without restrictions? That's the jackpot.

Why This Is the Ultimate DTGD Scenario

- No financial guardrails: They get full access to marital assets and future income by default.
- State laws favor them: Divorce courts do not care how wealth was accumulated, they only prioritize "fair division."
- Maximum payout, minimum effort: Unlike business fraud or financial scams, this strategy requires no skill—only patience.
- Built-in legal enforcement: They don't have to fight for money, as the state enforces the wealth transfer for them.

A no-prenup marriage means the DTGD's job is done the moment you say, *"I do."* All they have to do is stay married long enough to ensure that when the separation comes (and it always does), they are entitled to the largest possible payout.

Why Affluent Individuals Keep Falling for This Con

Despite its predictability, the no-prenup trap continues to ensnare high-net-worth individuals throughout the generations. Why? Because it doesn't feel like a trap at the time.

1. "They love me, not my money."
    - Victims believe emotional connection outweighs financial risk.
    - DTGDs frame prenups as a betrayal, making their targets hesitant to push the issue.

2. "Prenups are unromantic."
    - DTGDs will convince their targets that marriage is about trust, not contracts.

- This emotionally reframes legal protections as an attack on the relationship.

3. "It won't happen to me."
    - Many victims assume their relationships are different.
    - Cognitive dissonance keeps them from seeing the financial risk clearly.

4. The pressure of time and social expectations.
    - DTGDs often rush engagements and weddings to limit time for legal negotiations.
    - DTGDs will encourage family members and their friends to reinforce the urgency, making a prenup discussion feel unnecessary or even inappropriate.

By the time the wedding day arrives, the DTGD has already won. The only legal contract they need is already signed and filed with the state, and their financial extraction strategy is guaranteed to pay out when the marriage ends. Postnuptial agreement? Forget it. You walked right into this trap and you've been had.

How DTGDs Extract Maximum Wealth in a No-Prenup Marriage

Once inside the marriage, the DTGD doesn't have to be in a rush to leave—because the longer they stay, the bigger the payout becomes.

Key DTGD Tactics Post-Marriage

- Accumulating assets under marital property laws: Encouraging home purchases, joint investments, and shared financial accounts to blend assets and maximize their claim.
- Avoiding career progression: Ensuring they remain financially dependent, increasing potential spousal support entitlements.

- Weaponizing emotional and psychological manipulation: Manufacturing guilt, obligation, or "partner responsibilities" to justify financial reliance.
- Delaying the exit until financial leverage is absolute: DTGDs know that divorcing too soon might result in a lower payout, so they wait until the maximum asset transfer is secured.

By the time they file for divorce, their targets are already financially entangled beyond repair. The law will enforce the financial split—whether or not the victim agrees to it.

The Baseline for All Other DTGD Strategies

Every other DTGD archetype builds upon this foundational strategy. When a no-prenup marriage is off the table, they adapt and escalate, using different forms of legal, financial, and emotional entrapment.

In the next few chapters, you will see how DTGDs evolve their tactics when faced with resistance. These include:

- No-Prenup Marriage + Kids: The "Entitlement Accelerator" (locking in child support for guaranteed financial extraction).
- Prenup-Protected Marriage: The "Workaround" (finding loopholes to render prenups useless).
- The Permanent Fixture: A DTGD who never plans to leave, but instead drain resources for life.
- The Grave Robber: Targeting inheritances and estate manipulation as their financial strategy.

Each of these variations stems from the same fundamental blueprint. If a DTGD can't take everything up front, they will find alternative ways to extract wealth over time.

Final Thought: The No-Prenup Marriage Is Not Just a Mistake—It's an Invitation to Be Exploited

A DTGD doesn't need to be a master manipulator if their target voluntarily leaves the door wide open. If there is no prenup in place, the battle is already lost.

In the next chapter, we will explore how DTGDs escalate their financial entrapment even further—securing both spousal and child support to create a lifetime income stream at their victims' expense.

17

Archetype #2: The No-Prenup Marriage + Kids (aka "The Entitlement Accelerator")

A Greedy Double Dip

Marriage is supposed to be a partnership—a union built on love, trust, and mutual growth. When children are brought into that partnership, they are meant to be cherished, nurtured, and protected. But for a DTGD, marriage isn't about love and children aren't about family. They are strategic assets—a means to establish the most lucrative financial entanglement available *as quickly as possible.*

For a DTGD, the goal isn't just divorce with a payout—it's about maximizing financial gain through the legal system. What better way to achieve that than by securing not one, but two streams of decades-long financial support? Spousal support locks in post-divorce income, while child support guarantees a separate, often untouchable monthly payment. It's the ultimate greedy double dip, executed under the guise of caregiving and victimhood.

How DTGDs Weaponize Parenthood

For most people, having children is a life-altering decision that comes with deep emotional, financial, and ethical considerations. For a DTGD, it's an economic strategy—one that begins long before the child is even conceived.

DTGDs accelerate discussions about having children, insisting that "starting a family" is a natural progression of the relationship. They frame it as an act of love, a deepening of commitment, or even fate. But, beneath the surface, it's a calculated financial maneuver designed to create a lifelong entitlement pipeline.

An alarmingly high number of DTGDs will even resort to reproductive coercion, secretly tampering with birth control or feigning infertility struggles to push their partners into parenthood before they're ready. Others will manipulate emotions, saying things like:

- *"A baby will bring us closer together."*
- *"You'll be such an amazing parent—I can't wait to raise a family with you."*
- *"We're soul mates. Why wait?"*

It sounds romantic and it feels like love, but the reality is that, once that child is born, the financial framework changes forever.

The Financial Jackpot: Spousal and Child Support

Once a child enters the equation, the DTGD's financial entrenchment strategy is fully activated. Spousal support alone is a lucrative win, but child support is the real jackpot. Unlike alimony, which can sometimes be modified or terminated, child support is nearly untouchable. It's calculated based on income, often without strict accountability for how the funds are actually used.

Spousal Support: A Long-Term Investment

DTGDs know that spousal support entitlements typically increase based on the length of the marriage. Many legal systems have a sliding scale for alimony, which means a DTGD might need to stay married for years to accrue their maximum spousal support entitlement (which typically maxes out at 50% of the ex-spouse's income—often indefinitely). Child support, on the other hand, is an instant jackpot.

The Instant Payoff of Child Support

Unlike spousal support, which requires years of legal entrenchment, child support entitlements begin the moment a child is born. There is no waiting period. There is no time-based threshold to meet. A DTGD who has a child instantly secures court-enforced financial entitlements—and the more children they have, the larger their monthly payout becomes.

- More kids, more cash: With each child, the amount of child support increases, creating a scalable financial windfall.
- Income-based calculation: The higher the income of the paying parent, the higher the mandated payments—regardless of actual child-rearing expenses.
- No oversight: There is little to no regulation on how child support money is spent, meaning funds can be funneled into luxury items, vacations, or personal expenses, rather than the child's actual needs.

The system rewards this kind of financial abuse. The more children a DTGD produces, the more leverage they have in the courts. And, because child support is seen as sacrosanct, challenging or modifying these payments—even in cases of financial hardship—can be an uphill battle.

Emotional and Generational Consequences

The financial impact of a DTGD's double dip is massive, but the emotional cost is just as devastating. Children become bargaining chips, used to control, punish, and manipulate the targeted parent.

The Weaponization of Custody

A DTGD doesn't see co-parenting as a shared responsibility. Instead, they see it as a battleground. They know that primary custody equals larger financial entitlements in most cases, so they weaponize custody battles to their advantage.

- Parental alienation: DTGDs manipulate children to turn them against the other parent, fostering resentment and emotional distance.
- Fabricated physical abuse and neglect claims: False allegations of abuse or neglect are used to gain leverage in custody disputes, ensuring sole custody and maximum financial gain.
- Fabricated alcohol and drug abuse claims: False or embellished allegations of alcohol and drug abuse are often used to secure the additional financial windfall that comes with being awarded sole custody.
- Litigation as a weapon: By dragging out custody battles, DTGDs create emotional and financial exhaustion, making it easier to force settlements in their favor.

How to Protect Yourself: Ironclad Birth Control

The best way to prevent financial entrenchment is to eliminate unintended parenthood as a vulnerability. If someone is pushing for children early in a relationship, that alone should be a red flag.

For those who want to ensure they retain control over their reproductive choices, there are ironclad birth control measures that can prevent reproductive coercion:

- For men: A vasectomy is the single most effective way to prevent unwanted paternity. It's a permanent (albeit potentially reversible) solution that removes any chance of birth control sabotage or "accidental" pregnancies.
- For women: Long-acting reversible contraceptives (LARCs) such as an intrauterine device (IUD) or hormonal implants are highly effective, nearly impossible to tamper with, and last for years.
- For both: Combining multiple forms of birth control (e.g., condoms plus a LARC) ensures the highest level of protection.

A Calculated Evolution

DTGDs who exploit both spousal and child support systems represent the most dangerous iteration of financial predation. They aren't just opportunists, they are strategists, engineering a system that entraps their targets for decades while bringing children into the mix for economic gain rather than for the love and joy of raising a family.

Recognizing these tactics, taking proactive legal measures, and standing firm when it comes to financial and emotional boundaries is the only way to safeguard your future. The good news? Awareness is power. When you see the game for what it is, you can refuse to play.

In the next chapter, we'll explore how DTGDs circumvent even the most airtight prenuptial agreements—and what you can do to stop them before they start.

18

Archetype #3: The Prenup-Protected Marriage with Kids (aka "The Workaround")

When a Shield Becomes a Paper Wall

A well-crafted prenuptial agreement should act as an ironclad defense—a protective barrier ensuring financial fairness and clarity. But DTGDs are nothing if not adaptable. When faced with a prenup that limits their financial windfall, they don't admit defeat—they pivot. They seek out loopholes, manipulate legal gray areas, and, when all else fails, deploy the ultimate workaround: child support entitlements.

This chapter dives into the tactics DTGDs use to circumvent even the most airtight prenuptial agreements—from strategic pregnancies to emotional warfare—and what you can do to fortify your financial defenses against their relentless pursuit of economic control.

The Prenup Illusion: Why It's not Always Enough

Many high-net-worth individuals breathe a sigh of relief once a prenup is signed. They believe it's a done deal—a final safeguard ensuring their wealth remains protected. But what they fail to understand is that a prenup is only as strong as the legal system enforcing it—and that system has holes big enough for a DTGD to waltz right through.

Prenups can limit or eliminate spousal support, define asset distribution, and even put restrictions on shared finances, but they cannot override child support laws. And that's where DTGDs find their workaround.

Tactic #1: The Pregnancy Power Play

The moment a child enters the equation, the legal landscape shifts entirely in the DTGD's favor. They now have:

- An instant financial claim: Child support payments kick in regardless of the circumstances of conception.
- Guaranteed long-term payments: Child support often lasts 18+ years. In some cases, it continues through college.
- A weaponized custody battle: The DTGD can use custody as leverage to demand higher payments or gain further legal entitlements.

Reproductive Coercion as a Strategy

For many, an unplanned pregnancy is a life-altering event. For a DTGD, it's a career move. Reproductive coercion—the act of tampering with birth control, lying about contraception use, or outright deception around fertility—is a tactic many DTGDs use to create an irreversible financial link to their target.

Common DTGD pregnancy manipulation tactics include:

- Tampering with birth control (e.g., poking holes in condoms or stopping the use of oral contraceptives without informing their partner).
- Self-insemination with post-intercourse condoms (i.e., offering to "dispose of" a condom after intercourse and disappearing to the bathroom for a "long shower.")
- Feigning infertility to gain a false sense of trust around "safe" unprotected sex.
- Sabotaging medical decisions (e.g., lying about taking emergency contraception).
- Deliberate "accidents" (convincing their partner that conception was purely coincidental when, in reality, it was premeditated).

Tactic #2: Weaponizing Child Custody Laws

Even if a DTGD only manages to secure a single child, that child becomes the ultimate financial anchor—a lifelong connection to their victim's bank account.

The Custody Battlefield

DTGDs understand that primary custody equals financial control. Courts are often biased toward awarding primary custody to the parent who has historically been the "primary caregiver," which gives DTGDs every incentive to construct a narrative of being the more "nurturing" parent while strategically excluding their partner from parenting roles.

Once custody is secured, they can:

- Demand higher child support payments under the guise of "ensuring the child's standard of living."
- Use the child as a legal pawn to continue controlling their ex-spouse's decisions and finances.
- Prevent modifications to child support agreements by creating

legal roadblocks, such as fabricating emotional distress in the child.

The Never-Ending Financial Connection

Child support obligations are notoriously difficult to modify, even in cases where the recipient parent is misusing the funds or the payer's financial situation has changed. Courts tend to err on the side of "protecting the child's interests," which means that a DTGD can ensure a consistent financial pipeline with minimal accountability.

Some DTGDs take it a step further by pushing for additional financial entitlements beyond child support:

- Extraordinary expenses: Courts often grant additional support for "extraordinary expenses" like private school tuition, extracurricular activities, or medical treatments, further increasing financial obligations.
- Extended dependency: In some jurisdictions, child support can be extended beyond 18 years if the child pursues higher education or has special needs—another potential DTGD exploitation tactic.
- Life insurance mandates: Some DTGDs push for legal orders requiring the paying parent to maintain a life insurance policy with them as the beneficiary, ensuring continued financial gain even after death.

Closing the Loopholes

DTGDs who target prenup loopholes are playing a long game—one designed to outmaneuver legal protections and ensure a lasting financial windfall. The only way to counteract these tactics is through rigorous legal preparation, ironclad financial structures, and unwavering personal boundaries. The FFT proactively addresses this highly predictable DTGD attack vector by providing US-resident males who haven't had a vasectomy to have a qualifying domestic asset protection trust (QDAPT) *regardless* of whether the SO agrees to a qualifying prenuptial agreement (QPA). The QDAPT effectively caps the income amount available for consideration by family courts in calculating combined spousal support + child support to a modest amount, thereby dramatically reducing the economic incentive for spousal support or an "accidental" pregnancy. When a male FFT-settlor has children by choice, the settlor-appointed trust protector can modify or eliminate this requirement.

Recognizing their strategies, taking proactive legal steps, and never allowing emotional manipulation to dictate financial decisions is the key to remaining in control of your future.

19

Archetype #4: The Permanent Fixture

A Life of Luxury, Without Love

For some DTGDs, the objective isn't a dramatic divorce settlement or a calculated breakup—it's a lifetime of effortless indulgence. These individuals don't just want a payout—they want status, financial security, and a lavish lifestyle that never ends. They aren't plotting an exit strategy. Instead, they are digging in for the long haul and securing their place as a permanent fixture in their victims' lives while giving as little genuine affection as possible in return.

Their game is not about the high-stakes courtroom battle—it's about sustained, calculated manipulation, ensuring that their victims remain trapped in loveless, transactional marriages, too financially or socially entangled to leave. The emotional toll on the victims is profound. Over time, they realize that the love they thought they had was never real—that they are, in essence, nothing more than human bankrolls keeping their spouses in designer clothes, elite social circles, and unlimited spending privileges.

The Long Con: A Relationship Built on Appearances

Permanent Fixture DTGDs have one overarching goal: To establish themselves in marriages that grant them financial freedom without requiring them to work or give genuine emotional investment. To achieve this, they follow a methodical approach.

Step 1: The Illusion of Love and Partnership

In the beginning, they seem like the perfect partners—attentive, affectionate, and deeply committed. They study their targets, mirroring their values and interests while ensuring they present themselves as people who "belong" in their worlds.

But from the very start, the relationships are transactional. Everything they do is an investment—a carefully crafted image designed to secure the lifestyle they crave. Unlike other DTGDs looking for a fast exit strategy, Permanent Fixture DTGDs see marriage as the real prize—a long-term arrangement that guarantees them instant status and financial security without the inconvenience of work.

Step 2: The Gradual Withdrawal of Affection

Once the relationship is secure, the emotional connection fades. Intimacy becomes rare, if not non-existent. Quality time is replaced with excuses, distractions, and strategic coldness. When questioned, DTGDs expertly deflect:

- *"I'm just really stressed lately."*
- *"You're imagining things—we're fine."*
- *"I don't feel as connected because you've been so busy with work."*

At this stage, the victim starts to notice the shift, but the relationship remains intact—largely because leaving would mean untangling a complex web of financial, social, and familial ties.

Step 3: Establishing the Trap

DTGDs ensure that their victims feel like leaving is impossible. They remind them—explicitly or implicitly—that a divorce would be financially ruinous, humiliating, or disruptive to their public image. They weaponize the potential fallout, playing on fears of social scandal, financial devastation, and even damage to their children's well-being.

Some tactics include:

- Exaggerating the cost of divorce: *"You know how much a divorce would cost you—are you sure you want to throw everything away?"*
- Social leverage: *"Do you really want people talking about how you failed at marriage?"*
- Using the kids as a shield: *"We need to stay together for the children."*
- Financial entanglements: Joint investments, shared properties, and luxury purchases that make disentangling assets a legal and logistical nightmare.

At this point, the victims feel trapped—not just financially, but psychologically. They may begin rationalizing the arrangement. *"At least I get to keep my family intact." "Maybe this is just how marriage is." "I've already invested so much—starting over would be too difficult."*

The Emotional Toll on the Victims

The slow realization that their marriages are one-sided financial arrangements is deeply painful. Unlike other DTGD victims who endure a sudden betrayal, this suffering is prolonged—a slow erosion of self-worth and happiness.

Victims often feel:

- Emotionally starved: They crave real love and connection, but their spouses remain emotionally unavailable.
- Trapped in a gilded cage: They have material wealth, but their personal freedom and joy feel nonexistent.
- Socially isolated: The DTGDs ensure they remain the primary connection in their spouses' lives, discouraging close friendships or external support systems.
- Helpless to change their reality: Divorce, while an option, feels too costly, too complicated, or too humiliating to pursue.

Many victims of this DTGD archetype remain stuck for years—sometimes for life.

The Psychological Warfare of the DTGD

To maintain their grip, Permanent Fixture DTGDs carefully manage expectations. Their greatest tool isn't aggression or blatant manipulation—it's passive control. They ensure that their spouses never quite reach the breaking point by offering just enough affection, interaction, or validation to keep them tethered.

- Financial reminders: They remind their spouses what they stand to lose in a divorce.
- Occasional affection: Small gestures of love keep hope alive, but are never enough to satisfy.
- Subtle shaming: They mock or dismiss concerns, making their victims feel irrational for wanting more from the relationship.

By keeping their victims in a perpetual state of dissatisfaction without resolution, they ensure their financial security remains unchallenged.

Breaking Free: Finding the Courage to Choose Happiness

Victims of Permanent Fixture DTGDs don't suffer a dramatic betrayal—they suffer a slow death of joy, passion, and self-worth. The realization that their marriages are built on nothing but financial utility can be crushing, but the most dangerous trap is the one in their own mind—the belief that they have no way out. Fortunately, they do.

The first step is recognizing the reality of the situation—acknowledging that they are in a transactional relationship that no longer serves their emotional or personal well-being.

The second step is seeking support from a trusted friend, a therapist, or a financial advisor—someone who can provide perspective and clarity.

The final step is reclaiming autonomy. That doesn't always mean divorce, but it does mean consciously deciding what happiness looks like—and whether their marriage is truly a life worth living.

Life Is Too Short to Live Trapped

There is no reason to stay locked in a loveless marriage, trapped by fear of financial loss or social consequences. For victims of Permanent Fixture DTGDs, the real prison isn't the relationship—it's the belief that they must endure it.

This book does not advocate for reckless decisions or unnecessary conflict, but it does challenge its readers to ask themselves one question:

If you only have one life to live, is this how you want to spend it?

For those who see themselves in this chapter, the answer may be painfully clear—and that answer might be the first step toward freedom.

20

Archetype #5 (and #5.5): "The Grave Robber" and the "DTGD Grand Slam"

A Calculated Long Game

DTGDs are relentless strategists who exploit unique dynamics to maximize financial gain. In significant age-gap marriages, DTGDs employ tactics designed to secure not just a portion of their victim's wealth through divorce, but potentially all of it upon their partner's passing. This strategy is referred to as the "Grave Robber."

For some Grave Robber DTGDs, this isn't the endgame. They escalate even further to the "DTGD Grand Slam," combining the financial windfalls of age-gap marriages with the additional entitlements of child support and inheritance tied to having children with their older victims. This chapter examines both strategies, highlighting how DTGDs exploit these vulnerabilities and outlining countermeasures to protect assets, family legacies, and emotional well-being.

The Grave Robber: Exploiting Age-Gap Marriages

Age-gap marriages often come with inherent power imbalances, where one partner holds significantly more financial resources while the other wields emotional or relational influence. DTGDs thrive in these dynamics, exploiting both financial and emotional vulnerabilities.

Key Motivations for DTGDs

1. Access to Wealth
    - Older partners are more likely to have amassed significant assets, such as properties, investments, and business interests.
    - DTGDs target these resources as the ultimate prize.

2. Inheritance Windfalls
    - Remaining married until their partners' death positions DTGDs to inherit substantial portions of the estates, especially when wills and trusts are outdated or poorly structured.

3. Long-Term Security
    - If the relationship ends before death, divorce remains a fallback option to secure wealth through asset division and spousal support (and potentially child support).

Tactics Used in Age-Gap Marriages

1. Feigned Devotion
    - Caretaker role: Presenting themselves as indispensable, DTGDs step into caregiving roles to establish emotional and practical dependence.
    - Appealing to legacy: They convince their partners to steer estate planning decisions in their favor.

2. Estate Interference
    - Encouraging will changes: Persuading their partners to alter wills or trusts to benefit the DTGDs.
    - Alienating family: Creating rifts to exclude children or other heirs from inheritance plans.
    - Exploiting vulnerability: Taking advantage of cognitive decline or emotional dependence to secure financial control.

The Financial Impact of the Grave Robber

- Estate depletion: Significant portions of the estate may go to the DTGD, bypassing intended heirs.
- Asset liquidation: Family businesses or properties may need to be sold to meet financial obligations imposed during or after the marriage.
- Legal disputes: Heirs often contest wills or trusts influenced by DTGDs, leading to lengthy and costly battles.

The DTGD Grand Slam: Adding Children to the Equation

When Grave Robber DTGDs introduce children into age-gap marriages, they combine the strategies of the Grave Robber with child support entitlements, creating a financial "Grand Slam."

Why DTGDs Seek Children in Age-Gap Marriages

1. Guaranteed Financial Entitlements
    - Child support payments are legally mandated, ensuring a long-term income stream independent of marital status.
    - Even with a prenuptial agreement, child support obligations remain enforceable and non-negotiable.

2. Inheritance Leverage
    - DTGDs leverage their roles as the parents of the victims' children to secure an even larger share of the estate.
    - Provisions for children in estate plans often indirectly benefit the DTGDs.

3. Emotional Vulnerabilities
    - Older partners may feel a heightened desire to leave a legacy, making them more susceptible to manipulation.
    - Health concerns or fear of mortality often cloud judgment, leading to hasty financial decisions favoring the DTGDs.

The Financial Impact of the Grand Slam

1. Child Support Obligations
    - Monthly entitlements become payable if a divorce occurs before the victim's death.
    - If the DTGD and victim are still married when the victim passes, expect child support claims (18+ years' worth) against the estate to displace (and dramatically reduce) other beneficiaries' entitlements (potentially millions per child).
    - Additional claims often include private schooling, medical care, and extracurricular activities.

2. Estate Depletion
    - Estate provisions for children frequently benefit DTGDs, who position themselves as custodial parents.
    - Trust manipulations or will alterations further erode wealth meant for other heirs.

3. Long-Term Burdens
    - Non-expiring entanglements, such as trust funds or ongoing legal disputes, perpetuate financial strain.

Emotional Fallout: The Ripple Effects

The combined strategies of the Grave Robber and the DTGD Grand Slam leave emotional scars on both the victims and their families.

For the Victim

- Isolation: DTGDs often alienate their partners from trusted advisors and family.
- Emotional fatigue: Prolonged financial and legal battles drain the mental health and emotional resilience of the victims or their families in mourning.
- Guilt: Victims frequently feel trapped by a sense of responsibility toward their children, further empowering the DTGDs.

For the Family

- Disruption of legacy: Wealth intended for future generations is redirected to the DTGDs.
- Familial conflict: Adult children may feel betrayed or alienated, leading to long-lasting discord.
- Emotional turmoil for children: Exposure to manipulative dynamics often results in anxiety, trust issues, and poor relationship modeling.

Countermeasures: Protecting Against the Grave Robber and the Grand Slam

1. Estate Planning Safeguards
    - FFTs: Shield assets and future income from manipulation by securing them prior to marriage.
    - No-contest clauses: Deter challenges to wills or trusts by disinheriting contesting parties.
    - Regular reviews: Update estate plans to reflect current intentions and prevent undue influence.

2. Financial Planning
    - Separate accounts: Keep premarital and personal assets distinct to prevent co-mingling.

3. Reproductive planning
    - Reproductive awareness: Use reliable contraception to avoid unplanned pregnancies that could be exploited financially.

4. Professional guidance
    - Engage experienced advisors: Legal and financial experts can monitor for red flags and protect assets.
    - Financial guardianship: Consider designating an independent advisor to manage finances, particularly in the event of incapacitation.
    - Therapeutic resources: Seek counseling for emotional recovery and resilience.

Safeguarding Wealth and Legacy

The Grave Robber and DTGD Grand Slam are masterclasses in financial manipulation, leveraging the vulnerabilities of age-gap marriages to secure wealth through inheritance, divorce, and child support. By understanding these tactics and implementing robust safeguards, individuals can protect their assets and ensure their financial intentions are honored. Proactive planning, open communication, and professional support are critical to mitigating these risks and preserving family legacies.

Recognizing these tactics and implementing the countermeasures discussed above ensures that wealth and legacies are protected against exploitation and preserved.

21

Dishonorable Mentions in DTGD Sub-Archetypes: Unique Risks in the DTGD Playbook

While most DTGDs fall into well-defined patterns of financial manipulation, some operate within specific subcultures that make their tactics appear socially acceptable, and at times even aspirational.

This chapter highlights two particularly noteworthy environments where DTGDs thrive:

- The tradwife movement: A nostalgic return to "traditional" gender roles, which conveniently offers DTGDs the perfect cover to disguise laziness and financial opportunism as old-fashioned virtue.
- The sugar baby/sugar daddy economy: A financial transaction masquerading as a relationship, where some DTGDs leverage

the blurred lines of "mutual arrangement" to entrap high-value targets for long-term paydays.

While these dynamics often overlap with the previously discussed DTGD angles of attack, they present unique risks that deserve special mention.

The Tradwife Movement: A Gold Digger's Dream Setup

The tradwife movement—short for "traditional wife"—gained traction in recent years as a countercultural response to modern feminist ideals. The movement glorifies a return to 1950s-style gender roles, where the wife is a devoted homemaker and the husband serves as the sole financial provider.

On the surface, this seems like a personal choice or even a lifestyle preference. But scratch beneath the carefully curated social media aesthetic and you'll find a gold-plated invitation for DTGDs to embed themselves into a financially dependent dynamic.

Why the Tradwife Movement Attracts DTGDs

1. Built-in financial dependence: The tradwife model involves full economic reliance on a spouse. For a genuine traditional wife, this might be a meaningful choice. For a DTGD, it's a fast track to passive income, with zero accountability or intention to contribute meaningfully.

2. A socially acceptable excuse for laziness: A DTGD tradwife isn't a homemaker—she's a luxury consumer disguised as one. Instead of actually cooking, cleaning, and running a household, she outsources everything to nannies, meal deliveries, and housekeepers—all paid for by her devoted husband.

3. Weaponized divorce tactics: The tradwife narrative strengthens spousal support claims in divorce. The DTGD tradwife will argue that she "sacrificed" her career, securing a larger settlement in court. Key manipulation tactics include:

   - *"I stayed home to support his dreams."*
   - *"I gave up my career for this marriage."*
   - *"I have no marketable skills—he owes me."*

The endgame is decades of spousal support and a massive financial severance package that rivals some executive bonuses.

4. The ultimate "lifestyle upgrade" shortcut
A DTGD tradwife isn't looking for love—she's looking for a luxury lifestyle on someone else's dime. The strategy is simple:

   - Find a high-earning target looking for a "wholesome" woman.
   - Embed oneself into his life under the guise of "traditional values."
   - Secure legal entitlements by marriage.
   - Cash out in divorce.

Reality check: If a prospective spouse is adamantly opposed to a prenup and cites "traditional values" as the reason, the risk that they are a DTGD is off the charts.

The Sugar Baby/Sugar Daddy Economy: The Softcore DTGD Pipeline

At a glance, the sugar baby/sugar daddy dynamic appears transparent, transactional, and voluntary. The sugar daddy provides financial stability, gifts, and lifestyle perks, while the sugar baby offers companionship, affection, or more.

That's the sales pitch.

In reality, it's a DTGD's training ground. While not all sugar babies evolve into full-blown DTGDs, the platforms and cultural norms surrounding sugar dating reinforce entitlement, materialism, and manipulative relationship dynamics.

How DTGDs Leverage the Sugar Economy

1. Sugar dating as DTGD training camp: Platforms like Seeking.com and Sugarbook.com normalize the idea that relationships are fundamentally financial transactions. Many sugar babies start out with clear boundaries, but quickly learn how to extract maximum financial benefits with minimum effort. By the time they graduate from sugar dating to a long-term DTGD strategy, they've honed their skills in manipulation, entitlement, and high-end gold digging.

2. The strategic evolution from temporary arrangement to permanent payday: A DTGD sugar baby isn't looking for a temporary allowance—she's auditioning for a long-term financial attachment.
   - Step 1: Establish a sugar relationship with a wealthy, naive provider.
   - Step 2: Rebrand the dynamic into something "more meaningful."
   - Step 3: Leverage the emotional bond to transition into marriage, where they can demand far more than just a monthly allowance.

3. Grooming targets for legal financial extraction: Once a sugar baby DTGD secures a more permanent position in her target's life, she uses the same tactics as other DTGDs.
   - Resistance to prenups
   - Strategic pregnancies

- False promises of partnership, while quietly locking in financial claims

4. Endgame—from sugar daddy to ATM machine: Once the marriage (or legal partnership) is secured, the money flow doesn't stop. It just shifts from "gifts" to legal entitlements. The DTGD sugar baby isn't just dating for perks—she's hunting for an enforceable financial contract.

Final Takeaways: Why These Two Archetypes Matter

- Both the tradwife DTGD and the sugar baby DTGD present unique risks because their tactics appear socially acceptable.
- Both dynamics offer the illusion of legitimacy.
- One dresses up financial dependence as "traditional values."
- The other brands it as an "empowered choice."
- Both create legal leverage for DTGDs to exploit later.
- Tradwives use family court sympathy.
- Sugar babies use relationship rebranding to upgrade their financial stake.
- Both rely on obscuring their true intentions until the financial entanglement is locked in.

At the end of the day, whether it's a tradwife or a sugar baby, they almost always fit into one of the previously mentioned angles of attack used by DTGDs. These are variants, not exceptions.

The solution remains unchanged:

- Always require a prenup.
- Always secure assets within an FFT.
- Always recognize the warning signs of strategic financial dependence.

Whether they enter your life claiming "traditional values" or "mutual arrangement," the outcome remains the same.

They're here for the money—and if you're not protected, they'll take it.

DTGD Timeline Exposed: "The Long Con"

22

Phase 1: Scanning and Selecting the Ideal Prey

The Hunt Begins

A DTGD doesn't stumble into wealth—they hunt for it. Every move they make, every conversation they have, and every setting they place themselves in is carefully calculated to lead them to their next financial conquest. Unlike casual opportunists, who might date someone wealthy by chance, DTGDs design their entire social strategies around one goal: embedding themselves into the lives of high-value targets.

Understanding how DTGDs scan and select their prey is essential to dismantling their tactics. Let's step into their mindset and see the world through their predatory lens.

The DTGD's Hunting Grounds: Where Wealth and Influence Gather

A DTGD's success is directly tied to their ability to blend into spaces where wealth is abundant and approaching potential targets feels organic. They don't operate in places where affluence is spread thin. Instead, they infiltrate ecosystems where high-net-worth individuals gather in significant numbers.

1. Social and Professional Circles

DTGDs are chameleons, mastering the art of fitting into affluent social groups and exclusive environments. They are drawn to spaces where wealth and influence create a sense of built-in trust—places where people assume that anyone present must belong there.

- Upscale events: Charity galas, art exhibitions, luxury product launches, and political fundraisers are prime locations where DTGDs can seamlessly integrate. They curate an image of someone who is socially conscious, well-connected, and cultured, ensuring they are perceived as an equal rather than an outsider.
- Industry networking events: DTGDs focus on high-paying fields such as finance, law, medicine, and technology. They observe ambitious professionals on the rise and assess financial trajectories before their targets reach peak wealth.
- Private clubs and membership-only venues: Gaining access to country clubs, yacht clubs, equestrian circles, and exclusive gyms is a major advantage for DTGDs. These venues create an aura of exclusivity, making it easier for them to position themselves as legitimate members of the elite class.

2. Digital Arenas: The New Frontier of Manipulation

Technology has given DTGDs unparalleled access to their targets before they ever meet them.

- Elite dating apps: High-net-worth individuals often turn to platforms like Raya, Luxy, or The League to find partners within their social bracket. DTGDs tailor their profiles with highly curated aesthetics, portraying themselves as ambitious, sophisticated, and "the perfect match" for successful people.
- Social media data mining: Instagram and LinkedIn are like goldmines of information. DTGDs analyze luxury travel photos, designer purchases, and networking posts to determine financial status and social positioning.

3. Public Displays of Wealth

DTGDs don't rely solely on exclusive memberships or digital research. They also embed themselves in locations where affluence is on display.

- Luxury retail and services: High-end shopping districts, five-star hotels, and first-class airport lounges are playgrounds for DTGDs looking for relaxed, open targets.
- Exclusive fitness studios: Boutique gyms, private Pilates studios, and upscale tennis clubs provide casual, organic interactions where trust can be built naturally.

The Science of Selection: How DTGDs Evaluate Marks

Once inside a high-value environment, DTGDs begin their assessment phase, narrowing in on potential targets based on financial stability, emotional pliability, and long-term exploitability.

1. Wealth Indicators: Measuring Financial Stability

DTGDs don't waste time on speculation. They look for concrete indicators of wealth before engaging.

- Material possessions: They scan for designer watches, luxury cars,

tailored suits, and high-end jewelry, all of which signal disposable income.
- Behavioral clues: They pay attention to how individuals spend, tip, and discuss money—gauging whether their targets see wealth as something to be shared or protected.
- Social circles: DTGDs identify targets with connections to power and influence, knowing that one conquest could lead to broader financial access.

2. Detecting Emotional Vulnerabilities

A wealthy target alone isn't enough—DTGDs also seek emotional entry points that make manipulation easier and the chance of compliance higher.

- Loneliness and social isolation: High-net-worth individuals who travel frequently or lack close family ties are prime candidates.
- Naivety and generosity: Overly trusting and generous individuals can be persuaded into financial entanglements under the guise of love or partnership.
- Validation-seeking behavior: Someone who craves admiration, validation, or companionship is more likely to overlook red flags in a DTGD's tactics.

Target Identified: Locking in on the Prey

Once DTGDs select their targets, they transition from passive observation to active engagement. This stage is highly customized, meticulously crafted to fit the targets' specific personalities, needs, and aspirations.

1. Building the Dossier: The DTGD's Research Phase

DTGDs do not approach blindly. Before making their move, they conduct extensive research to ensure their engagement is flawless.

- Social media deep dive: They analyze social media posts—often going back years—to construct a psychological and financial profile.
- Public records search: Some will investigate real estate holdings, corporate affiliations, and legal disputes to confirm financial status.
- Casual inquiry through mutual acquaintances: They subtly extract information through indirect questioning, presenting their curiosity as harmless interest.

2. Crafting the Perfect Persona

Armed with knowledge, DTGDs shape their identities to mirror their targets' ideal partners.

- Mirroring interests and values: They adopt hobbies, speech patterns, and aspirations that perfectly align with their targets.
- Creating a "meant to be" narrative: They plan staged encounters that appear fated, reinforcing an illusion of destiny.
- Deploying emotional availability: They become attentive, understanding, and engaging companions, strengthening the illusion of compatibility.

3. Engineering the Approach

DTGDs don't leave first impressions to chance. They orchestrate encounters in pre-planned, high-impact ways.

- Strategic timing: They initiate contact when targets are emotionally receptive, such as after a breakup or a major career shift.
- Social proofing: They build credibility by ensuring mutual connections vouch for their presence.
- Staged "coincidental" meetings: They appear at just the right places and just the right times, making it seem as though fate—not strategy—brought them together.

Recognizing the Early Red Flags

Despite their meticulous planning, DTGDs often reveal small inconsistencies early on. Recognizing these warning signs can prevent deeper entanglement.

- Over-the-top charm: Their attention and affection feels too intense, too soon.
- Excessive interest in finances: They ask too many pointed questions about income, assets, and future plans.
- Resistance to boundaries: They subtly push against financial or personal boundaries, testing compliance levels.

The First Steps of a Long Con

DTGDs' hunting and target identification phase is not reckless—it is strategic, patient, and adaptive. Understanding their scanning process, selection criteria, and tactics of infiltration is the first step to avoiding entrapment. Awareness is your first and best line of defense against a predator in disguise.

23

Phase 2: Making Their Move

The Illusion of Chance

Most people believe that love, attraction, and connection are governed by fate—a chance meeting, a serendipitous conversation, an unexpected spark. But for a DTGD, nothing is left to chance. Their entire game is built on meticulous planning, where every encounter is carefully staged to appear natural and every conversation is scripted to create a sense of deep, effortless connection.

Once DTGDs have compiled their dossiers—psychological and financial profiles of their targets—they transition into the next phase: making their move. This is when they engineer their introduction, ensuring that, when they do cross paths, it feels like the universe itself has conspired to bring them together. Their goal is to create an immediate sense of familiarity, trust, and destiny, ensuring that their target never questions the too-good-to-be-true nature of the connection.

Understanding the illusion of chance is essential for preventing entanglement. When you recognize that fate is being *manufactured*, you regain control over your own story.

Orchestrating the Encounter: When "Coincidence" Isn't Coincidence

DTGDs rarely leave their first impressions to fate. They ensure that their introduction to their targets feels effortless, organic, and inevitable—when in reality, it's anything but. Every setting, every mutual connection, and every casual encounter has been strategically designed to break down skepticism and establish trust quickly.

Positioning Themselves in the Right Place at the Right Time

DTGDs embed themselves in places their targets frequent, ensuring they can manufacture "chance" encounters that feel genuine.

- They study routines, tracking where their targets get coffee, exercise, or socialize.
- They synchronize their presence with the targets, arriving at these locations just often enough to seem familiar but not suspicious.
- They leverage mutual connections to gain access to social or professional gatherings where their presence will feel natural.

In some cases, DTGDs will go as far as relocating their lives to align with their targets'. They may suddenly take an interest in a new gym, a specific charity, or a professional networking group—anything that places them squarely in the orbit of their intended victims.

Staging Serendipity: The Art of the Engineered Introduction

When the moment is right, DTGDs make their moves. But they rarely approach directly—they ensure their introduction feels like fate doing its work.

- They "bump into" the target during a morning jog or an elevator ride in an exclusive building.
- They join the same class, club, or seminar, ensuring repeated exposure under the guise of shared interests.
- They orchestrate a mutual friend's introduction, framing their meeting as casual and unplanned.

Everything about DTGDs' approach is subtle but intentional—just enough familiarity to lower defenses, but enough coincidence to make the encounter feel special.

Building the Connection: The Art of Rapid Bonding

The first meeting is just the beginning. From there, DTGDs carefully nurture the relationships, ensuring that what starts as *coincidence* quickly deepens into *attachment.*

They mirror their targets—adopting their hobbies, mimicking their speech patterns, and subtly aligning with their values. The goal is to create the illusion that they are a *perfect match*—someone who just so happens to share the same dreams, ambitions, and outlook on life.

- They validate their targets' goals and insecurities, positioning themselves as the one person who truly understands them.
- They escalate interactions, increasing the frequency of "accidental" meetings.

- They seamlessly integrate into the targets' social circles, reinforcing their presence as a natural part of their lives.

What feels like *deep compatibility* is often just calculated manipulation—DTGDs' ability to become exactly what their targets want them to be.

Recognizing the Signs of Manipulation

No matter how sophisticated their tactics, DTGDs often leave subtle clues that expose their game. Recognizing these red flags early can prevent deeper entanglement.

- Too much knowledge, too soon: If someone you just met seems to know an uncanny amount about your interests, past experiences, or preferences, ask yourself how they could possibly have that information.
- An overly convenient connection: If a new acquaintance mirrors your personality, passions, and goals almost *too* perfectly, it may not be an accident.
- Frequent "chance" meetings that feel calculated: If you seem to keep running into the same person, especially in unexpected places, consider the possibility that it's by design, not coincidence.

How to Disrupt Their Strategy

The best way to stop a DTGD from embedding themselves in your life is to break the illusion of chance before they gain a foothold.

- Question coincidences: If a meeting feels too perfect, take a step back. Ask yourself how and why this person suddenly appeared in your life.

- Control the pace: DTGDs want to accelerate emotional bonding as quickly as possible. Slow things down. Be wary of anyone who pushes for exclusivity, deep emotional intimacy, or financial entanglement early on.
- Introduce new acquaintances to trusted allies: DTGDs thrive in one-on-one interactions, where they control the narrative. Involve your close friends or family in early stages of a relationship and seek their perspectives. They may spot inconsistencies or red flags you have missed.

The Turning Point: When Illusion Becomes Entrapment

If left unchecked, this stage of the DTGD's playbook paves the way for deeper manipulation and financial entrenchment. Once trust is established, they shift from courtship to control, weaving their way towards cohabitation, joint financial decisions, major life choices, and the personal vulnerabilities of their target.

What begins as a series of coincidences becomes an inescapable trap—unless the target recognizes the illusion for what it is and takes back control before it's too late.

Understanding this phase is crucial. Awareness dismantles deception. Questioning breaks the spell. Once the illusion of chance is shattered, the DTGD's carefully laid foundation begins to crumble.

You have more power than they want you to believe. The key is recognizing it before they make their next move.

24

Phase 3: Pulling You Into Their Web

The Deepening of the Game

At first, DTGDs seem like a dream come true. They are attentive, interested, and seem to understand you on a deep level. But beneath the charm, DTGDs are not merely getting to know you—they are gathering data, testing boundaries, and identifying vulnerabilities. This is the phase where they shift from surface-level interactions to embedding themselves into their targets' lives.

By this point, they have done their research. They know your routines, your goals, your financial standing, and your emotional triggers. What they need now is confirmation—a real-time assessment of how much control they can establish, how much access they can secure, and what (or who) stands in their way.

This is where they test the waters.

The Covert Interview Process: Masking Manipulation as Curiosity

DTGDs do not interrogate their targets outright. Instead, they pose as engaged and empathetic partners, using subtle questions, careful observations, and strategic vulnerability to assess the landscape.

They will probe for emotional weak points, financial status, and external safeguards—all while ensuring that their curiosity feels like genuine concern rather than reconnaissance.

Emotional Probing: Finding the Cracks

DTGDs are on the lookout for emotional soft spots—areas of insecurity, past trauma, or loneliness that can later be manipulated. They will often engage in conversations designed to create emotional intimacy—but, in reality, they are scouting for leverage.

- *"What's been the hardest part of your journey so far?"*
- *"Is there anyone you can truly rely on when things get tough?"*
- *"I hate seeing you stressed—do you feel like people understand the pressure you're under?"*

Their goal is to map out where you feel unsupported or misunderstood. These are the areas they will later exploit, positioning themselves as the one person who truly *gets* you.

Financial Probing: Gauging Wealth Without Asking Directly

Rather than bluntly inquiring about bank balances, DTGDs frame their questions in ways that appear casual and innocuous.

- *"What inspired you to pursue your career?"* (Assessing ambition and financial trajectory.)

- *"What are your long-term financial goals?"* (Looking for access points into future wealth.)
- *"I love your place—how long have you lived here?"* (Gathering information on property ownership and assets.)

Each question serves a purpose. They are building a financial profile, determining what kind of lifestyle you maintain, and assessing if you have the disposable income they seek.

Support System Evaluation: Identifying Threats to Their Influence

DTGDs don't just target individuals—they must also neutralize the external forces that could detect and disrupt their manipulation. Advisors, close friends, and financially savvy family members are obstacles that must be assessed.

- *"Who do you usually spend your time with?"* (Assessing how socially isolated or connected you are.)
- *"Do you talk to your family often?"* (Determining if familial input will be a challenge.)
- *"Have you ever worked with a financial planner or lawyer? That sounds so smart."* (Gauging awareness of financial safeguards.)

If they detect strong external influences—advisors, friends who ask questions, or family members who have experienced manipulation before—they will begin subtle strategies to isolate you.

Testing Influence and Boundaries

Once they have assessed their targets' vulnerabilities, DTGDs will begin subtly exerting control, testing just how much influence they can wield.

Planting Suggestions: Low-Risk Compliance Testing

Small, seemingly harmless recommendations are their first step in establishing control over decisions.

- *"You should try this restaurant, it's amazing. I think you'd love it."*
- *"Have you thought about changing your investment strategy?"*

They will watch carefully to see how their targets respond. If the targets comply easily, they will increase the weight of their suggestions, eventually steering major life decisions—where to live, where to invest, and even which friendships to maintain.

Boundary Pushing: How Far Will You Let Them Go?

DTGDs don't immediately overstep boundaries. Instead, they test the waters with small encroachments that seem harmless.

- *"Let me hold onto your keys, I'll let the tradesperson in for you."*
- *"Why don't I cover this Amazon order? It's no trouble at all."*

What they are looking for is resistance. If none is met, they will escalate, working their way into financial control and decision-making authority, and eventually entrenching themselves into their targets' daily lives.

Identifying Safeguards: Spotting the Obstacles to Control

The more protection targets have—legally, financially, and socially—the harder it is for DTGDs to embed themselves. That's why they are constantly on the lookout for safeguards that could block their paths.

- Trusted advisors: They will attempt to discredit financial planners, attorneys, or friends who are financially literate.
- Legal protections: If they detect a partner is generally supportive of prenuptial agreements, trusts, and other financial safeguards, they will reframe them as barriers to trust and intimacy.
- *"Advisors sometimes make things more complicated than they need to be."*
- *"Do you think they really understand your unique situation?"*
- *"Prenups feel so transactional—don't you think love is bigger than that?"*

If they identify legal obstacles, they will pivot, attempting to extract resources in ways that bypass these protections.

How to Counteract Phase 3 Tactics

By this stage, subtle red flags begin to emerge.

- They are too interested in your personal details too soon.
- They insert themselves into your life and routines quickly.
- They subtly undermine trusted friends, advisors, or protective structures.

This is a pivotal moment in DTGDs' long con. Recognizing the manipulation early is key to maintaining control over your emotions, your finances, and your future.

- Maintain control over information: Keep personal and financial details private until trust is well-established.
- Strengthen your support network: Keep trusted friends and advisors in the loop—outside perspectives are invaluable.
- Set firm boundaries: Decline unnecessary involvement in your finances, property, or decision-making.

- Mention you have an FFT: Casually bringing up financial protections deters opportunists early on.
- Document interactions: If something feels off, keep a record of conversations and behavioral patterns.

Consolidating Control: Preventing Further Entrenchment

Phase 3 is a turning point. This is when DTGDs shift from surface-level charm to active manipulation. By recognizing their tactics of testing, probing, and boundary-pushing, you can prevent deeper entanglement before real damage is done.

25

Phase 4: Love Bombing to Close the Deal

The Final Push to Lock in Financial Entrenchment

By the time DTGDs reach this stage, their plans are in full motion. They have tested the waters, assessed vulnerabilities, and begun embedding themselves into their targets' lives. Now, they go all in.

This phase is about sealing the deal before external obstacles—legal safeguards, trusted advisors, or second thoughts—can derail their strategy. They do this through a calculated mix of love bombing, emotional manipulation, and, when necessary, reproductive coercion. It is an all-encompassing push to gain permanent legal and financial entrenchment.

This is the last opportunity for a target to recognize what's happening and step away before the entanglement becomes legally binding.

Love Bombing: The Grand Illusion of Devotion

Love bombing is not affection—it's an overwhelming psychological assault designed to disarm and consume. It creates an emotional high that fosters dependency, making targets more compliant and less likely to question the rapid acceleration of relationships. DTGDs want their victims to be intoxicated by the fantasy of love, swept up in the intensity of "once-in-a-lifetime" devotion.

Their tactics unfold with stunning intensity. There are extravagant gifts that seem too generous for the stage of the relationship, surprise getaways meant to sweep targets off their feet, and declarations of eternal love that escalate far too quickly. The purpose isn't just to impress—it's to create a dynamic where targets feel the need to reciprocate, match the enthusiasm, and fall headfirst into something that feels too magical to question.

The relationship accelerates at a breakneck pace. DTGDs don't have the patience for a natural progression. Instead, they push for exclusivity, cohabitation, and engagements that feel thrilling in their urgency. They frame the rush as romantic destiny. *"When you know, you know."* The words roll off their tongues effortlessly, planting the idea that questioning the speed of it all is somehow cynical. They paint vivid images of the future—a dream home, shared adventures, and the perfect family. It's a fantasy carefully designed to keep targets focused on what could be rather than what actually is.

If doubts creep in, DTGDs don't confront them directly. Instead, they pivot, turning hesitation into an attack on the relationship. *"Why are you doubting what we have?"* they ask, their voices laced with hurt. *"I've never felt this way before. Have you?"* They don't argue—instead, they make their targets question their own instincts. If friends or family express concern, DTGDs subtly plant seeds of doubt about their intentions. *"It's just jealousy,"* they say. *"Some people don't want others to be happy."* They chip away at external influences, ensuring that, when the time comes to take the final plunge, targets feel like there's no one left to question it.

Reproductive Coercion: The Ultimate Insurance Policy

When emotional manipulation alone isn't enough, DTGDs escalate to the ultimate trap: forced parenthood. A child ensures long-term financial connection, guaranteeing legal ties and monetary entanglements that last for decades. It's not about family—it's about leverage.

The pregnancy is never truly an accident. Birth control is tampered with, or simply "forgotten." When the test comes back positive, the reaction is carefully rehearsed. *"This must be fate."* They lean into the social pressure of responsibility, the weight of expectation that dictates a partner must stay, must support, must build a life around this unplanned reality.

Even if their targets question it, even if they hesitate, societal narratives make escape difficult. DTGDs play into them seamlessly. They talk about family values, doing what's right, and how they can make this work together. The conversation isn't about choice—it's about inevitability.

The Wedding Rush: Eliminating Escape Routes

For DTGDs, an expedited wedding is the ultimate victory. The faster the marriage happens, the less time there is for prenuptial agreements, second thoughts, or financial precautions.

Hesitation is met with guilt. If a target suggests waiting, DTGDs make it about trust, love, and proving commitment. *"If you love me, why would we wait?"* they ask. *"What could possibly change between now and then?"* They weave doubt into romance, making it feel like a betrayal to pause and think.

The wedding itself becomes a distracting spectacle. The focus is on dress fittings, venue selections, elaborate guest lists—everything but the legal reality of what's happening. Any mention of financial protections is dismissed outright. *"Prenups are for people who don't believe in love,"* they scoff. *"You're already planning for failure."* They turn security into cynicism, ensuring that, by the time vows are exchanged, there's no barrier left between them and their financial goal.

Recognizing the Red Flags and Resisting Entrenchment

At this stage, there are ample warning signs—if the targets are willing to see them. If affection feels excessive, if the relationship timeline feels rushed, if external influences are dismissed as jealous or controlling, these are not quirks. They are signs of a deliberate strategy.

The key to resistance is slowing down. Love does not need urgency to be real. Taking time to evaluate the foundation of a relationship is not fear—it's wisdom. Seeking the perspective of trusted friends and family is not disloyalty—it's self-protection. Insisting on financial protections like prenuptial agreements is not planning for failure—it's planning to protect your autonomy.

For those who already have safeguards in place, such as an FFT or a legal requirement for a prenup due to business interests, this is the moment to disclose it. Letting DTGDs know that financial access is restricted can be enough to deter them entirely. They thrive on the presumed vulnerabilities of their intended victims, and a preemptive show of strength disrupts their entire playbook.

A Crucial Turning Point

This is it—the moment when DTGDs either lock in their financial entrenchment or lose control of their targets. Love bombing, reproductive coercion, and emotional manipulation are powerful weapons, but awareness is the ultimate defense. Recognizing these tactics and taking decisive action during this phase is critical to avoiding lifelong financial and emotional entrapment.

26

Phase 5: Marriage and the "Happy Couple" Façade

Marriage: The Foundation of Control

For DTGDs, marriage is not about love, commitment, or partnership—it is a legally binding financial contract that cements their control over their victims. Unlike casual relationships, where financial entanglements remain optional, marriage grants DTGDs automatic legal leverage, creating a structure where wealth transfer is not just possible, but enforced by law.

Once the vows are exchanged, the ability to walk away without catastrophic financial and emotional damage diminishes significantly. This is when DTGDs shift from building the illusion of love to securing long-term entitlements. What was once a whirlwind romance becomes a calculated process of deepening control, manipulating perceptions, and laying the groundwork for eventual extraction.

The "Perfect Couple" Image: A Strategic Illusion

One of the most insidious tactics DTGDs use after marriage is maintaining the appearance of the happy, devoted spouse while subtly shifting the power dynamic behind the scenes. This is not an accidental shift—it is part of the long-term game plan.

In the public eye, the DTGD continues to play the doting partner. They engage in high-profile social displays of affection, host lavish gatherings, and ensure that mutual acquaintances see them as the epitome of a supportive spouse. But behind closed doors, they begin a measured withdrawal of emotional and physical intimacy, a process so gradual that the victim often doesn't recognize it for what it is.

This phase serves two crucial purposes:

- Social and legal positioning: By maintaining a positive public image, they make it harder for the victim to seek support or raise concerns. If the victim eventually tries to escape, the DTGD can weaponize public perception, portraying themselves as the blindsided, devoted spouse.
- Financial integration without resistance: The illusion of stability allows the DTGD to push for financial decisions that might otherwise be met with skepticism. Joint accounts, post-marital asset acquisitions, and estate planning conversations are framed as "trust-building" exercises, making the victim feel guilty for resisting.

The Gradual Shift from Passion to Emotional Neutrality

Unlike the later sabotage phase, the happy couple phase is not overtly hostile. Instead, the relationship shifts from passionate and affectionate to neutral and routine. DTGDs ensure that their victims remain emotionally invested while subtly lowering expectations over time.

- Less enthusiasm for shared activities: Where they once eagerly participated in hobbies or date nights, they now show disinterest, offering lukewarm engagement at best.
- Physical intimacy declines, but without conflict: Instead of outright rejecting their partner, they use excuses like exhaustion, stress, or not being "in the mood" to gradually lower the frequency of intimacy.
- Emotional availability diminishes: Conversations shift from deep, engaging discussions to surface-level interactions. If questioned, DTGDs frame it as normal relationship evolution: "This is just what happens after the honeymoon phase."

During this period, DTGDs are not pushing for divorce—they are settling into marriage, ensuring they remain legally entitled to financial benefits for the required period before making their next moves. The victims often rationalize these changes, attributing them to work stress, personal struggles, or the natural progression of long-term relationships.

The Early Warning Signs of Future Sabotage

Although the DTGD is not yet actively case-building, there are telltale signs that something is off. Perceptive victims might notice:

- Inconsistent affection: The DTGD provides just enough warmth and reassurance to keep their partner from questioning the relationship too deeply.
- Shifts in financial discussions: They bring up shared assets, inheritance, or long-term financial planning more frequently, even if it feels premature.
- Subtle isolation tactics: While not overtly controlling, they make it harder for the victim to maintain strong outside relationships by feigning disinterest in social events or subtly discouraging certain friendships.

At this stage, the victim still believes the relationship is fundamentally solid. Because the DTGD does not yet display overt hostility, there is no obvious trigger for the victim to take action.

The Calm Before the Storm

The "happy couple" façade can last years, depending on how long DTGDs need to hit their economic entitlements targets. Some DTGDs remain in this phase until they have accrued legal rights to a specific level of spousal support or property division (or indirect access to inheritances). Others move more quickly if they can succeed in maxing out their 50% entitlements to their victims' post-divorce income by having children, entitling them to child support.

However, some DTGDs are content to extend this phase indefinitely if their victims provide a sufficiently comfortable lifestyle. If they are living in luxury, with access to high-status social circles and an effortless existence funded by their partners' labor, there is little incentive to move on until financial benefits start to plateau. They will delay the case-building phase until:

- They perceive better financial opportunities elsewhere (i.e., a new target with greater wealth or influence).
- They reach legal milestones where alimony or asset division become more favorable in a divorce.
- Their victims begin to push back on financial decisions, making future entitlements harder to secure.

For some victims, this means enduring a decade or more of a hollow, transactional marriage before DTGDs finally pull the trigger on their exit strategies. The longer the victims remain unaware, the more marital assets accumulate in ways that benefit the DTGDs upon exit.

But make no mistake—this phase always ends for DTGDs who have a goal of economic extraction. DTGDs are not content with neutrality. Their ultimate goal *is* financial extraction. When they decide that the time is right, they begin their turn toward active case-building, setting up their victims for the final act of the con.

What follows is the start of Phase 6—"The Turn"—where DTGDs shift from passive withdrawal to active sabotage. The happy couple illusion cracks and victims find themselves in a carefully laid psychological and legal trap—one designed to ensure that, when the marriage ends, the DTGDs walk away victorious.

27

Phase 6: Baiting, Case-Building and Reduction of Intimacy in "The Turn"

The Illusion Cracks: DTGDs' Shift from Neutrality to Sabotage

The "happy couple" phase does not last forever. At some point, DTGDs decide it is time to shift gears. The transition from passive financial entrenchment to active case-building is what we call "The Turn"—when DTGDs begin systematically sabotaging their relationships while rewriting history to portray themselves as the victims.

This is not a natural drifting apart or a couple struggling through ordinary relationship difficulties. This is a calculated, strategic effort to create a legal and social framework that maximizes their financial and reputational benefit when they leave. They are building a carefully crafted narrative to use against their victims in divorce proceedings.

For the victims, this shift can feel sudden, but in reality, the DTGDs have been planning it for a long time. The kindness is gone, the warmth dissipates, and small, manipulative digs become a daily occurrence. The victims, often blindsided, believe they are simply going through a rough patch, unaware that they are being set up for a future courtroom battle.

Baiting and Conflict Engineering: The Psychological Trap

DTGDs know that a clean, amicable divorce will not maximize their financial gain. They need a legal justification to demand higher settlements, spousal support, or child custody advantages. This is why they begin engineering conflicts that will serve as "evidence" for their upcoming legal maneuvering.

Some of their favorite tactics include:

- Strategic provocation: They push their targets into reactive emotional responses by picking fights at inopportune times—during business stress, at family events, or in front of witnesses.
- Gaslighting and distortion: DTGDs twist words and memories to make their victims question reality. If confronted, they will say, *"I never said that. You're remembering it wrong."*
- Playing the long game: They accumulate months of "incidents," ensuring a pattern of behavior emerges that they can later present as justification for their separation demands.
- Weaponized documentation: They record arguments, save text messages, and collect "evidence" that, when taken out of context, paints them as the reasonable party and their victims as unstable or aggressive.

By the time the victims realize what is happening, the DTGDs have already assembled an arsenal of complaints and grievances. The victims are left bewildered, trying to "fix" relationships that were never truly broken—just set up for collapse on the DTGDs' terms.

The Social Smear Campaign: Controlling the Narrative

Parallel to creating a case within the home, DTGDs start shaping public perception. This is crucial because when the relationship finally implodes, they want friends, family, and even the legal system to side with them instantly.

The smear campaign typically follows a predictable pattern:

- Soft launch of doubt: DTGDs start dropping hints to mutual friends: *"I don't know what's going on lately. I feel like we're drifting apart."*
- Subtle victimization: Without directly accusing their partners, they plant seeds of concern: *"I just feel like I'm walking on eggshells sometimes."*
- Public performance of suffering: Social media posts about "self-care," "healing," and "toxic relationships" appear. DTGDs ensure that anyone observing their relationships from the outside believe that something is deeply wrong, even if the victims have done nothing out of the ordinary.
- Gathering supporters: Mutual acquaintances are quietly recruited as allies so that when the victims inevitably push back, they are met with disbelief: *"I don't know, they seemed so unhappy for a while now."*

The goal is to preemptively destroy the victims' credibility, ensuring that, if they later claim they were manipulated or deceived, no one will believe them.

The Financial Setup: Preparing for Maximum Extraction

Alongside emotional and social manipulation, DTGDs begin making subtle but significant financial moves. This phase is about creating as many economic entanglements as possible, ensuring that, when the split happens, victims are financially compromised.

- Encouraging major purchases: They push for unnecessary home renovations or new vehicles—purchases that will later be leveraged in settlement negotiations.
- Shifting financial responsibilities: In the unusual event that DTGDs are still working by this point, they reduce their hours or "get fired." They reduce personal contributions to expenses while ensuring their partners pay for more, making it appear that they have been "financially dependent."
- Positioning for spousal and child support: If children are involved, DTGDs begin shifting more parenting responsibilities onto themselves while documenting their partners' "absence"—creating the illusion that they are the primary caregivers.
- Consulting divorce attorneys in secret: Well before victims suspect anything, DTGDs are already planning their exit strategies, consulting legal experts to determine how to maximize their payouts.

The Emotional Toll: Keeping the Victim in the Dark

Overwhelmed by the shift in behavior, victims often internalize the blame. They try harder to fix things, unaware that they are being manipulated into a legal and financial noose.

Key signs that "The Turn" is happening:

- Arguments feel orchestrated, not spontaneous.

- DTGDs start portraying themselves as "exhausted" or "unappreciated" partners.
- Sudden financial shifts begin happening, but they appear reasonable at first.
- Mutual friends begin distancing themselves from victims, already influenced by DTGDs' narratives.

Recognizing the Turn and Taking Action

If victims recognize the signs early enough, they can start protecting themselves before DTGDs fully execute their final moves.

- Stop reacting emotionally to baiting tactics. DTGDs want outbursts that they can use against their victims. Deny them that.
- Secure independent legal counsel immediately. Do not wait until divorce is mentioned—by then, DTGDs will already be 10 steps ahead. If asset and income protection are a consideration, talk to an asset protection lawyer *before* talking to a divorce lawyer (See Resources).
- Prepare financially. If the advice of an asset protection lawyer aligns with your outlook, start moving assets into protected legal structures to prevent financial ambush.
- Preserve evidence in reverse. If DTGDs are documenting victims, then victims must document DTGDs. Save messages, record financial contributions, and maintain a record of events.
- Rebuild outside relationships. DTGDs thrive on isolation. Strengthen bonds with friends and family who can offer support.

The Next Phase: The Divorce Filing and Legal Assault

Once the case-building is complete, DTGDs move into their final act: filing for divorce or baiting their victims into doing it first. This is where everything they've engineered comes together, ensuring that, when the split happens, they hold all the cards.

Understanding this phase is critical. Once "The Turn" begins, the time to act is now. Waiting too long can mean walking into a courtroom already labeled as the aggressor—a battle that is lost before it even begins.

28

Phase 7: Filing for Divorce or Baiting You to Do It

The Orchestrated Exit

Filing for divorce is not just an end—it is the grand finale of a long, calculated con. For DTGDs, this moment is not an emotional decision but a carefully executed strategy that has been in motion for years. By this point, they have crafted narratives, planted the necessary evidence, and ensured that, when the curtain falls, they are seen as the innocent party, while their targets are left scrambling to defend themselves. Whether they initiate the divorce themselves or manipulate their victims into filing first, the objective remains the same: Control the narrative, maximize financial extraction, and secure long-term entitlements.

The months leading up to this moment are filled with orchestrated chaos. DTGDs manufacture "final straw" events—engineered moments of conflict or crisis designed to justify their exit in the most advantageous way possible. They provoke, antagonize, and document, ensuring that, when they walk away, they do so as the aggrieved party, with an entire case file of "proof" to back their claims. Their performance is flawless, their timing impeccable, and their ability to manipulate public perception nearly perfect. By the time victims realize what has happened, DTGDs have already laid the foundation for legal and financial dominance.

Setting the Stage for the Final Blow

DTGDs never walk away without first ensuring that they control the storyline. By the time they file—or force the victims' hands—they have already primed their audiences. They have spent months carefully curating conversations, dropping hints about being unhappy, subtly suggesting mistreatment, and strategically enlisting friends and acquaintances to support their versions of events. This is not an emotional reaction—it is a carefully built framework designed to solidify their roles as victims and ensure sympathy and support from those around them.

Once they are ready to make their moves, they stage events dramatic enough to justify their exit. Perhaps it's a public argument that escalates just enough to be witnessed, but not enough to be questioned. Maybe it's an exaggerated act of suffering, where they collapse under the weight of their "miserable" circumstances, confiding in others about how they can't take it anymore. For more extreme DTGDs, it might be a false accusation—carefully planned and executed to maximize damage and force victims into immediate defensive mode.

No matter the method, the goal is clear: Dictate the terms of the separation before victims even realize what is happening.

Baiting the Victim to File

For some DTGDs, filing first gives them the control they desire. For others, baiting victims into filing is the preferred tactic—allowing the DTGDs to maintain their roles as reluctant spouses who "tried everything."

To accomplish this, they turn relationships into living nightmares.

They withdraw affection, sabotage routines, and create unbearable environments. They oscillate between cold detachment and calculated cruelty, making it clear that nothing victims do will ever be enough. When frustration mounts, they provoke emotional reactions, then use those reactions as further proof of why their marriages must end.

This technique is highly effective. The victims, drained and defeated, begin to feel like there is no choice but to walk away. When they do, DTGDs capitalize on it, framing themselves as the devastated partners who "did everything they could to make it work."

Weaponizing the Legal System

Divorce is not just a personal battle for DTGDs—it is a high-stakes negotiation in which every move is designed to secure financial and emotional dominance. Once proceedings begin, their strategy shifts to leveraging legal tools to their fullest extent.

They bring carefully curated documentation—texts, emails, and witness statements—each reinforcing their version of events. If necessary, they escalate to legal intervention, filing restraining orders, making allegations of emotional mistreatment, or ensuring that custody fights become battlegrounds for financial leverage.

Victims typically enter the proceedings in a reactionary state, scrambling to defend themselves against accusations they never saw coming. Meanwhile, DTGDs remain composed, working within a system they spent months preparing for.

The Psychological Toll: Breaking the Victim Down

Beyond financial and legal entanglements, DTGDs' strategy involves a heavy psychological component. Their goal is to fracture victims' confidence and stability, ensuring that, even outside of court, they remain emotionally tethered to the DTGDs' influence.

They create public narratives of heartbreak and survival, ensuring that mutual friends, social media connections, and even professional circles see them as the innocent parties. They launch quiet smear campaigns, eroding victims' reputations just enough to make them doubt whether fighting back is even worth it.

They sometimes dangle the possibility of reconciliation, drawing out the process with vague promises and mixed signals. They do just enough to keep victims second-guessing themselves, prolonging the emotional fallout and ensuring that their control extends far beyond the legal proceedings.

Protecting Yourself in the Final Phase

Once DTGDs enter the divorce crescendo, the only way to counter their strategy is to stop reacting and start strategizing. Emotional responses play into their hands, while measured, calculated decisions disrupt their momentum.

- Reduce all direct contact and keep communication documented and professional.
- Secure strong legal representation early to counter any fabricated claims or manipulations.
- Strengthen financial protections and anticipate attempts to manipulate settlements.
- Engage trusted allies to provide clarity and support during the inevitable character attacks.
- Prioritize emotional resilience, recognizing that this phase is designed to break you down so that you give in.

The Grand Finale Looms

The final phase of DTGDs' con is not about walking away—it is about extracting the highest possible return before they move on. Understanding that the separation itself is part of their long game is crucial to surviving it with your finances, reputation, and sanity intact.

In the next chapter, we will explore "The Grand Finale"—the stage where DTGDs execute their final moves, leveraging every emotional, legal, and financial tool they've set up in the preceding phases. Recognizing these tactics before they reach their peak is the only way to step out of the storm with at least partial control over your future.

29

PHASE 8: THE DIVORCE TRIAL OR OUT-OF-COURT SETTLEMENT NEGOTIATIONS

The Grand Finale of the Long Con

DTGDs don't just walk away—they stage an exit designed for maximum impact. Phase 8 is the final act of their con, the culmination of every manipulation, deception, and setup that came before. Whether through a dramatic divorce trial or a coercive settlement negotiation, their singular focus is to extract as much financial gain as possible while ensuring they suffer no reputational damage.

For DTGDs, the ideal outcome is clear: a lucrative settlement wrapped in the secrecy of a non-disclosure agreement (NDA), allowing them to vanish into the next opportunity unscathed. For victims, this is the most treacherous phase, where financial security, personal reputation, and emotional stability are all on the line.

This is not just a breakup—it is a war.

Pre-Trial Offensive: The DTGD's Path to Leverage

In the months leading up to the formal separation, DTGDs escalate their emotional, financial, and social warfare to set the stage for their financial coup. They are no longer pretending to be loving partners—they are assembling their legal arsenals.

They start with a smear campaign, ensuring that, by the time legal proceedings begin, they have already positioned themselves as the wronged party. Publicly, they float narratives of mistreatment, neglect, or even abuse. Privately, they whisper in the ears of mutual friends and family, carefully shaping the perception that they are victims trapped in untenable situations. Their goals? Sympathy, support, and credibility.

False allegations are their weapon of choice. Some DTGDs file restraining orders based on fabricated incidents, ensuring there is legal documentation of supposed abuse. Others report fictitious claims of misconduct to employers, law enforcement, or social circles. Their goal is not just to damage the victims' reputations, but also force them into weakened legal positions where they are more likely to settle quickly.

Financial pressure is another tool in their arsenal. They deliberately drag out proceedings, filing frivolous motions, requesting excessive discovery, and escalating demands for support. The goal is not justice—it is exhaustion. They know that the more time and money their victims spend fighting, the more likely they are to accept settlements just to end the misery.

But perhaps the most gut-wrenching blow comes when the victims are ordered to pay their abusers' legal fees.

Funding the Attack: When the Court Makes You Finance Your Own Destruction

Few injustices feel as cruel as being forced to finance the very legal team working to destroy you. Yet, in many cases, family courts require the higher-earning spouse to cover legal costs for the lesser-earning spouse.

While framed as a mechanism to ensure fairness, this becomes an economic weapon in the hands of DTGDs.

What this can mean:

- Victims are paying for DTGDs' legal assaults, funding the lawyers who will pick apart their finances, character, and credibility.
- DTGDs are incentivized to prolong proceedings, knowing they don't have to foot the bills for their legal teams' endless tactics.
- Psychological distress intensifies, as the idea of funding one's own destruction adds another layer of despair to an already crushing ordeal.

For victims, this is financial and emotional double jeopardy. It is not enough to defend themselves—they must do so while simultaneously bankrolling the very forces working to dismantle them.

The Settlement Trap: Baiting the Target into Compliance

For many DTGDs, a private settlement is preferable to a public trial. The payout is substantial, and, just as crucially, it comes without the risk of public scrutiny. The ideal mechanism? A settlement that includes an NDA.

An NDA is not just about financial secrecy—it is also about ensuring that DTGDs' manipulations remain hidden. Once the documents are signed, victims are legally bound to silence, unable to share their stories or expose the truth. Meanwhile, DTGDs walk away with their reputations intact, free to repeat the same cycle with their next unsuspecting victims.

To ensure compliance, they exploit their victims' desperation for peace. They frame settlement as the "mature" option and the best way to move forward. At the same time, they subtly threaten escalation, making it clear that choosing to go to trial will be a long, ugly, and expensive war. The victims, exhausted, financially drained, and eager to move on, often sign away their rights to tell the truth in exchange for an end to the nightmare.

The Trial: A High-Stakes Gamble

If victims refuse to settle, DTGDs' tactics shift toward making the trial as excruciating as possible. This is not about fairness, it is about scorched-earth warfare.

They manipulate the system to ensure:

- Sky-high legal costs (filing unnecessary motions and creating obstacles that require costly countermeasures).
- Public character assassination (ensuring that the victims' personal and financial matters are dragged into the spotlight).
- Relentless emotional attrition (forcing their victims to relive every manipulated moment of the relationship under brutal cross-examination).

For some, trial represents a chance to expose the truth, but for many, it is simply too costly to endure. DTGDs count on this. They count on fatigue winning over justice—and too often, it does.

Surviving the Grand Finale

Escaping this phase unscathed is nearly impossible, but minimizing damage is critical. The key lies in foresight, documentation, and resilience.

- Secure the best legal representation available. Family courts are not always fair, but a skilled attorney can dismantle false claims and mitigate financial damage.
- Document everything. Keep records of all interactions, conversations, and financial transactions. Truth without proof is useless in court.

- Guard your reputation fiercely. DTGDs thrive on destroying credibility. Stay composed, stay factual, and avoid public outbursts that can be weaponized against you.
- Protect your mental health. Therapy, support groups, and close allies can be the difference between surviving and succumbing to the psychological toll.

The Aftermath: What Comes Next?

For DTGDs, divorce is just business. Once the ink dries, they will move on without looking back, ready to repeat the cycle with their next target. For the victims, however, the scars remain—financially, emotionally, and reputationally.

30

Phase 9: Rinse and Repeat on the Next Victim

The Endless Cycle of Exploitation

For DTGDs, the end of one relationship isn't a loss—it's a reset. It's the closing of one profitable chapter and the beginning of a new scheme, executed with sharper precision and a more polished approach. They don't mourn. They don't reflect. They simply move on, armed with the financial spoils from their last victims, a carefully curated image, and the advantage of experience.

While their previous targets are left picking up the pieces—emotionally, financially, and legally—DTGDs are already laying the groundwork for their next conquests.

They refine their strategies with each victim, fine-tuning their ability to manipulate, extract, and discard. And because NDAs and settlements protect them from exposure, their reputations remain intact, ensuring their next targets see only the versions of them they want to be seen.

This is not just a pattern. It's a system—an endless loop of deception that can only be broken by awareness, education, and proactive defense.

Weaponizing the "Winnings"

When DTGDs exit marriages or long-term relationships, they rarely do so empty-handed. Their financial windfalls from divorce settlements, spousal support, and child support don't just sustain them—they fund their next opportunities.

They use these financial gains to manufacture the illusion of success. With liquid assets at their disposal, they present themselves as self-sufficient, well-off, and independent. But the stability they project is a façade—one that is carefully maintained to attract wealthy, emotionally vulnerable individuals who will sustain their lifestyles for the long haul.

DTGDs with significant settlement payouts can continue to circulate within affluent social circles, leveraging their appearance of financial security to gain access to their next targets. They upgrade their images, dress impeccably, vacation in high-end destinations, and attend elite networking events—posing not as outsiders looking for benefactors, but as people who belong there.

Because their previous victims are legally bound to silence, there is nothing standing in the way of their carefully rewritten narratives. The truth of what happened is sealed away behind legal documents, while the DTGDs position themselves as wronged parties, strong survivors, and independent success stories. They lean into their victimhood when necessary, hinting at exes who were "controlling" or "emotionally unavailable," but they never reveal the truth—that they engineered the relationships' collapse for financial gain.

Scouting the Next Target

Often, the next victim is identified long before the last relationship officially ends. DTGDs never allow for "downtime" between relationships—they are always preparing for the next stage of the con.

While still legally or emotionally entangled with their previous victims, they begin testing the waters—identifying new marks in spaces designed to attract wealth and influence.

If they ever stopped, they resume frequenting charity galas, private clubs, high-end networking events, and luxury fitness studios—places where affluent individuals gather in relaxed social environments. They blend even more seamlessly into these spaces, using their well-crafted personas to cultivate and deepen connections with potential targets.

Some DTGDs begin preparing their next targets while still married, strategically positioning themselves as needing a trusted friend or confidant. What starts as "harmless" emotional support, often in the form of sympathetic conversations about their failing marriages, gradually transitions into something more. By the time their divorces are finalized, their next victims already feel emotionally invested, seeing themselves as potential saviors rather than pawns in a calculated game.

Refining the Playbook

Each completed con provides valuable lessons. DTGDs are always learning and adapting.

If they encountered resistance in their previous relationships—perhaps a prenuptial agreement limited their financial extraction—they take note. They begin strategizing around that obstacle, refining their approach to ensure that their next victims won't make the same demands.

If their previous marks hesitated before committing, they accelerate the manipulation timeline, recognizing that a faster pace leaves less room for skepticism.

Each target is a stepping stone to the next, and with each cycle, DTGDs become more adept, more convincing, and more dangerous.

Breaking the Cycle

The most terrifying part of DTGDs' endless cycle is how seamlessly they move from victim to victim, unburdened by consequences. With each fresh start, they leave a trail of financially and emotionally devastated individuals—people who never saw it coming, and who may never recover fully.

But the cycle can be interrupted.

Recognizing the patterns is the first step. Understanding that DTGDs do not operate in isolated incidents—but rather within a carefully crafted system of deception, extraction, and reinvention—is critical.

They thrive in darkness, secrecy, and plausible deniability. By bringing awareness to their tactics, exposing their cycles, and ensuring that potential targets see the red flags before the damage is done, it is possible to diminish the ability of DTGDs to operate unchecked.

Each time a potential victim recognizes the warning signs and walks away, the cycle weakens.

Each time a survivor refuses to be silenced and shares their experience—even in general terms, and anonymously—another layer of their shield of secrecy is chipped away.

Each time a legal structure like an FFT, a well-drafted prenup, or an AI-powered screening tool is used to protect wealth before the con can begin, DTGDs' opportunities shrink.

The Grave Robber Timeline

The Grave Robber Timeline is slightly different, diverging from the classic DGTG timeline, starting at Phase 7. (See Appendix A)

DTGD Psychology: Know Thine Enemy

31

Personality Disorders, Pathological Laziness, and Entitlement

The Dark Mindset of a Predator

DTGDs are not just opportunistic manipulators—they are predators driven by a morally bankrupt worldview. Their attitudes, shaped by elements of personality disorders, pathological laziness, and a deep sense of entitlement, fuel their ability to exploit others without remorse. For DTGDs, relationships are not about connection or partnership. Rather they are calculated transactions designed to extract maximum value.

Understanding the psychological framework of DTGDs is critical to recognizing their manipulative strategies and preventing exploitation. This chapter explores how they think, their defining attitudes, and the red flags that signal their predatory nature.

The DTGD Worldview: Entitlement and Exploitation

At the core of the DTGD mindset is an unshakable belief that they are entitled to the wealth and resources of others. This belief underpins their manipulative behavior and justifies their morally corrupt actions.

Entitlement Complex

DTGDs operate with an inflated sense of self-worth, seeing their entitlement to luxury and comfort as inherent. In their minds, this is the result of:

- Unfounded superiority: They view themselves as inherently deserving of wealth, rationalizing that others' success or fortune is a resource meant to be redistributed in their favor.
- Exploitation as justice: DTGDs frame their actions as justified rebalancing, perceiving themselves as being "owed" a life of ease and indulgence. This belief allows them to exploit others without guilt.

Pathological Laziness

A hallmark of DTGDs is their aversion to hard work or self-sufficiency.

- Avoidance of effort: DTGDs prefer manipulation over traditional paths to wealth, viewing careers or entrepreneurship as beneath them.
- Façade businesses: Many maintain pseudo-businesses—ventures that exist solely to create the illusion of independence. These are often shallow and lack economic viability, serving as props in their manipulative act.
- Career instability: Colleagues and employers often see through their lack of authenticity, leading to job-hopping or professional failure.

Fear of Exposure
DTGDs thrive in secrecy and panic under scrutiny.

- Obsessive secrecy: They avoid transparency in financial or emotional matters, knowing that public scrutiny could unravel their schemes.
- Visible discomfort under scrutiny: Asking detailed questions about their pseudo-businesses or financial independence often exposes inconsistencies in their narratives.
- Panic responses: When faced with reasonable questions about their families, education, or career backgrounds, evasive or untruthful responses are common.

Key Attitudes That Define DTGDs

Understanding the attitudes that define DTGDs helps in recognizing their manipulative behaviors. These attitudes not only reveal their predatory nature, but also serve as warning signs for potential victims.

Transactional Thinking
For DTGDs, relationships are purely transactional.

- People as assets: They evaluate others based on financial value and exploitability, investing affection, charm, or feigned vulnerability solely to secure returns.
- Lack of genuine connection: Emotional depth is absent. Every interaction is a calculated move to advance their agendas.

Moral Flexibility
DTGDs operate with a belief that the ends justify the means.

- Rationalizing deceit: Lying, cheating, and manipulating are tools in their arsenal, justified as necessary for achieving their goals.

- Selective empathy: They can feign compassion, but lack genuine concern for the harm they cause.

Hyper-Adaptive Behavior
DTGDs excel at adjusting their personas to suit their targets.

- Chameleon-like personas: They mirror their targets' values, interests, and aspirations, creating the illusion of compatibility.
- Precision exploitation: DTGDs quickly identify emotional vulnerabilities and use charm or manipulation to gain trust.

A Checklist for Recognizing DTGD Attitudes

Use this checklist to identify warning signs of DTGDs before becoming entangled in their manipulation:

- ❑ Do they seem overly interested in your financial status early in the relationship?
- ❑ Do they resist discussions about financial boundaries or protective measures like prenups?
- ❑ Do their stories about their past or achievements seem inconsistent or exaggerated?
- ❑ Do they display entitlement to your resources without contributing equally?
- ❑ Do they isolate you from friends, family, or advisors under the guise of protecting the relationship?
- ❑ Do their pseudo-business ventures appear unsubstantiated or lack economic substance when probed for details?

Predators Behind the Mask

DTGDs operate with a deeply ingrained sense of entitlement and moral flexibility, justifying their manipulations as a means to an end. Their inability to sustain viable careers or credible ventures further underscores their reliance on exploitation to achieve their goals. By recognizing their attitudes and identifying red flags, you can protect yourself from becoming a target. These predators thrive on secrecy and deception, but knowledge of their playbook is your best defense.

In the next chapter, we will take a closer look at how narcissism drives manipulation and exploitation in narcissistic-leaning DTGDs.

32

Understanding Dark Triad Traits in Depth: Narcissistic-Leaning DTGDs

The Narcissistic Core

While DTGDs exhibit elements of all three Dark Triad traits—narcissism, Machiavellianism, and psychopathy—some lean more heavily toward one trait than the others. For narcissistic-leaning DTGDs, their entitlement and manipulative strategies are deeply rooted in an inflated sense of self-importance and relentless craving for admiration.

This chapter explores how narcissism shapes the attitudes and tactics of DTGDs, offering insights into their psychological framework, strategies for exploitation, and the red flags that reveal their true nature. By understanding these traits, you can identify and counter their manipulation before becoming ensnared.

Narcissism in the Dark Triad Cluster

Narcissism is characterized by an inflated sense of self-importance, a craving for admiration, and a lack of empathy. Narcissistic DTGDs excel at creating compelling personas that obscure their self-serving motives. Their behaviors are driven by entitlement, a fixation on appearances, and emotional shallowness.

Inflated Entitlement

Narcissistic DTGDs operate with an unyielding belief that they deserve wealth and adoration, even though they haven't earned it.

- Unrealistic expectations: They view relationships as a means to secure luxury and status, justifying their entitlement as inherent to their perceived superiority.
- Zero-sum thinking: For narcissistic DTGDs, relationships are competitions. Their gain is inherently justified, while their targets' losses are dismissed as irrelevant.

Obsession with Image

Appearances take precedence over substance in the lives of narcissistic DTGDs.

- Curated personas: They meticulously craft social media profiles, wardrobes, and public personas to project success, charm, and desirability.
- Reputation management: Hyper-aware of how they are perceived, narcissistic DTGDs go to great lengths to suppress criticism and control narratives, often preemptively discrediting others who threaten their image.

Emotionally Shallow

A lack of emotional depth defines their relationships and decisions.

- Absence of empathy: They cannot genuinely understand or care about the emotional consequences of their actions on others.
- Self-centered decision-making: Every choice is filtered through the lens of personal benefit, with no regard for fairness or equity.

Tactics of Narcissistic-Leaning DTGDs

Narcissistic DTGDs excel at strategies that elevate their status, secure admiration, and extract value from their targets. Their tactics are calculated to manipulate perceptions and reinforce their superiority.

Love Bombing with a Narcissistic Twist

- Grandiose displays: Extravagant dates, over-the-top compliments, and declarations of love are used to overwhelm targets' defenses. These gestures are performative, designed to reinforce DTGDs' dominance rather than cultivate genuine connection.
- Transactional affection: Narcissistic DTGDs expect admiration or financial benefits in return for their displays of affection. Any imbalance is reframed as their targets' failure to appreciate them.

Manipulating Social Perceptions

- Narcissistic DTGDs carefully curate their images to maintain control over how they are perceived:
- Cultivating admiration: They appear as the "perfect partners" to friends, family, and the public, creating networks of supporters who are quick to discredit their targets' concerns.
- Smear campaigns: When confronted, they preemptively discredit their targets, portraying them as ungrateful, controlling, or abusive in order to shift blame and maintain sympathy.

Exploiting Vulnerabilities

- Targeting insecurities: Narcissistic DTGDs excel at identifying emotional weaknesses and using validation or strategic withdrawal to manipulate their targets.

- Leveraging admiration: They often choose targets who admire their confidence or charm, using this admiration to gain emotional and financial leverage.

How Narcissistic Traits Enhance Manipulation

Narcissistic DTGDs are uniquely equipped to deceive and exploit because their psychological traits amplify their manipulative capabilities.

A Grandiose Shield

- Confidence as camouflage: Their unshakable self-belief makes them appear credible and trustworthy. Targets often mistake their bravado for competence or stability.
- Immunity to criticism: Narcissistic DTGDs deflect criticism with charm or aggression, maintaining control over the narrative and silencing dissent.

Strategic Charm

- Charismatic personas: Narcissistic DTGDs use wit, confidence, and social finesse to disarm skepticism and build trust quickly.
- Weaponized vulnerability: They occasionally feign vulnerability to evoke sympathy and deepen emotional bonds, making their targets more invested in "helping" or "saving" them.

Lack of Emotional Consequences

- No remorse: Their lack of empathy allows them to manipulate without guilt, focusing solely on their own gain.
- Rationalizing harm: Narcissistic DTGDs reframe the harm they cause as necessary or deserved, often portraying themselves as the victims.

What Happens When They Turn on You

When their control is threatened or their egos are wounded, narcissistic DTGDs eventually escalate their manipulation into overt abuse and malice.

Weaponized Rage

- Explosive reactions: Criticism or exposure triggers intense anger, often disproportionate to the situation. This rage is designed to intimidate and silence their targets.
- Emotional attacks: They exploit deeply personal vulnerabilities to inflict maximum emotional damage, reframing conflicts as evidence of the targets' faults.

Vengeful Manipulation

- Revenge narratives: Narcissistic DTGDs construct stories that paint them as victims and their targets as abusive or unworthy, rallying mutual connections to their side.
- Sabotage: They undermine their targets' professional or social standings through rumors, misinformation, or public outbursts.

Escalation of Control

- Withholding affection: Narcissistic DTGDs withdraw emotionally and physically, framing this as punishment for their targets' perceived offenses.
- Financial retaliation: If they have financial access, they may drain accounts, run up debts, or manipulate joint resources to inflict economic harm.

Psychological Insights into Narcissistic DTGDs

Research offers key insights into why narcissistic DTGDs are so effective at manipulation.

Narcissistic Supply

- Narcissistic DTGDs thrive on attention, admiration, and validation. They see their targets as sources of this "supply."
- Targets are often chosen for their wealth and ability to affirm DTGDs' superiority, creating a dual incentive for exploitation.

Fragile Ego Beneath the Surface

- False confidence: Beneath their bravado lies deep insecurity, masked by overcompensation and grandiosity.
- Aggressive defense mechanisms: Challenges to their images provoke hostility, as they perceive criticism to be a direct threat to their carefully constructed facades.

Red Flags of Narcissistic DTGDs

Spotting a narcissistic DTGD early can help prevent entanglement. Warning signs include:

- Excessive focus on appearance: Constant validation-seeking for their looks, lifestyle, or achievements.
- Resistance to boundaries: Defensive or dismissive reactions to discussions about financial or emotional boundaries.
- Deflection and gaslighting: Redirecting blame or invalidating concerns to maintain control.
- Rapid intimacy: Pushing for quick commitment to bypass scrutiny and establish dominance.

Protecting Yourself from Narcissistic DTGDs

Proactive measures are essential to avoiding entanglement with narcissistic DTGDs. Recommended strategies include:

- Questioning grandiosity: Look for inconsistencies in their claims of success or achievements. Pay attention to how they handle criticism or setbacks.

- Setting and Enforcing Boundaries: Be firm about financial and emotional boundaries, even if they attempt to dismiss or challenge them. Insist on transparency in financial matters.
- Signaling the existence of financial safeguards: Casually mention the existence of an FFT or a domestic asset protection trust (DAPT) or foreign asset protection trust (FAPT). Present these as family policies rather than personal choices to signal a unified front.
- Reinforcing the family narrative: Frame financial safeguards as part of a broader family legacy, emphasizing shared values and protection across generations. This discourages opportunistic behavior by portraying resources as well-guarded.
- Consulting trusted advisors: Share your observations with friends, family, or professionals who can provide objective insights. Rely on legal and financial advisors to implement protective measures like prenuptial agreements.

The Narcissistic Manipulator

Narcissistic DTGDs are uniquely dangerous predators, combining charm, entitlement, and emotional shallowness to exploit their targets. Their reliance on admiration and control makes them formidable manipulators, but understanding their tactics and psychological framework can offer crucial defenses. By recognizing the traits and warning signs of narcissistic DTGDs, you can safeguard your emotional and financial well-being and avoid becoming their next source of exploitation.

33

Understanding Dark Triad Traits in Depth: Psychopathic-Leaning DTGDs

Calculated and Remorseless Manipulation

DTGDs with pronounced psychopathic tendencies are the most dangerous. They take a cold, calculated approach to relationships, viewing people as tools to exploit for financial and emotional gain. Lacking empathy, remorse, and emotional attachment, they operate with a fearless and calculated mindset, which allows them to manipulate, deceive, and exploit without hesitation.

This chapter examines how psychopathy manifests within the DTGD cluster, emphasizing their predatory behaviors, psychological framework, and strategies for exploitation. By understanding their tactics and the psychological mechanisms they exploit, you can recognize the hallmarks of their manipulations and defend yourself effectively.

Psychopathy in the Dark Triad Cluster

Psychopathy is defined by emotional detachment, callousness, and a lack of moral restraint. These traits make psychopathic DTGDs uniquely dangerous, enabling them to manipulate with surgical precision and exploit without hesitation.

Emotional Detachment
Psychopathic DTGDs lack the emotional capacity for genuine connections.

- Absence of empathy: They cannot understand or feel the emotional consequences of their actions. Emotional pain, fear, or disappointment in others are merely tools for manipulation.
- Mechanical charm: Their charm is calculated and mechanical, deployed strategically to disarm skepticism and gain trust. This charm feels compelling, but often lacks depth or sincerity.

Fearless Exploitation
Psychopathic DTGDs adopt risky, high-reward schemes that most people would avoid.

- Risk-taking behavior: They pursue bold and reckless plans to extract maximum financial and social advantage, undeterred by potential consequences.
- Total moral flexibility: Traditional ethical constraints mean nothing to them. Lying, cheating, and even criminal activity are justified by their unwavering focus on self-interest.

Absence of Remorse
A lack of guilt allows psychopathic DTGDs to escalate their schemes without hesitation.

- Cold calculations: They harm others emotionally, financially, and socially without a second thought. To them, damage to others is merely a byproduct of achieving their goals.
- Shifting blame: When confronted, they skillfully deflect blame onto their victims or external circumstances, portraying themselves as misunderstood or victimized.

Tactics of Psychopathic-Leaning DTGDs

Psychopathic DTGDs operate with a cunning approach that leverages charm, deception, and fearlessness to dominate their targets. Their tactics are characterized by precision and a lack of emotional constraints.

Strategic Deception

Psychopathic DTGDs excel at creating false personas to manipulate their targets.

- Mastering the mask: They create personas that align perfectly with their targets' desires, from shared interests to fabricated backgrounds. This adaptability enables them to embed themselves seamlessly into their targets' lives.
- Fabricated histories: To gain trust, they construct elaborate backstories that portray them as successful, altruistic, or victimized. These stories are carefully curated to manipulate their targets' emotions and beliefs.

Gaslighting and Psychological Domination

To maintain control, psychopathic DTGDs use psychological tactics that distort reality and create dependency.

- Undermining reality: Gaslighting is a core tool. Psychopathic DTGDs distort facts, rewrite events, and manipulate perceptions to make their victims doubt their own judgment.

- Eroding self-worth: Subtle insults and strategic criticisms are used to weaken their targets' confidence, fostering dependency and compliance.

Financial Exploitation
Psychopathic DTGDs are adept at extracting financial resources while minimizing detection.

- Invisible drains: They siphon resources gradually through joint accounts, unauthorized withdrawals, or forged documents, often avoiding immediate suspicion.
- Extravagant schemes: Framing costly purchases or investments as "opportunities for both of us," they ensure that victims bear the financial burden while they reap the benefits.

What Happens When They Turn on You

When psychopathic DTGDs perceive threats to their control or financial access, their response is cold, calculated, and often devastating. Unlike narcissistic DTGDs, who respond emotionally, psychopathic DTGDs escalate strategically.

Strategic Retaliation

- Preemptive strikes: Psychopathic DTGDs initiate smear campaigns, spreading lies and distortions to discredit their victims and gain public sympathy.
- Sabotage: They target professional, social, or familial relationships, isolating their victims and weakening their support systems.

Emotional Manipulation

- Weaponizing vulnerabilities: Psychopathic DTGDs exploit their victims' insecurities or emotional connections, amplifying guilt or fear to regain control.

- Calculated abandonment: If they see no further utility, they abruptly end relationships, leaving financial and emotional devastation in their wake.

Escalation of Exploitation

- Legal battles: Psychopathic DTGDs often escalate to legal claims, using fabricated evidence or emotional narratives to bolster their positions in court.
- Economic devastation: Draining accounts, maxing out credit lines, or forcing the sale of assets are common tactics employed to secure additional gains.

How Psychopathic Traits Enhance Manipulation

Psychopathic DTGDs leverage their traits to exploit with unparalleled efficiency. Their core characteristics amplify their ability to deceive, control, and harm.

Emotional Insulation

- No guilt, no hesitation: Their lack of remorse allows them to pursue manipulative tactics without the emotional barriers most people experience.
- Unmoved by emotion: Targets may struggle with emotional fallout, but psychopathic DTGDs remain cold and focused, unaffected by their victims' pain.

Tactical Thinking

- Anticipating reactions: They excel at predicting their targets' moves, allowing them to stay one step ahead.
- Backup plans: Psychopathic DTGDs prepare contingency strategies, ensuring they maintain control even when their initial schemes fail.

High-Stakes Risk Tolerance

- Confidence under pressure: They thrive in high-stakes situations, using their composure to outmaneuver opponents.
- Relentless focus: Their single-minded pursuit of gain makes them relentless and difficult to deter.

Psychological Insights into Psychopathic DTGDs

Experts and studies offer valuable perspectives on the manipulative capabilities of psychopathic DTGDs

Manipulative Superficiality

- Dr. Robert Hare (author of *Without Conscience*): "Psychopaths are emotionally shallow, which makes them adept at mimicking emotions to manipulate others."
- Psychopathic DTGDs use emotional mimicry to feign connection, exploiting their targets' trust and empathy while remaining entirely self-serving.

Fearlessness and Risk-Taking

- Dr. Kent Kiehl (author of *The Psychopath Whisperer*): "Psychopaths exhibit reduced activity in the amygdala, the brain region responsible for fear and empathy."
- This fearlessness enables psychopathic DTGDs to execute high-risk schemes with unnerving confidence, often succeeding where others would hesitate.

Red Flags of Psychopathic DTGDs

Identifying psychopathic DTGDs early is crucial to avoiding financial and emotional devastation. Key warning signs include:

Inconsistencies in Behavior

- Shifting demeanor: Sudden transitions from charming to cold

when their control is challenged.
- Discrepant backstories: Fabricated histories that unravel under scrutiny.

Hyper-Control of Finances
- Demanding access: Insistence on joint accounts or asset control.
- Avoiding oversight: Resistance to financial transparency or independent review.

Emotional Manipulation
- Persistent guilt-tripping: Using fear, obligation, or guilt to secure compliance.
- Gaslighting: Manipulating facts and perceptions to erode confidence and self-trust.

Protecting Yourself from Psychopathic DTGDs

To counter the calculated tactics of psychopathic DTGDs, proactive measures are essential.

Demand Transparency
- Verify claims: Scrutinize their background, accomplishments, and financial independence.
- Avoid early commitments: Delay merging finances or making significant joint purchases.

Set and Enforce Firm Boundaries
- Maintain financial independence: Keep personal accounts separate and limit shared financial responsibilities.
- Reject high-pressure tactics: Be wary of urgency or coercion to commit financially or emotionally.

Signal That Financial Safeguards Exist
- Disclose protections early: Casually mention the existence of an

FFT, including your legal requirement to either have a prenup or establish a DAPT/FAPT. Present these as family policies rather than personal choices to signal a unified front.
- Reinforce a family narrative: Frame financial safeguards as part of a broader family legacy, emphasizing shared values and protection across generations. This discourages opportunistic behavior by portraying resources as well-guarded.

Involve Trusted Advisors
- Consult professionals: Work with financial planners and legal advisors to establish safeguards such as prenuptial agreements or trusts.
- Seek outside perspectives: Share concerns with trusted friends or family who can offer objective insights.

The Calculated Predator

Psychopathic DTGDs are the most calculated and remorseless predators within the Dark Triad cluster. Their emotional detachment, fearless risk-taking, and tactical brilliance make them uniquely dangerous. When their control is threatened, they escalate their manipulative tactics to inflict maximum damage with cold precision.

Understanding their traits, tactics, and psychological framework is essential for recognizing red flags and protecting yourself. By implementing robust defenses and maintaining vigilance, you can safeguard your financial and emotional well-being against these calculated predators.

34

Understanding Dark Triad Traits in Depth: Machiavellian-Leaning DTGDs

The Master Manipulators

DTGDs who lean heavily on Machiavellianism are the ultimate strategists. Machiavellian DTGDs operate with a calculated, long-term approach to manipulation, using cunning, charm, and meticulous planning to extract maximum value from their victims.

This chapter explores how Machiavellianism manifests within the DTGD cluster, detailing their strategies, tactics, and the impact of their manipulative behaviors. It also examines what happens when these DTGDs feel cornered or betrayed, offering insights into their retaliatory nature and the hallmarks of their malice when their illusion of control is threatened.

Machiavellianism in the Dark Triad Cluster

Machiavellianism is defined by a focus on manipulation, strategic thinking, and the exploitation of others for personal gain. Machiavellian DTGDs are the most patient and adaptable, willing to play the long game to secure their objectives.

Calculated Opportunism

- Machiavellian DTGDs carefully assess their targets, prioritizing individuals with high financial value or emotional vulnerability.
- Strategic targeting: They identify victims who are affluent, socially influential, or emotionally isolated, using patience to observe their habits and vulnerabilities before making a move.
- Long-term vision: Unlike impulsive manipulators, Machiavellian DTGDs invest months or years into schemes, meticulously planning their approach to minimize risk and maximize reward.

Emotional and Social Mastery

- Machiavellian DTGDs excel at navigating social dynamics and tailoring their behavior to fit their targets' expectations.
- Cold reading: By carefully observing body language, tone, and social cues, they gather critical information to adapt their tactics.
- Subtle influence: Their manipulation often feels natural, as they nudge their targets toward desired outcomes without overt pressure.

Detached Rationality

These DTGDs maintain emotional distance from their targets to ensure clear, objective decision-making.

- Transactional thinking: Relationships are viewed as strategic exchanges, devoid of genuine emotional investment.
- Risk assessment: Every decision is calculated for potential benefits and consequences, ensuring they maintain control at every stage.

Tactics of Machiavellian-Leaning DTGDs

Machiavellian DTGDs are defined by their ability to manipulate subtly and effectively, often leaving their targets unaware of their exploitation until it's too late.

Strategic Infiltration

- Building credibility: They establish themselves as trustworthy and indispensable, often positioning themselves as problem-solvers or confidants.
- Embedding in networks: By integrating themselves into their targets' social or professional circles, they gain influence and legitimacy, making their manipulations harder to detect.

Controlled Narratives

- Machiavellian DTGDs craft elaborate narratives to justify their actions and maintain control.
- Crafting stories: They weave convincing backstories and explanations that align with their targets' values or beliefs, securing trust and admiration.
- Information control: By selectively sharing or withholding information, they manipulate perceptions and maintain a strategic advantage.

Financial Engineering

- Subtle asset access: Unlike overt manipulators, Machiavellian DTGDs quietly gain access to finances through joint accounts, shared investments, or legal agreements.
- Framing as mutual benefit: They present financial decisions as collaborative efforts, ensuring targets feel complicit in their own exploitation.

How Machiavellian Traits Enhance Manipulation

Machiavellian DTGDs combine intelligence, patience, and adaptability to execute their strategies with precision. These traits make them exceptionally difficult to detect and counter.

Hyper-Adaptive Behavior

- Dynamic personas: They adjust their behavior and attitudes to align with their targets' expectations and values, blending seamlessly into different environments.
- Social versatility: Their ability to shift between personas enables them to exploit various social and professional contexts.

Mastery of Deception

- Convincing lies: They construct detailed, believable fabrications to maintain their façades, often reinforcing these lies with consistent, calm delivery.
- Feigning vulnerability: By appearing vulnerable or victimized, they disarm skepticism and elicit sympathy, creating a protective shield against scrutiny.

Emotional Detachment

- Objective decision-making: Their lack of emotional attachment allows them to exploit others without guilt or hesitation.
- Risk management: They meticulously calculate risks, ensuring their manipulations remain undetected while maximizing rewards.

What Happens When They Turn on You

When Machiavellian DTGDs perceive a loss of control or threat to their plans, their retaliation is strategic, cold, and devastating. Unlike the emotional outbursts of narcissistic DTGDs or the calculated malice of psychopathic DTGDs, Machiavellian DTGDs approach revenge as a methodical dismantling of their targets' lives.

Tactical Smear Campaigns

- Reputation destruction: They systematically spread false or exaggerated claims to damage their targets' reputations.
- Influencing allies: By manipulating mutual friends, colleagues, or family members, they isolate their targets and erode their support systems.

Legal and Financial Retaliation

- Weaponizing agreements: They exploit joint financial agreements, legal loopholes, or ambiguities to drain resources or create liabilities.
- Deliberate delays: In cases of divorce or separation, they use stalling tactics to exhaust their targets emotionally and financially.

Psychological Manipulation

- Planting doubts: They gaslight their targets into questioning their own decisions, ensuring they remain unsure and compliant.
- Rebuilding control: Through subtle acts of kindness or reconciliation, they reassert influence over their targets, prolonging the exploitation.

Psychological Insights into Machiavellian DTGDs

Experts and studies provide valuable perspectives on how Machiavellianism enhances manipulation and control.

The Art of Deception

- Dr. Richard Christie (Machiavellianism Researcher): "Machiavellians excel at understanding the motives of others and using that knowledge to their advantage."
- This insight highlights how Machiavellian DTGDs tailor their tactics to exploit their targets' specific vulnerabilities.

Social Maneuvering

- Dr. Caroline Watt (Psychologist, Expert on Manipulation): "Machiavellians are masters of social engineering, capable of influencing group dynamics to serve their purposes."
- Machiavellian DTGDs often exploit social networks to reinforce their legitimacy and gain leverage.

Red Flags of Machiavellian DTGDs

Spotting Machiavellian DTGDs requires vigilance and a keen eye for patterns of manipulation. Key warning signs include:

Overly Polished Personas

- Their behavior feels rehearsed or too perfect, lacking genuine spontaneity.
- They adapt their personalities to match their targets' preferences with uncanny precision.

Strategic Avoidance of Accountability

- They deflect responsibility for conflicts or mistakes, often blaming others.
- When questioned, their answers are evasive or overly complicated.

Persistent Information Gathering

- They probe for personal or financial details under the guise of casual curiosity.
- Their questions often seem disproportionately focused on vulnerabilities or decision-making processes.

Protecting Yourself from Machiavellian DTGDs

Proactive measures are essential for countering the calculated tactics of Machiavellian DTGDs.

Demand Transparency

- Verify their claims about their background, intentions, and financial independence.
- Avoid sharing sensitive information early in the relationship.

Set Firm Boundaries

- Clearly define emotional and financial boundaries, and enforce them consistently.
- Be wary of efforts to merge living arrangements and finances, or to make joint investments prematurely.
- If an FFT is in place, disclose its existence early.

Involve Trusted Advisors

- Consult legal and financial professionals to establish safeguards, such as prenuptial agreements or independent account oversight.
- Share concerns with trusted friends or family for objective perspectives.

The Strategic Predator

Machiavellian DTGDs are master manipulators, relying on their intelligence, adaptability, and long-term planning to exploit their targets. When their control is threatened, they respond with cold, calculated malice, dismantling their victims' support systems and financial security piece by piece. Understanding their traits and tactics is essential to recognizing red flags, protecting yourself, and disrupting their schemes.

35

DTGDs' Dark Shadows and the Lies They Tell Themselves

The Self-Deceptive Narratives of DTGDs

DTGDs do not see themselves as manipulators, predators, opportunists. To do so would require self-awareness, and self-awareness is the enemy of their survival. Instead, they weave a carefully curated web of self-deception, convincing themselves—and often those around them—that they are not just justified in their actions, but somehow *virtuous* in them.

They do not believe they are taking from their victims—they believe they are *owed.* They are not exploiting—they are *balancing the scales.* They are not lying—they are *protecting themselves* from the injustices of an unfair world. These narratives serve as the foundation of their psychological armor, allowing them to move through relationships with no guilt, no hesitation, and no accountability.

This chapter delves into the internal monologue of DTGDs—the mental gymnastics they perform to avoid confronting the darkness within themselves—and what happens when the fragile walls of their self-deception start to crack.

The Delusion of Entitlement

At the heart of every DTGD's mindset is the unwavering belief that they deserve what they take. In their world, wealth, privilege, and comfort are not things to be earned through effort, perseverance, or merit—they are *entitlements*, owed to them simply because they exist.

They see their victims' financial success as unjustly accumulated wealth, something that should be shared, redistributed, or simply absorbed into their own lifestyles. DTGDs reframe their actions not as exploitation, but as rectification—a self-serving delusion that turns their manipulations into a perverse kind of justice.

They whisper to themselves:

- *"They wouldn't have this success without people like me."*
- *"I bring so much to the relationship—this is just my fair share."*
- *"They owe me for everything I've put up with."*

This entitlement fuels their actions, making it easy to justify financial manipulation, extravagant spending, and even outright fraud. They are not taking advantage—they are simply *getting what is rightfully theirs.*

The Survival Narrative

When challenged, DTGDs lean more heavily into the victim narrative. They are never the aggressor, the schemer, or the opportunist—they are simply someone who has had to do what was necessary to survive.

In their minds, life has been unfair to them. They've suffered, they've struggled, and they've had to fight for everything they have. If that means leveraging someone else's wealth to secure their own future, so be it. Survival justifies everything.

This is how they excuse deception. They aren't lying—they are *navigating a world that has never given them a fair chance.* They aren't manipulative—they are *doing what they must to protect themselves.*

- *"If I don't look out for myself, who will?"*
- *"Other people don't have to struggle the way I did. This is just leveling the playing field."*
- *"They have plenty—what's wrong with me taking a little?"*

Through this lens, exploitation becomes a necessity, while morality becomes a luxury they cannot afford.

The Mask of Love

One of the most insidious lies DTGDs tell themselves is that they are in it for love. Even as they meticulously plan their financial extraction—even as they manipulate, gaslight, and entrench themselves into their victims' lives—they convince themselves that *this is a real relationship.*

They tell themselves that their feelings are genuine, and that their material motivations are secondary to their emotional connection. Even when faced with their own calculated actions—when the unvarnished truth is that they have stayed because the prenup was weak, or because the asset division would be in their favor—they push away the truth.

- *"I really do care about them."*
- *"If I didn't love them, I wouldn't still be here."*
- *"They're just paranoid—I'm not here for the money."*

The mask of love is a self-preservation tool, allowing them to suppress any lingering doubts that their relationships might be purely transactional. This is essential, because to acknowledge that would mean acknowledging something far worse: They are cold, calculating predators incapable of genuine intimacy. They are gold diggers.

The Role of the Dark Shadow

Beneath their façade lies DTGDs' "Dark Shadow"—a term borrowed from Carl Jung's concept of the shadow self, representing the repressed and unacknowledged parts of their psyche. For DTGDs, this shadow is defined by insecurity, fear of abandonment, and a deep-seated belief in their own unworthiness.

The Fear of Exposure

Deep down, behind the delusions and justifications, there is fear. DTGDs know—whether consciously or unconsciously—that if their true motivations were exposed, their world would crumble.

They fear the moment someone sees through them—when the carefully constructed illusion of love, devotion, and partnership is shattered by legal structures, financial boundaries, or the dawning realization of their victims.

Protective measures like prenups and financial trusts serve as more than just legal barriers—they are mirrors that force DTGDs to see themselves as they truly are when confronted with impenetrable obstacles to their goals of unjust enrichment. This realization often triggers rage, malice, and desperate retaliation. It is not just about losing financial access—it is about losing the ability to pretend.

What Happens When the Mask Slips

When DTGDs are forced to confront their Dark Shadow—either through external boundaries or the dissolution of their relationships—their manipulative façades often give way to anger, malice, and desperation.

Protective measures like FFTs and prenuptial agreements do more than block financial schemes—they deliver a direct blow to DTGDs' inflated sense of entitlement. These individuals operate under the unshakable belief that they are owed access to their partners' wealth. When they encounter airtight legal and economic barriers that preempt their plans to dodge or water down a prenup, they are forced to confront a reality they never anticipated: They are *not* truthfully "in it for the right reasons," and now they have nothing to gain.

The psychological impact of this realization triggers cognitive dissonance—a deep internal conflict between their self-perception as a deserving partner and the irrefutable evidence that their motivations have been financial all along. Rather than face this truth, they react with disproportionate fury, scrambling to rewrite the narrative before anyone else does.

This is when the distorted breakup narrative takes shape—a self-serving version of events where they cast themselves as the aggrieved party. They cannot allow the story to be that they walked away because their economic extraction strategy failed. Instead, they paint their former partner as cold, controlling, or untrusting. In their twisted version of events, they were the one who suffered—betrayed by a partner who refused to fully "commit" or "invest" in the relationship.

Getting Ahead of the Story

DTGDs live in constant fear of exposure. The very idea of being labeled for what they truly are—financial opportunists who were never emotionally invested—is unbearable. When they realize that bulletproof legal protections have closed every loophole they intended to exploit, their instinct for self-preservation kicks in.

Their new mission? Divert attention away from the inconvenient "coincidence" that they left immediately after discovering they had no financial path forward. They fabricate a more dramatic and sympathetic exit story, one that drowns out the real reason they walked away.

To outsiders, it looks like a sudden change of heart. To their former partners, it's an infuriatingly obvious deflection—an attempt to shift focus from the fact that they lost the financial game before it even began.

The Dark Shadow Exposed

DTGDs operate in the shadows of self-deception, crafting narratives that justify their actions and suppress their inner darkness. But when confronted with truth—whether through protective structures, exposure, or self-inflicted failure to effectively deceive their intended victims—their lies begin to crumble.

And once the mask slips, there is no putting it back on.

36

Why DTGDs Fear Exposure

Thriving in the Shadows

DTGDs do not thrive in the light. Their power lies in secrecy, deception, and controlling the narratives around them. Exposure is their kryptonite. It threatens their ability to manipulate, extract wealth and resources without question, and maintain the illusion of being something they are not. They are master illusionists, carefully curating their public personas to avoid scrutiny while moving through their prospective targets' circles undetected.

Understanding how DTGDs avoid exposure, manipulate perceptions, and weaponize secrecy is critical to dismantling their tactics. Bringing them into the light strips them of the control they so desperately cling to and, more importantly, makes it significantly harder for them to repeat the cycle with new victims.

DTGDs' Dependence on Secrecy

Secrecy is not just a convenience for DTGDs—it is a necessity. Without it, their manipulations unravel. Their carefully constructed identities rely on a lack of documentation, a controlled social narrative, and the ability to silence anyone who might challenge their versions of events.

They craft elaborate stories, tailoring their pasts to fit the expectations of their current targets. They offer just enough detail to be believable, while avoiding anything that might invite deeper scrutiny. The inconsistencies in their histories are explained away with charm or vague deflections: "It's complicated" or "You wouldn't understand." Their goal is to keep their victims focused on the present, never the past, because too many questions will expose too many cracks.

This is why DTGDs avoid crossing social circles. They compartmentalize their relationships, ensuring that people from different areas of their lives don't interact or compare notes. Their histories are fragmented, and their entire personas are based on who they need to be in the moment. The more disconnected their social networks are, the easier it is to maintain the illusion of credibility.

Fear of Exposure: The Achilles' Heel of DTGDs

DTGDs' biggest fear is being unmasked. Exposure threatens not only their financial gains, but also their entire senses of self. They have built their identities on deception, and the possibility of being seen for who they truly are is an existential threat.

Being publicly labeled gold diggers can destroy the foundation of their con. In the circles they target, reputation is everything. Wealthy individuals share information—and once the warning signs are out there, finding the next target becomes exponentially harder.

Beyond mere financial loss, exposure unravels the false reality they have constructed for themselves. DTGDs believe their own lies—they have to, in order to sell them convincingly. But when confronted with undeniable evidence of their manipulation, the illusion collapses. And with it, so does their ability to maintain control.

Fear of Being Exposed as Mentally Ill

For many DTGDs, the possibility of being labeled mentally unstable is just as terrifying as being exposed as a financial predator. Their manipulative tactics depend on maintaining an image of composure, competence, and control. If they are seen as emotionally unhinged, unstable, or suffering from a diagnosable personality disorder, they risk losing the trust and credibility that allow them to infiltrate wealthy social circles.

- Shame and stigma: DTGDs carefully construct images of power and success. Being labeled as mentally ill shatters that illusion, forcing them to face the reality that their behaviors stem from deep psychological dysfunction rather than strategy alone.
- Loss of leverage: The perception of mental instability weakens their ability to manipulate. DTGDs who are seen as emotionally erratic will have difficulty persuading others to see them as victims or worthy recipients of financial support.
- Fear of accountability: If their behavior is categorized as a symptom of malignant narcissism, psychopathy, or borderline personality disorder, they risk being viewed not just as manipulators, but as people who need psychological intervention rather than financial rescue.

How DTGDs Avoid Exposure

Because exposure is their greatest fear, DTGDs invest significant energy into ensuring it never happens. They employ a range of tactics designed to deflect scrutiny, control the narrative, and neutralize threats before they arise.

They gaslight their victims, making them question their own reality and instincts. When someone gets too close to the truth, DTGDs shift the focus, making their victims feel paranoid or overly suspicious. They might say:

- *"You're being ridiculous—why are you always looking for problems?"*
- *"You're making things up in your head."*
- *"I can't believe you don't trust me."*

If gaslighting fails, they turn to social manipulation. Preemptive smear campaigns are a favorite tool. They discredit their victims before the victims can expose them. DTGDs whisper half-truths to mutual friends, subtly positioning themselves as the true victims. When the real victims finally speak up, they are met with skepticism. The DTGDs have already laid the groundwork to frame them as bitter, jealous, or even unstable.

When all else fails, they run. Relocation is their final escape hatch. When DTGDs' deceptions are close to being exposed, they disappear from one social circle and reinvent themselves in another. New cities, new groups of friends, new wealthy targets—the cycle begins again.

Why Documentation and Transparency Are Their Worst Nightmare

If secrecy is DTGDs' strongest weapon, documentation is their greatest weakness. Paper trails expose inconsistencies, and transparency forces accountability. This is why they avoid formal agreements, contracts, and anything that can be used against them later. It's also why they fear the obligatory premarital financial disclosures that must be made in conjunction with prenups. False narratives of financial stability come undone with the requisite disclosures.

Instead, they rely on verbal agreements, knowing that words can be twisted and denied. They avoid shared financial records, ensuring there is no clear evidence of what was given versus what was taken. The less documentation there is, the easier it is for them to rewrite history when their relationships inevitably collapse.

But when confronted with hard evidence, their manipulations fall apart. Contracts, financial statements, written messages—these are the tools that render their gaslighting ineffective. They cannot deny what is in writing.

Transparency in relationships is equally powerful. Bringing in trusted advisors, maintaining open financial discussions, and ensuring major decisions involve third-party oversight creates a hostile environment for DTGDs. They cannot manipulate a system that refuses to function in secrecy.

Bringing DTGDs Into the Light

Knowledge is power. The more you understand about how DTGDs operate, the less power they have over you.

37

The Chameleon Effect

How DTGDs Evolve to Avoid Detection

DTGDs are not static predators. They do not rely on a single approach or a predictable pattern of manipulation. Instead, they are masters of adaptation, constantly refining their tactics, modifying their personas, and adjusting their strategies based on the failures and successes of their past. Much like a chameleon changes color to blend into its surroundings, DTGDs shift their personas to match their targets' expectations, avoiding scrutiny and ensuring their continued ability to exploit without detection.

If this book ever becomes an accidental bestseller, it won't just be because potential victims have sought to educate themselves. It will be because DTGDs themselves are reading it just as carefully, devouring every word in an effort to study how their playbook has been laid bare. Aware that exposure is their greatest enemy, they seek to adapt their methods of deception, ensuring their tactics can still fly under the radar.

This chapter explores how DTGDs refine and evolve their manipulative techniques, the ways they respond to exposure, and the steps that can be taken to counteract their ever-adapting strategies.

Tailoring the Perfect Persona

DTGDs do not present the same face to every target. Their greatest skill is their ability to tailor their personas to the unique vulnerabilities of each new mark. They become what their targets wants to see.

If their next target is a philanthropist, they adopt the façade of someone deeply passionate about charitable work. If their target is a successful entrepreneur, they pose as an ambitious self-starter with grand business ideas. If they are pursuing someone who values stability and family, they lean into a narrative of traditional values and a longing for deep emotional connection.

They are not just skilled manipulators—they are method actors, perfecting their performances until they become indistinguishable from authenticity. Every conversation, shared interest, and mirroring of values is a strategic play to deepen trust and establish themselves as irreplaceable.

But what makes them especially insidious is their ability to sustain these performances for extended periods. Unlike ordinary fraudsters, who rely on short-term deception, DTGDs play a long con—one that unfolds over years. Their patience is calculated, as their investment in the relationship is a means to an end.

Technology as a Weapon: How DTGDs Leverage Digital Tools

The modern world provides DTGDs with an arsenal of technological advantages. Social media, online databases, and networking platforms have supercharged their ability to target, study, and manipulate victims with unprecedented efficiency.

They use social media as a surveillance tool, analyzing their targets' posts to gather insights into their routines, interests, and values. A simple

Instagram story can reveal a preferred restaurant, a business trip destination, or the kind of emotional validation their targets crave. Armed with this data, they tailor their interactions, ensuring that every conversation feels eerily serendipitous.

They also use technology to refine their own digital images. Their social media profiles are carefully curated, filled with carefully chosen posts that reinforce whatever persona they are currently crafting. They may fabricate job titles, manufacture social proof by surrounding themselves with equally superficial acquaintances, and erase digital traces of previous failed attempts at deception.

They are also students of their own craft. DTGDs actively seek out resources like this book, as well as online forums and relationship psychology articles to refine their tactics. They are aware that exposure is their enemy, and they proactively adapt to ensure they remain undetectable to the untrained eye.

How Public Exposure Forces DTGDs to Adapt

For all their cunning, public exposure is the single greatest threat to DTGDs' survival. When they sense it looming, they move quickly to adapt their approaches.

When books, online communities, or articles dissect their tactics, DTGDs take notes. They learn which red flags are becoming well-known and adjust their behavior accordingly. They abandon tactics that have become too recognizable and refine their scripts to appear more authentic. If the world learns to watch for one type of manipulation, they simply pivot to another.

Community awareness forces DTGDs to work harder, but it also makes their manipulations more sophisticated. In affluent circles where reputations are currency, they know how to rebrand themselves—leaving one social group and emerging in another with a new backstory and a fresh batch of unsuspecting targets.

The Bloodline Alliance's Response: A Living Repository of DTGD Tactics

Recognizing that DTGDs are constantly evolving, The Bloodline Alliance has established a living repository for tracking DTGD tactics in real time.

A growing network of victims, advocates, and researchers are contributing crowdsourced intelligence, including detailed accounts of manipulative behaviors, emerging red flags, and evolving DTGD strategies. This ensures that, no matter how much they adapt, their tactics are always being documented and exposed.

As new editions of this book emerge, they will include the latest iterations of DTGD behavior, ensuring that awareness keeps pace with their ever-changing playbook.

Staying Ahead: How to Recognize DTGDs, No Matter How They Adapt

Despite their evolution, there are constants in DTGDs' methodology—patterns that persist no matter how much they refine their approach. Recognizing these enduring traits is key to outmaneuvering them.

- They always tailor their personas to their targets. If someone seems *too perfect, too aligned with everything you value*, take a step back.
- They avoid transparency. Whether it's finances, past relationships, or personal history, there will always be a fog of vagueness surrounding key details.
- They resist scrutiny. DTGDs will always find a way to make *you* feel guilty for asking too many questions, shifting the focus away from their inconsistencies.
- They resist financial boundaries. Whether it's trust structures or prenups, they will put up extraordinary resistance, usually paired with negative and highly manipulative portrayals of you as a jerk for even suggesting the idea.

The Battle Against an Evolving Predator

DTGDs are not static. They evolve, they refine, and they stay ahead of those who are not paying attention. But no matter how much they adapt, the steps to protecting yourself remains the same: Understand their playbook, recognize the patterns, and never let deception masquerade as authenticity.

Education is the first line of defense. Awareness is the weapon they fear most. By sharing knowledge, documenting experiences, and maintaining collective vigilance, we ensure that, no matter how much they try to evolve, they will never again go unseen.

Common DTGD Exploitation Tactics

38

Exploiting Generosity to Build Dependence

Generosity as a Double-Edged Sword

Generosity is often seen as one of the noblest human qualities, a sign of kindness and selflessness. Yet, in the hands of DTGDs, generosity becomes a weakness to be exploited. DTGDs are experts at identifying and leveraging their targets' goodwill to create financial and emotional dependency. They use generosity as a tool, turning acts of kindness into opportunities for manipulation and control.

This chapter examines how DTGDs exploit their targets' generosity to build dependence, highlighting the tactics they employ and the psychological impact on their victims. Practical strategies for maintaining healthy boundaries while protecting your finances and emotional well-being are also provided.

How DTGDs Exploit Generosity

DTGDs view generosity not as an admirable quality, but as a resource to be mined. They capitalize on their targets' desire to help, turning acts of kindness into obligations and opportunities for exploitation.

Establishing Patterns of Giving

From the beginning, DTGDs subtly test the limits of their targets' generosity. They may start with small requests—a favor here, a loan there—but gradually escalate over time. These initial asks often seem harmless and even endearing, as they frame their needs as temporary hurdles. Once the targets prove willing to give, DTGDs set the stage for larger demands.

Weaponizing Empathy and Guilt

DTGDs often portray themselves as struggling under extraordinary circumstances, crafting narratives designed to elicit sympathy. They might claim they are victims of an unfair system, bad luck, or unresolved trauma. By framing their financial dependence as a result of external forces, they make their targets feel morally obligated to help.

Statements like "You're the only one I can count on" or "If I don't get this money, I'll lose everything" create a sense of urgency and guilt, compelling targets to act. Over time, the targets' generosity becomes less about choice and more about obligation.

Conflating Generosity with Love

For DTGDs, financial and emotional support are transactional. They blur the lines between generosity and affection, framing acts of giving as proof of love. Phrases like "If you really loved me, you'd help me with this" or "This is what partners do for each other" manipulate targets into equating financial sacrifice with emotional commitment.

Building Dependency Through Generosity

Once DTGDs establish a pattern of giving, they shift their strategy to build dependency, ensuring their targets become entangled in a cycle of support that is difficult to escape.

Financial Dependency
DTGDs use their targets' generosity to create financial enmeshment. By encouraging shared accounts, joint investments, or co-signed loans, they ensure their targets feel financially obligated to "see things through." For example, DTGDs might suggest co-signing on a new car or taking out a joint loan to "start a business" that rarely materializes into anything more than a drain on their targets' finances.

Emotional Dependency
DTGDs understand that generosity often stems from emotional connection. They weaponize this connection by intertwining their financial requests with their targets' sense of worth and value in relationships. The more the targets give, the more invested they become in "fixing" the DTGDs' fabricated struggles, creating a cycle of emotional dependency that is hard to break.

Normalizing the Asks
Asking for financial support becomes routine. Over time, targets begin to see these requests not as manipulative, but as a normal part of their relationships. DTGDs are adept at normalizing increasingly unreasonable demands, making their targets feel as though they are simply doing their part.

Examples of Exploitation in Practice

DTGDs adapt their tactics to suit their targets' personalities, values, and vulnerabilities. The following are common examples of how they exploit generosity to build dependence.

Fabricating Financial Crises

DTGDs often manufacture emergencies to elicit financial support. Whether it's a sudden medical bill, a "once-in-a-lifetime" investment opportunity, or a fabricated legal issue, these crises are designed to create urgency and compel their targets to act without question.

For instance, a DTGD might say, "I need $10,000 to cover an unexpected expense, and if I don't get it, I could lose everything." This scenario often plays on their target's sense of responsibility and compassion, forcing them to step in as the "savior."

Leveraging Guilt

When targets hesitate to provide financial support, DTGDs employ guilt-tripping tactics. They might remind targets of past gifts or sacrifices, framing their current requests as reasonable "payback." For example, "After everything I've done for you, I can't believe you'd question helping me this once."

Framing Generosity as "Shared Goals"

DTGDs often mask their financial demands as investments in their relationships. They might suggest starting a business together, upgrading to a more luxurious home, or taking a "dream vacation" that ends up being funded almost entirely by their targets. By framing these asks as "shared goals," they obscure their true intentions.

The Psychological and Financial Toll

The exploitation of generosity leaves lasting scars on both the emotional and financial well-being of the targets. Victims often experience feelings of betrayal, shame, and financial insecurity as they grapple with the realization that their kindness has been manipulated.

Emotional Impact

- Self-doubt: Victims may question their own judgment, wondering how they allowed themselves to be exploited.

- Guilt and shame: Many struggle with feelings of embarrassment or guilt for not recognizing the manipulation sooner.

Financial Fallout

- Depleted resources: Victims often face significant losses—ranging from drained savings to mounting debt—as a result of their misplaced trust.
- Erosion of future trust: The experience often leaves victims wary of future relationships, complicating their ability to rebuild emotional and financial stability.

Strategies for Protection

Recognizing and countering generosity exploitation requires a proactive approach to setting boundaries and maintaining financial autonomy. The following are practical steps to safeguard your emotional and financial well-being.

Set Clear Boundaries

- Establish limits: Decide in advance how much financial support you are willing to provide (if any) and stick to these boundaries.
- Avoid co-mingling funds: Keep your finances separate until the relationship has been established over a significant period.
- Avoid living together for *at least* a year: A classic DTGD manipulation is to fabricate some sort of "crisis" with their present living arrangement so their target feels obligated to take them in "temporarily." The DTGD's crystal clear (albeit unstated) intent is to install themselves in your home and never leave. They want to make it impossibly awkward for you to break up with them, while concurrently blocking any possibility of a competing romantic interest. If living together is sprung on you as some form of "urgent crisis," nine times out of 10, you're dealing with a bona fide DTGD who is laying a trap to ensnare you.

Verify the Crisis

- Fact-check requests: Ask for documentation or evidence before agreeing to financial assistance. Genuine needs will withstand scrutiny.
- Seek a second opinion: Consult trusted friends, family, or advisors to validate the legitimacy of financial requests.

Maintain Emotional Independence

- Resist guilt-tripping: Recognize emotional manipulation for what it is and refuse to be swayed by guilt or obligation.
- Encourage self-sufficiency: Offer advice or resources instead of direct financial support, empowering the other person to solve their own problems.

Generosity Without Exploitation

Generosity is a strength, but in the hands of DTGDs, it becomes a tool for exploitation. By recognizing their tactics and establishing firm boundaries, you can protect your emotional and financial resources while maintaining your capacity for genuine kindness. Healthy relationships are built on mutual respect and reciprocity, not manipulation disguised as need.

39
Intermittent Reinforcement: Calling Out Ham-Handed Manipulations

The Power of Intermittent Reinforcement: Psychological Entrapment

Love should be a source of connection and security, but for DTGDs, it is used as a tool—a calculated mechanism for control, manipulation, and financial extraction. Nowhere is this more apparent than in their masterful use of intermittent reinforcement, a psychological strategy that mirrors gambling addiction. Just as a slot machine doles out occasional rewards to keep players hooked, DTGDs cycle between affection and withdrawal, ensuring that their victims remain emotionally invested even in the face of neglect, cruelty, or exploitation.

Victims caught in this cycle desperately chase the fleeting moments of kindness, ignoring the emotional wasteland in between. This form of manipulation is not accidental—it is deliberate, time-tested, and devastatingly effective. The unpredictability of their affection strengthens the emotional bond, ensuring that victims cling to illusions of love while excusing the suffering they endure.

"The Rules": A DTGD's Guide to Manipulative Courtship

Few cultural artifacts so perfectly capture the DTGD's psychological playbook as the book *The Rules: Time-Tested Secrets for Capturing the Heart of Mr. Right.* Originally marketed as a guide to help women attract men, this book is, in reality, a thinly veiled manual on emotional control. It advises women to be unavailable, play hard to get, and keep men in a constant state of pursuit. For an authentic partner looking for love, these tactics can be exhausting and counterproductive. For DTGDs, however, this is the ideal structure to entrap a target and secure long-term financial gains.

Key tactics from *The Rules* that align perfectly with DTGD strategies include:

- Scarcity tactics: DTGDs understand that value is often associated with rarity. By making themselves seem exclusive or difficult to attain, they create an artificial sense of urgency in their targets' minds.
- Controlled access: Keeping interactions brief, refusing to initiate contact, and feigning disinterest forces targets to work harder to gain approval.
- Pushing the pursuit: The more effort targets invest, the less likely they are to walk away. DTGDs manipulate this by requiring constant validation while offering little in return.
- Random rewards: DTGDs will occasionally provide intense affection, romantic gestures, or words of affirmation to keep their victims emotionally addicted, much like a gambler chasing a jackpot.

Weaponized Distance and Re-Engagement

DTGDs rarely maintain a steady emotional baseline in their relationships. Instead, they carefully balance detachment with bursts of affection, engineering an emotional rollercoaster designed to maximize dependence.

- The cold shoulder: DTGDs will often pull away for seemingly no reason, making the target question their own actions and scramble to regain favor.
- Hot and cold: They alternate between being intensely affectionate and distant, ensuring their targets remain emotionally destabilized and desperate for their approval.
- The re-engagement trap: When victims start to pull away, DTGDs suddenly become the partners they were at the beginning, reigniting hope just long enough to reset the cycle.

This method ensures that victims remain emotionally invested, often ignoring red flags in the hope of rekindling the rare, euphoric highs they once experienced.

Why It Works: The Psychological Hook

Intermittent reinforcement is so effective because it plays on a fundamental aspect of human psychology: The uncertainty of rewards increases addiction.

Studies in behavioral psychology show that when people are given rewards at random intervals rather than at predictable times, they are far less likely to give up—even when those rewards are outweighed by negative experiences. DTGDs exploit this relentlessly.

- Oxytocin manipulation: The chemical associated with bonding and trust floods victims' brains during affectionate moments, making them dismiss warning signs.

- Dopamine traps: The unpredictable highs trigger the same neural pathways as gambling addiction, reinforcing the victims' pursuit of fleeting emotional rewards.
- Cognitive dissonance: Victims rationalize mistreatment by focusing on the good moments, convincing themselves that the relationship is worth saving.

How to Throw DTGDs off Balance

If you suspect that someone is using *The Rules* or intermittent reinforcement tactics to manipulate you, the best strategy is not to take the bait when they pull away.

Instead of chasing them or questioning their behavior, flip the dynamic. Make *them* be the one to revisit *you* (and eat crow). When they do re-engage, subtly acknowledge their tactics with an offhanded, innocent-yet-devastating remark that exposes the game without direct confrontation:

"Oh, I thought you were busy...or were testing 'The Rules' on me (chuckle). Have you ever read it?"

This accomplishes three things:

1. It signals that you see through the manipulation. By calling it out humorously, you strip away their power and put them on the defensive.
2. It forces them to reassess their strategy. If they realize their game isn't working, they may either drop the act or escalate, making their intentions even more obvious.
3. It positions you as the one in control. Instead of being the pursuer, you become the prize—someone who is self-aware, confident, and unwilling to engage in childish emotional games.

The key here is not to be angry, defensive, or confrontational—but instead to remain lighthearted, amused, and in control. DTGDs thrive on emotional responses. Deprive them of that, and their grip begins to weaken.

The Path to Breaking Free

Recognizing the cycle of intermittent reinforcement is the first step in breaking free. Awareness disrupts the psychological grip of DTGDs, allowing victims to see patterns for what they truly are: manipulative tactics designed to extract resources and maintain control.

Steps to Escape DTGDs' Emotional Grip

1. Identify the pattern: Document interactions, noting when affection is given and when it is withdrawn. Seeing the cycle on paper eliminates the illusion of unpredictability.
2. Don't take the bait: This signals their attempted manipulations won't work on you.
3. Seek support: Friends, therapists, and financial advisors can provide objective perspectives on your observations.
4. Prioritize logic over emotion: Look at the facts of the relationship. How much emotional and financial effort have you given compared to what you have received?
5. Understand that love should not be a rollercoaster: Healthy relationships are stable, predictable, and supportive. Anything else is manipulation.

The Reckoning: A Collective Response

DTGDs rely on society's reluctance to call out manipulative behavior for what it is: financial and emotional exploitation. By exposing these tactics, we strip them of their power. This is why sharing knowledge is one of the greatest weapons against their deception.

Every time a victim shares their story, recognizes the cycle, or walks away, it is a direct blow to the DTGD system.

- Spread awareness: Talk openly about how intermittent reinforcement is used as a weapon.
- Reject false narratives: Challenge cultural myths that normalize manipulative tactics like those in *The Rules*.
- Fortify boundaries: Protect yourself and others by ensuring financial autonomy and emotional security.

The more people recognize the hallmark tactics of their game, the fewer victims there will be—and that is a future worth fighting for.

40

The Role of Isolation in Control

Isolation as a Weapon

Isolation is one of the most insidious tools in the DTGD arsenal. By cutting their victims off from supportive networks—friends, family, and trusted advisors—DTGDs erode external perspectives that could expose their manipulation. Through subtle tactics and calculated strategies, they foster a dynamic of dependency, ensuring that their victims have no one else to rely on but them.

This chapter examines how DTGDs use isolation to control their targets, the psychological impact on victims, and actionable steps to rebuild connections and escape their manipulative grip. Understanding these dynamics is critical for identifying red flags and preventing further harm.

How DTGDs Isolate Their Victims

The process of isolation begins subtly, often cloaked in affection or concern, but eventually escalates to complete control. DTGDs know that, in order to gain full dominance, they must sever their victims' ties to outside influences, leaving them vulnerable and reliant.

Undermining Relationships
DTGDs plant seeds of doubt about the motives of friends and family, framing them as unsupportive, jealous, or even hostile. Comments like "Your best friend seems really judgmental about us" or "I don't think your family understands what makes you happy" create subtle rifts over time. These remarks accumulate, leading victims to question the intentions of those around them.

Monopolizing Time
By insisting on constant companionship and discouraging independent activities, DTGDs ensure that victims' worlds shrink to revolve solely around them. Invitations to social events are often declined on victims' behalf with excuses like "We need some time for ourselves" or "I thought it would be nice to have a quiet evening together." This steady erosion of external connections deepens victims' dependence.

Controlling Communication
DTGDs often intercept or discourage communication with others. They might "forget" to pass along messages from friends or frame conversations with family members as intrusive. Conflict is another tool in their arsenal. By fabricating disputes or exaggerating minor disagreements, they create friction between victims and their support networks, making reconciliation more difficult.

The Psychological Impact of Isolation

The consequences of isolation are profound, affecting victims' emotional well-being, self-perception, and decision-making abilities. Without external perspectives, victims become increasingly reliant on DTGDs' versions of reality.

Erosion of Confidence

Isolation strips victims of feedback loops that validate their instincts and decisions, leaving them doubting their own judgment. They begin to rely exclusively on DTGDs' narratives, which are often distorted to serve the manipulator's agenda. This lack of perspective makes it difficult for victims to recognize manipulation or take steps to protect themselves.

Emotional Dependence

As isolation deepens, emotional dependence grows. Victims come to see DTGDs as their sole source of support and validation. This dynamic often leads to a fear of abandonment, which DTGDs exploit to maintain control. Subtle threats like "I don't know what I'd do if you ever left me" reinforce victims' sense of responsibility for DTGDs' well-being, further entrenching the manipulative dynamic.

Social Disconnection

Fractured relationships with friends and family leave victims feeling alone and unsupported. Even if they recognize DTGDs' manipulation, the prospect of rebuilding these connections can feel daunting, creating a sense of helplessness.

Why Isolation Strengthens DTGDs' Control

Isolation is more than a tactic—it's a strategy for consolidating power. By removing external influences, DTGDs ensure that their targets' decisions are shaped entirely by their manipulative input. This control extends to both emotional and financial aspects of the relationship.

Emotional Control

Without outside perspectives, victims are less likely to question DTGDs' intentions or actions. The absence of trusted confidants allows DTGDs to dictate the narrative unchallenged, reinforcing their version of reality as the only truth.

Financial Exploitation
Isolation removes critical safeguards, such as trusted advisors or family members who might encourage protective measures. DTGDs often discourage trusts, prenuptial agreements, estate planning, or financial transparency, framing them as unnecessary or distrustful. This lack of oversight enables them to gain unimpeded access to resources, which they exploit for their own gain.

Rebuilding Connections After Isolation

Escaping DTGDs' grip requires more than recognizing their tactics—it involves actively rebuilding the relationships and support systems that were eroded. While this process can be challenging, it is essential for regaining independence and emotional stability.

Acknowledging the Isolation
Victims must identify the ways in which their connections were severed and challenge the narratives that justified it. This may involve revisiting past interactions with friends or family to recognize where DTGDs' influence distorted their perceptions.

Reaching Out to Loved Ones
Rebuilding connections requires vulnerability and honesty. Victims may need to explain their circumstances and ask for understanding. While not all relationships can be fully repaired, many people are willing to offer support when they understand the manipulative dynamics at play.

Setting Boundaries
As victims rebuild their networks, they must protect their spaces and prioritize their well-being. This includes limiting DTGDs' influence over

their time, communication, and decisions. Professional support from therapists, legal advisors, and financial planners can provide additional guidance and structure, helping victims regain control over their lives.

Reclaiming Independence

Isolation is one of DTGDs' most effective weapons, allowing them to manipulate their targets without interference. However, by recognizing their tactics and taking deliberate steps to rebuild connections, victims can break free and reclaim their independence. Healthy relationships thrive on mutual respect and shared connections, qualities that no DTGD can truly offer.

41

USING AI TO MANIPULATE

The Digital Deception: How DTGDs Use AI to Manufacture Love and Manipulate You

Love, when it's real, is a rare and powerful thing. It's not just about attraction or compatibility—it's about seeing the soul of another person and choosing them, flaws and all. It's about connection—the kind of bond that makes life richer, deeper, and more meaningful.

But what happens when that connection is a lie? What happens when you've spent months, maybe even years, falling in love with a fiction, a manufactured persona crafted by artificial intelligence? When every deep conversation, every perfectly timed reassurance, every vulnerable confession wasn't real, but instead generated to control you, trap you, and financially entangle you?

This is no longer a hypothetical question. AI-driven seduction tools like Blush, LoveGenius, and custom-built AI chatbots are being used by DTGDs to manufacture emotional bonds with surgical precision. These tools don't just assist with dating—they create entire romantic illusions designed to bypass your defenses and embed themselves in your heart and mind. And once you believe you've found the perfect partner? That's when the financial extraction begins.

This is full-scale deception. AI-driven romance isn't just dishonest—it's an act of psychological and emotional fraud.

The AI Playbook: Weaponizing Technology

In the past, DTGDs had to rely on natural charm, intuition, and manipulation skills to infiltrate their targets' lives. They had to be quick thinkers, skilled at mirroring, and adept at emotional exploitation. Now, AI does the heavy lifting for them.

Step 1: Using AI to Craft the "Perfect Partner" Persona

When DTGDs begin their hunts, they first create data profiles of their targets. They use AI tools to analyze your communication style, personality, and emotional triggers. These AI systems collect and interpret vast amounts of data from:

- Your social media activity (likes, comments, posts, shared interests)
- Your texts and messages (word choice, emotional tone, response timing)
- Your online behaviors (articles you read, videos you watch, topics you engage with)

Using this data, AI-powered tools then craft perfectly tailored romantic responses.

- Every "spontaneous" love message? Pre-optimized.
- Every flirtation? Fine-tuned by an algorithm.
- Every deep conversation? Scripted to elicit maximum emotional engagement.
- Every moment that makes you feel understood and deeply

connected may not actually be real. It may be AI analyzing and manipulating you in real time.

Step 2: AI-Generated Emotional Bonding

Once DTGDs have shaped their personas into the ideal partners, they move into emotional engineering. This is where they embed themselves into your psyche, making it nearly impossible for you to distinguish between real love and an AI-manufactured illusion.

They use AI-generated deep conversations in texts and messenger apps that appear vulnerable and sincere. They don't have to bare their souls—they can let an algorithm do the work.

They optimize responses for maximum attachment, knowing exactly when to pull back, when to show affection, and when to create distance for maximum psychological reinforcement.

In person, they follow AI-powered scripts to mirror your emotional needs. They become the person you've been looking for—because AI has taught them how to play the role.

You might feel like you've found your soulmate, but in reality, you've found someone who has weaponized AI to manipulate your emotions.

How to Defend Yourself: Spotting AI-Driven Manipulation

The terrifying thing about AI-generated romance is that it's designed to feel indistinguishable from real human connection. But if you know what to look for, you can disrupt the illusion before they have a chance to control you.

1. The In-Person Mismatch

If the person you've been texting with seems wildly different in real life, take notice.

- Do they struggle with spontaneous, unscripted conversations?
- Do they seem less articulate, less engaging, or less emotionally perceptive in person?

- Do they fail to recall past online discussions that were deeply emotional?

AI-crafted personas often collapse under real-world conditions. Trust your instincts—if something feels off, it probably is.

2. Test for AI-Generated Text
Use AI-identifying tools like

- CopyLeaks
- GPTZero
- Originality.ai

If the messages that made you feel so "seen" turn out to be generated by a machine, you have your answer.

3. Disrupt Their Algorithm
AI thrives on patterns. Disrupt them by:

- Changing your texting style frequently.
- Asking deeply personal, unpredictable questions.
- Introducing random, unexpected topics and seeing if they can keep up.

If their responses feel generic, repetitive, or overly polished, you may be dealing with an AI-assisted manipulator.

Final Thoughts: Protecting the Sanctity of Real Love

Love is meant to be authentic. It should be built on truth, trust, and raw human connection. When DTGDs use AI to manufacture affection, they commit the ultimate betrayal—not just against you, but against the very concept of love itself.

They are not just lying—they are stealing something sacred.

By understanding how AI is used to manipulate relationships, you can arm yourself with knowledge, test for deception, and ensure that your connections are built on genuine trust rather than algorithmic precision.

Real love is not a script or an algorithm—and it is certainly never a con.

42

Do You Want a Dependent Spouse?

Allergic to Work

Most people walk into marriage expecting partnership. They assume that both individuals will contribute in ways that keep the relationship balanced—whether that means financially, emotionally, or practically within the household. But expectations don't always align with reality. If there's one universal truth about DTGDs, it's this: Work is not in their vocabulary.

For DTGDs, finding partners with financial means *is* their full-time job. Their career aspirations often start and end with securing someone else to foot the bill for their lifestyle. But they know better than to make that obvious at the outset. Instead, they present themselves as ambitious, independent, and even entrepreneurial—until the moment they no longer have to be.

Which brings us to the real question: Are you comfortable with a dependent spouse? If the answer is yes, that's your choice—but it should be an intentional one, not one you were manipulated into. If your answer is no, then it's imperative that you recognize the strategic ways DTGDs transition from "career-driven" to "financially dependent" before you become trapped in one of their webs.

This chapter explores how DTGDs slowly maneuver their way out of work, how they justify doing so, and how they ultimately set themselves up for long-term financial dependence—often culminating in permanent spousal support claims. More importantly, it outlines what you can do to protect yourself before that happens.

From Ambition to Retirement: The DTGD Playbook

When you first meet them, DTGDs often give the impression of being driven and successful. They may have jobs, "businesses," or vague but exciting-sounding career paths that suggest self-sufficiency. But this is simply part of the con—a mirage designed to make them seem like equal partners, when, in reality, they have no intention of pulling their weight in the long term.

The Career "Wind Down" Strategy

Watch for these telltale signs that DTGDs are laying the groundwork for financial dependence:

- They suddenly lose interest in their job or career path. What was once an exciting opportunity for them now "isn't fulfilling" or "doesn't feel right anymore."
- They frame stepping back as a sacrifice for the relationship. They might suggest that their "career shift" is about "prioritizing the relationship" or "supporting your goals."
- They create an economic dependency excuse. Maybe they insist their job was "too demanding" or "too stressful," or they say, "I

want to be more present in our life together."
- They let "temporary" breaks turn into permanent ones. What starts as a month or two off to "recharge" turns into years of inactivity—until they establish a baseline expectation that you will provide for them.

Once they've transitioned out of work, the next step is to cement their financial dependence.

Pregnancy: The Ultimate Retirement Plan

For DTGDs, having children is the perfect justification for leaving the workforce indefinitely.

Step One: Use pregnancy as an excuse to take time off work.
- DTGDs will insist that working while pregnant is "too much" or "too stressful."

Step Two: Extend their absence into the newborn years.
- Once the baby arrives, returning to work is "impossible." They claim their presence at home is essential, dismissing any suggestions of part-time work or outside childcare.

Step Three: Introduce additional children to reset the clock.
- The easiest way to never have to go back to work is to keep having kids. Each new pregnancy restarts the dependency cycle, ensuring they remain financially supported for another stretch of years.
- Conveniently, this strategy also accelerates post-divorce economic entitlements against your post-divorce income through child support.
- Even if there is a prior agreement (verbal or written) about returning to work after having children, DTGDs will gaslight you into believing that expecting them to honor their given

word on your mutual agreement is cruel, neglectful, or unreasonable. In divorce proceedings, they will paint themselves as the selfless parent who sacrificed everything for the family—a strategy designed to justify long-term spousal support and maximum child support payments.

The "No Marketable Skills" Argument

Fast forward to divorce proceedings, and you'll find yourself facing the ultimate DTGD trump card: "I have no marketable skills."

Make no mistake—this narrative is cultivated over time. DTGDs know the longer they can dodge rejoining the workforce, the more helpless they appear and the better chances they have of securing long-term financial support.

How they set this up:

- Refusing career development opportunities.
- Dismissing suggestions to re-enter the workforce.
- Insisting they're "better suited" to managing the household.

In family court, this translates into the perfect victim argument:

- *"I gave up my career for this marriage."*
- *"I sacrificed everything to support my spouse."*
- *"I have no skills to re-enter the workforce—I need financial support."*

The goal? Justify indefinite spousal support.

Spousal Support: The Longer They Stay, the More They Take

Spousal support entitlements increase over time. Typically, the longer the marriage lasts, the greater the percentage of your post-divorce income DTGDs can claim in spousal support. In many jurisdictions, spousal support can reach 50% of your after-tax income, *indefinitely.* In some states, that number can climb as high as 55%.

DTGDs know it can take a few decades to max out their spousal support entitlements at 50% of your income, but they also know how to shorten that timeline to 5 years or less. How? By having your children, with or without your consent.

Children are an economic multiplier in divorce proceedings. Not only do they make it harder for you to argue against spousal support, but they also introduce long-term child support obligations that further drain your resources. The moment children enter the picture, DTGDs have locked in financial entrenchment for decades—often while refusing to work altogether.

This legal reality underscores why having children with DTGDs is one of the riskiest financial decisions you can make. Chapters 45 to 47 cover the consequences in detail, including whether it's advisable to have them *at all* with DTGDs.

Prevention: Set Clear Expectations From the Start

You don't have to guess your way through this. Instead, decide what you're comfortable with *before* you commit to an engagement.

- Are you okay with being the sole provider?
- If not, what are your expectations for financial contribution?
- If your partner were to stop working, under what conditions would that be acceptable?

Put it in writing. A well-drafted prenup can address this before it ever becomes a problem. Prenups designed to proactively prevent later claims of dependency often have clauses providing for vocational training and childcare if the relationship ends, so there are no plausible excuses for being "unable to support themselves" or having "no marketable skills." People all over the world reinvent themselves every day—so can DTGDs.

43

Dodging Prenups: Definitely a DTGD

Prenup Resistance

This chapter examines the most common objections DTGDs use to avoid signing prenuptial agreements. These tactics are not just red flags—they are sirens blaring a warning that you are almost certainly dealing with a DTGD. By understanding their strategies, you can protect yourself from falling victim to their schemes.

Common Objections DTGDs Use to Avoid Prenups

When faced with the prospect of a prenup, DTGDs deploy an arsenal of emotional manipulations, often disguised as heartfelt objections. Their goal is to shift the conversation away from financial protection and frame the request as an attack on the relationship.

"You don't love me."

- DTGDs weaponize affection, implying that the very suggestion of a prenup undermines the foundation of the relationship.
- Statements like "If you really loved me, you wouldn't need this" or "I thought love was about trust, not contracts" are designed to guilt targets into abandoning the idea.

"You don't trust me."

- Trust is the next weapon in the arsenal, with DTGDs framing the prenup as a betrayal.
- They might say, "How can we build a future together if you don't trust me?" or "Do you think I'm only with you for your money?" These questions are rhetorical traps, designed to manipulate targets into proving their trust by forgoing the prenup.

"You're already planning for the end."

- DTGDs paint prenups as harbingers of doom, suggesting that they reflect a lack of faith in the longevity of the relationship.
- Phrases like "Why are you already planning for us to fail?" or "Are you expecting this marriage to end before it even begins?" attempt to shift focus from financial protection to emotional commitment.
- Interestingly, the person who is putting up resistance to signing a prenup is the party who is already planning for the end. They don't want a prenup getting in the way of their intended divorce windfall.

"I thought we were building a future together."

- By framing the prenup as a barrier to partnership, DTGDs position themselves as champions of unity and collaboration.
- Statements like "I thought we were supposed to share everything" or "A prenup makes it feel like we're not really in this together" are designed to undermine targets' resolve.

How DTGDs Escalate Manipulation

If emotional appeals fail, DTGDs often escalate their tactics, resorting to more overt forms of manipulation to avoid signing a prenup.

Feigning Offense

- DTGDs may react with exaggerated indignation, claiming that the request for a prenup is insulting or demeaning.
- By turning the conversation into an emotional confrontation, they hope to derail the discussion entirely.

Delaying the Conversation

- Procrastination is a common tactic, with DTGDs suggesting that the prenup discussion can wait until after the wedding planning or other milestones.
- This delay tactic creates time pressure, making it harder to finalize an agreement before the marriage.

Threatening to Leave

- In extreme cases, DTGDs may issue ultimatums, such as, "If you don't trust me enough to marry without a prenup, maybe we shouldn't get married at all."
- This high-stakes manipulation forces targets to choose between their emotional commitment and their financial security.

Why These Objections Are Red Flags

The intensity and persistence of DTGDs' objections to prenups often reveal their true motives. For a genuine partner, a prenuptial agreement is a practical tool to protect both parties and foster transparency. For DTGDs, it's an obstacle that threatens their financial ambitions.

Resistance to Transparency

- DTGDs thrive on ambiguity and secrecy. A prenup's requirement for full financial disclosure disrupts their ability to manipulate or misrepresent their own situation.

Fear of Accountability

- Prenups introduce clear boundaries and responsibilities, which limit DTGDs' capacity to exploit marital laws for personal gain.

Emotional Manipulation as a Defense

- Genuine partners engage in open, honest discussions about financial agreements. DTGDs, by contrast, rely on emotional manipulation to avoid accountability.

How to Handle Prenup Discussions with Potential DTGDs

Navigating a prenup discussion with a potential DTGD requires tact, preparation, and an unwavering commitment to your financial boundaries.

Introduce the Idea Early

- Bring up the topic of a prenup well before engagement or wedding planning begins. This allows time for honest discussions without the pressure of impending deadlines.
- If an FFT is in place, the requirement to disclose its existence (and share a copy) will make it evident that you have a legal obligation to either have a prenup or protect your assets and future income in a trust that protects them from future marital claims.

Frame It as a Mutual Benefit

- Emphasize that a prenup protects both parties and provides clarity, fostering trust and transparency in the relationship.

Involve Legal Counsel

- Encourage both parties to seek independent legal advice to ensure the agreement is fair and enforceable.

Stand Firm Against Emotional Manipulation

- Recognize and resist guilt-tripping or rhetorical traps. Reframe objections as opportunities to discuss values and expectations openly.

A Litmus Test for True Intentions

DTGDs' reactions to prenuptial agreements are often a telltale sign of their true motives. While genuine partners view prenups as practical and fair, DTGDs see them as barriers to their financial ambitions. By recognizing their objections for what they are—manipulative tactics—you can protect yourself from exploitation and ensure your relationship is built on genuine trust and respect.

By contrast, The Real Deal—someone genuinely invested in the relationship—approaches the idea of a prenup with curiosity rather than indignation. Even if they have no personal concerns about financial agreements, they are open to discussing the topic because they respect what is important to their partner. For them, customizing a fair set of possible outcomes is a reasonable and collaborative approach. Crucially, The Real Deal does not see the relationship as transactional, which makes the idea of planning for financial clarity a straightforward and unemotional process.

44

Invalidating Prenups: DTGDs' Covert Premarital Maneuvers

The DTGD Battle Against Prenups: How They Undermine Legal Safeguards

For DTGDs, a prenuptial agreement represents the single biggest roadblock standing between them and the wealth they aim to siphon—and they know it. This is why, from the very moment the idea of a prenup is introduced, DTGDs are already strategizing how to render them useless.

The mistake most people make is assuming that once a prenup is signed, it's ironclad. That belief is what DTGDs are counting on. They understand that prenups can be invalidated with alarming ease—as long as they carefully manipulate the circumstances leading up to the prenup. The real game isn't fought in the signing of the prenup—, it's fought in the way it was negotiated—in the timing, the optics, and the legal details that were either deliberately or accidentally overlooked.

Remember, DTGDs do most of their work in the pre-entrenchment phase, before the wedding even happens. They know that setting the right traps early makes it infinitely easier to invalidate prenups when the time comes. If they can manufacture just the right amount of pressure, just the right amount of uncertainty, and just the right procedural vulnerabilities, they can create scenarios where judges are more than willing to toss prenups out completely.

This chapter is about recognizing and defeating DTGDs' strategies before they have the chance to execute them. Remember, a prenup isn't just a document—it's a defense mechanism. But that defense is only as strong as its weakest point.

How DTGDs Set the Stage to Invalidate a Prenup

A prenup can be challenged and overturned in a number of ways, but nearly all arguments fall under one of five categories:

1. Coercion or duress: Claiming they were forced to sign under pressure.
2. Procedural errors: Exploiting loopholes or legal oversights in the execution of the agreement.
3. Unconscionability: Arguing that the agreement is so one-sided that it's inherently unfair.
4. Lack of independent legal advice: Claiming they did not have access to proper legal representation.
5. Incompetent legal counsel: Claiming that, although they had a lawyer, their legal advice was ineffective or negligent.

DTGDs don't just hope for one of these circumstances to occur by chance—they orchestrate them. Their strategy starts before the prenup is even introduced and continues until they have secured marriage.

Claiming Duress: The Art of Manufacturing Pressure

One of the simplest and most effective ways to challenge a prenup is by claiming it was signed under duress. DTGDs excel at creating narratives where they appear to be the reluctant, pressured parties, forced into signing something they never truly agreed with.

Parental Pressure: A Built-In Excuse for Duress

When parents insist on a prenup as a condition of marriage, they may believe they are doing the right thing by protecting their children's financial future. But DTGDs see this as an opportunity—a perfect excuse to later argue that they signed the agreement only to appease the family and avoid losing the relationship.

Even more upsetting, when parents attempt a seemingly gentler approach by offering financial incentives to signing prenups—such as offering to pay for the wedding or contributing to a house down payment—DTGDs can later claim coercion, stating that they only signed because they couldn't have afforded the wedding or the home if they "lost" access to those funds.

They will frame these conversations in a way that highlights emotional coercion:

- *"His family kept pushing the prenup on me. I felt like I had no choice."*
- *"I didn't want to sign it, but they were paying for our wedding and our house, and I didn't want to ruin our future."*

These are textbook duress coercion claims—ones that courts have historically been sympathetic to.

Spousal Pressure: Framing the Negotiation as Coercion

Another strategy DTGDs use is creating the illusion of being pressured by their partners. If you make the mistake of trying to "convince" them to sign a prenup, they *will* weaponize your enthusiasm against you later.

They might even strategically resist signing at first, forcing multiple conversations where you attempt to persuade them. Every email, text message, or discussion about the prenup then becomes evidence of undue pressure.

The solution is to never push. If a partner refuses to negotiate a prenup fairly, take it as a red flag. Do not argue or try to convince them. Instead, move your asset and income protection strategies into place before the wedding and be transparent about it. Or, better yet, move on entirely, now that they have shown you their true colors.

Lack of Independent Legal Advice: A Built-In Escape Route

DTGDs can attempt to invalidate prenups by arguing they were never given access to proper legal representation.

- They may claim they didn't fully understand the terms because they weren't given a lawyer.
- They might suggest they signed without knowing they had the right to consult an attorney.

Courts generally require written documentation proving that each party was given access to a lawyer. If DTGDs refuse legal counsel, it is extremely inadvisable to proceed with marriage unless you have fully protected your premarital assets and future income with an FFT, DAPT/FAPT, or both.

Incompetent Legal Counsel: A Deliberate Loophole

Even if DTGDs have lawyers, they may later claim that their attorneys were ineffective, inexperienced, or negligent. This is a separate issue from not having legal representation at all, and can be just as effective in challenging a prenup.

- They may hire a lawyer with little to no experience in family law, or one who has a reputation for rubber-stamping agreements.
- Even if they have a good lawyer, they might deliberately avoid seeking clarification on key points, ensuring they can later claim misunderstanding.

To counter this, ensure that both parties retain highly competent, independent legal counsel—and that this is well-documented. Courts take competent legal representation seriously, so making sure their lawyer is legitimate eliminates this potential loophole.

DTGDs' Perspective

To the outside world, DTGDs may appear somber or reluctant when signing prenups. In reality, they often laughing (inside, at least) all the way to the bank if their victims or victims' parents have made missteps they can leverage to have the prenups invalidated. Whether parents apply pressure (duress) or offer incentives (coercion), or whether the DTGDs have carefully constructed narratives of inadequate legal counsel, all approaches provide a clear path to invalidating prenups once they have secured marriage. This windfall handed to them on a silver platter often goes unnoticed by those attempting to protect their wealth, but the DTGD knows their prenup isn't worth the paper it's printed on.

How to Ensure Your Prenup Holds Up

The best defense against DTGDs' attempts to invalidate prenups is meticulous preparation and adherence to legal best practices. By anticipating their tactics, you can ensure your agreement withstands scrutiny.

Start Early

1. Begin discussions well in advance.

- Initiate conversations about a prenup long before engagement or wedding planning. This eliminates the argument that timing created duress.

2. Allow time for negotiation.
• Provide ample time for both parties to review and revise the agreement, ensuring no one feels rushed.

Ensure Independent Legal Advice

1. Hire qualified attorneys.
• Both parties should have their own experienced legal counsel to review and negotiate the agreement.

2. Document representation.
• Keep records proving that both parties received independent legal advice to counter future claims of inadequate representation.

Be Transparent About Finances

1. Provide full disclosure.
• List all assets, liabilities, and income sources comprehensively and accurately.

2. Verify accuracy.
• Have financial disclosures reviewed by a neutral third party, such as an accountant or financial planner, to ensure accuracy.

The Real Battle Happens Before the Wedding

As you can see, your greatest risk factors for being lined up for an expensive fall—even *with* a prenup—are happening right under your nose in the months and weeks leading up to a wedding. This is when DTGDs are doing the real work—laying legal traps, manufacturing pressure, and setting up procedural vulnerabilities that will allow them to shred prenups when they need to cash out.

If you know the red flags to watch out for, you'll also know whether to call off the wedding entirely. Remember, no piece of paper—not even the most well-crafted prenup—can save you if you walk into a marriage with someone whose sole objective is to dismantle your financial future from the inside.

Think Twice About Having Children

45

Do You Want Kids? Be Crystal Clear About This Going In

A Life-Altering Decision

Few decisions carry as much weight as the choice to have children. For some, it is a natural and joyous part of life. For others, it is a path they know they do not want to walk. Regardless of your preference, one thing is clear: You must be certain about this decision and communicate it unequivocally before entering into marriage or a long-term commitment. This conversation is not optional, as ambiguity can leave you vulnerable to manipulation, particularly by DTGDs, whose motives may not align with yours.

This chapter delves into why crystal-clear communication about having children is essential. It also looks closely at reproductive coercion—a tactic often employed by DTGDs to entrench themselves financially. Reproductive coercion is a serious issue that can strip you of autonomy and financial control.

Why Clarity About Children Matters

Marriage and long-term commitments are built on shared values and goals, and few topics are as fundamental as whether or not to have children. Misalignment on this issue can lead to emotional devastation, financial burdens, and lifelong regrets.

Aligning Expectations

If you want children, it's not just a matter of saying "yes" and moving forward. You need to discuss the logistics, including when you want to have them, how many, and how you envision raising them. Topics like education, religious upbringing, and shared parenting responsibilities must be addressed. These discussions ensure that both partners are on the same page and reduce the likelihood of future conflicts.

On the other hand, if you don't want children, it's equally critical to communicate this firmly and without ambiguity. Avoiding the topic or making vague statements can leave room for misunderstanding—and in the hands of manipulative DTGDs, that ambiguity can become a weapon against you.

Protecting Your Future

For individuals who do not want children, failing to communicate and assert this boundary leaves the door open to life-altering outcomes. Reproductive coercion—where one partner manipulates or deceives the other to achieve pregnancy—is a real and dangerous tactic employed by DTGDs. One "accident" can forever alter the trajectory of your life, tying you legally and financially to someone whose intentions were never genuine.

A critical part of this discussion must include clarity on what you would each want to do in the event of an unplanned pregnancy. If you and your partner have divergent wishes about whether to keep or terminate a pregnancy, this can lead to significant conflict and legal or emotional fallout. Be particularly wary of vague responses such as "We'll decide together if that ever happens," which signal a lack of accountability and leaves the door open for manipulation.

If You Do Want Kids: Having the Conversation

For those who want children, it's essential to have a thorough and honest discussion with your partner before entering into cohabitation or marriage. Clarity on timing, parenting values, and shared responsibilities is key.

Discuss the Details

- When and how: Agree on a timeline for having children. Are you looking to start a family immediately, or do you want to wait a few years?
- Parenting philosophies: Address topics like education, discipline, and religious upbringing. Differences in these areas can create significant friction if not resolved early.
- Financial planning: Prepare for the financial responsibilities of raising children by establishing savings goals, budgets, and resources for their future.
- Shared roles: Agree on how parenting responsibilities will be divided to avoid resentment or imbalance later on.

If You Don't Want Kids: Taking Control of Your Fate

For those who do not want children, safeguarding against reproductive coercion and maintaining control over your reproductive choices is paramount. It takes only one "accident" to permanently alter the course of your life.

Proactive Measures for Women

- Long-acting contraceptives: Options like IUDs or implants are less susceptible to user error or tampering.
- Consistency: Ensure that you are diligent with your chosen method of contraception and keep it under your control at all times.

Proactive Measures for Men

- Condoms and vasectomy: Condoms remain a critical line of defense, but are vulnerable to tampering. A vasectomy ensures that reproductive choices remain within your control.
- Reactions to vasectomy: Many DTGDs will react with anger or dismay if they learn you've had a vasectomy. This removes one of their most profitable angles of attack—the ability to secure child support through an "accident."
- Male birth control pills, injections, and gels: With clinical trials in advanced stages, these new products are set to come to market in the very near future. When they do, keep your chosen method of contraception under your control at all times to avoid tampering.

Communicate Firm Boundaries

- Be clear and firm: Do not leave room for ambiguity when discussing your decision not to have children. Phrases like "I'm open to the idea someday" can be misinterpreted or deliberately twisted by a manipulative partner.
- Discuss consequences: Make it clear that reproductive coercion is a dealbreaker and that you will not tolerate any attempts to circumvent your autonomy.

A Decision That Shapes Your Life

The decision to have or not have children is deeply personal, but it is also a decision that must be made with absolute clarity and intention. Ambiguity leaves you vulnerable, particularly in relationships with manipulative partners like DTGDs, who may see children as a means to financial entrenchment.

By asserting control over your reproductive choices and communicating your intentions clearly, you can safeguard your autonomy and build relationships based on mutual respect and shared goals. In this life-altering decision, clarity is your greatest defense.

46

Polluting Your Gene Pool with DTGD Hereditary Risks

A Legacy Worth Protecting

In contrast to reproductive coercion, consciously *choosing* to have children with a DTGD is a decision that should not be entered into lightly. Electing to have children is one of the most profound decisions of your life. It's about more than passing on your DNA—it's about the values, opportunities, and emotional foundation you provide for future generations. But what happens when one of the parents is a DTGD? The stakes become exponentially higher.

Children with DTGD parents face a double-edged sword of hereditary and environmental risks. While you may be hopeful about co-parenting and believe in giving your child the best, the reality is that DTGDs create environments so toxic that the damage often extends far beyond childhood. This chapter explores why the decision to have children with a DTGD is fraught with predictable dangers, generational consequences, and difficult truths—and why it's imperative to consider these risks before taking the leap.

The Double Threat: Biological and Environmental Risks

Dark Triad traits—narcissism, Machiavellianism, and psychopathy—don't just impact DTGDs' immediate relationships—they can echo throughout generations. Whether through genetics, environment, or both, DTGD parents' influence often leaves children at a significant disadvantage.

Biological Risks

Personality traits are influenced by genetics, and children of DTGDs may inherit predispositions that skew their moral compass.

- Narcissistic tendencies: Your child may develop a distorted sense of entitlement, an insatiable need for validation, and a lack of empathy.
- Machiavellian traits: Traits like manipulativeness, deceitfulness, and a talent for exploitation can surface, perpetuating DTGDs' toxic legacy.
- Psychopathy: The genetic inheritance of emotional detachment, impulsivity, and a lack of guilt or remorse can lead to harmful behaviors in adulthood.

Environmental Risks

Even if your child doesn't inherit DTGD traits genetically, they'll be shaped by the environment the DTGD creates—a world driven by manipulation, self-interest, and deceit.

- Normalization of exploitation: A DTGD parent models the idea that manipulation and exploitation are acceptable tools for getting ahead in life.

- Emotional neglect: DTGDs are masters of prioritizing themselves, often leaving their children's emotional needs unfulfilled.
- Instability: With DTGDs' constant scheming, financial irresponsibility, and propensity for conflict, households become a breeding ground for chronic anxiety and uncertainty.
- Parental alienation: DTGDs frequently weaponize children in conflicts, turning them against the other parent to gain sympathy or financial leverage.

Generational Consequences

Having children with a DTGD doesn't just complicate your relationship—it creates ripples that can damage future generations. The legacy of a DTGD's behavior doesn't end with the divorce decree—it becomes woven into the fabric of your child's identity and outlook on life.

Toxic Values Passed to the Next Generation

Children learn by observing their parents. DTGD parents teach, either directly or indirectly, that manipulation, deceit, and self-interest are tools for navigating the world. This creates a cycle of dysfunction that's difficult to break.

- Moral ambiguity: Children may struggle to distinguish right from wrong, having seen deceit and exploitation normalized at home.
- Entitlement mentality: With a parent who prioritizes their own needs above all else, children may grow up with a skewed sense of entitlement.

Emotional and Psychological Damage

The emotional fallout of growing up with a DTGD parent can be immense and long-lasting—often lifelong.

- Chronic anxiety: Living in an unstable and manipulative household fosters fear and hypervigilance.

- Low self-worth: A child subjected to guilt, shame, or conditional love often struggles with feelings of inadequacy.
- Trust issues: Witnessing deceit and exploitation within the family makes it difficult for children to form healthy relationships later in life.

Financial and Legal Burdens
The chaos created by DTGD parents often leaves children grappling with financial and legal issues well into adulthood.

- Inheritance conflicts: DTGDs frequently manipulate estate planning to secure advantages for themselves, leaving children to navigate contentious disputes.
- Debt or financial mismanagement: DTGDs' reckless spending and poor financial decisions can leave a legacy of debt for the next generation.

Protecting Yourself from Generational Risk

The decision to have children with a DTGD carries immense, predictable risks. Recognizing and addressing these risks is critical to breaking the cycle of dysfunction.

1. Understand the predictable outcomes.
Accept that the odds are stacked against you and your potential children. While not every child will inherit or adopt DTGD traits, the likelihood of emotional, financial, and psychological damage is alarmingly high.

2. Take preventative measures.
The most effective way to avoid these risks is to make the conscious decision not to have children with DTGDs.

3. Seek professional guidance.
Before making any life-altering decisions, consult with therapists, legal

advisors, and trusted loved ones. They can help you navigate the complexities of your relationship and provide clarity on what's best for you and your potential family.

4. Prioritize self-preservation.

Bringing a child into a toxic environment isn't just a personal risk—it's a generational one. By focusing on self-preservation and avoiding parenthood with DTGDs, you're also protecting future generations from unnecessary harm.

Think Twice Before Polluting Your Gene Pool

Having children with DTGDs isn't just a gamble—it's a guaranteed entry into a world of hereditary and environmental risks, emotional trauma, and generational fallout. While the idea of starting a family may seem appealing, the reality of co-parenting with DTGDs often leads to regret, conflict, and harm that extends far beyond your relationship.

The DTGD legacy doesn't have to define your family's future. By understanding the risks and making informed decisions, you can protect yourself, your children, and the generations that follow. Remember, your choices today shape the lives of tomorrow.

47

DTGDs Are Toxic Role Models as Parents

A Recipe for Anguish and Generational Chaos

We have already discussed child support manipulations ad nauseum, but what about DTGD parenting skills and role modeling? Parenting requires selflessness, stability, and a commitment to nurturing children's emotional and psychological development. For DTGDs, who are inherently entitled, selfish, morally compromised, and highly manipulative, these qualities are as foreign as honesty in a con artist's vocabulary. DTGDs are not merely bad parents—they are toxic role models who inflict deep and lasting damage on their children, perpetuating cycles of dysfunction and emotional harm that reverberate for generations.

Raising children with a DTGD is akin to planting seeds in poisoned soil. Their narcissistic tendencies, Machiavellian manipulation, and psychopathic detachment contaminate the home environment, ensuring that their offspring face significant psychological hurdles. Worse, this damage doesn't stop with one generation—it cascades into the future, perpetuating trauma and toxic values.

The Narcissistic Parent: All About the Spotlight

Parenting Through the Lens of Ego

Narcissistic DTGDs treat their children not as individuals, but as extensions of their own inflated sense of self. The children exists to serve the parents' ego, whether through achievements that reflect well on the DTGDs or through unwavering loyalty and adoration.

- Exploitation of achievements: Children are forced into high-pressure activities—elite sports, beauty pageants, or academic overachievement—solely to bolster the DTGD's image. The children's needs or desires are irrelevant. Only the parent's glory matters.
- Emotional vampirism: Narcissistic DTGDs often demand constant attention and validation from their children, leaving little room for the children's emotional growth.

Psychological Perspective

Dr. Karyl McBride, author of *Will I Ever Be Good Enough?*, highlights the fact that children of narcissistic parents often experience chronic self-doubt, as their worth is tied solely to their ability to serve their parents' needs. This leads to:

- Low self-esteem
- Difficulty setting boundaries
- A pattern of seeking validation through unhealthy relationships

The Machiavellian Parent: A Master Manipulator

Weaponizing Parenthood

For Machiavellian DTGDs, children are pawns in their never-ending game of manipulation. Every interaction is calculated to maximize control and minimize accountability.

- Turning children into pawns: Machiavellian parents weaponize their children to manipulate the other parent, often engaging in parental alienation. They will fabricate narratives to turn children against the victim parent, ensuring loyalty while deepening emotional wounds.
- Instilling deceit as a value: Machiavellian DTGDs teach their children that manipulation and deceit are tools for survival. Through observation and modeling, children learn that honesty and empathy are weaknesses to be exploited.

Psychological Perspective

Dr. Paul Babiak, co-author of *Snakes in Suits*, notes that Machiavellian parents condition children to adopt transactional worldviews, where relationships are built on exploitation rather than connection. This leads to:

- An inability to trust others
- Cynicism in relationships
- A heightened risk of becoming manipulative themselves

The Psychopathic Parent: Detached and Dangerous

Emotional Absence

Psychopathic DTGDs operate with chilling emotional detachment. They lack empathy, remorse, or genuine concern for their children's well-being, often leaving a void where unconditional love should be.

- Instability and chaos: Psychopathic DTGDs create volatile home environments, fostering insecurity and fear in their children. They thrive on control and chaos, ensuring their children never feel safe or grounded.

- Indifference to emotional needs: These parents dismiss or mock their children's emotional expressions, teaching them that vulnerability is a liability.

Psychological Perspective

Dr. Robert Hare, a leading expert on psychopathy, explains that children of psychopathic parents often experience long-term effects, such as:

- Emotional numbness
- Poor impulse control
- Increased likelihood of adopting antisocial behaviors

The Ripple Effect: Intergenerational Trauma

Toxic Values Passed to the Next Generation

Children learn by observing their parents. DTGD parents teach, consciously or unconsciously, that manipulation, deceit, and self-interest are tools for success. These toxic values can ripple through generations, perpetuating cycles of dysfunction and exploitation.

Children raised by DTGDs often face significant emotional and psychological challenges, including:

- Chronic anxiety: Growing up in an unstable and manipulative environment fosters fear and uncertainty.
- Low self-worth: A parent who uses guilt, shame, or manipulation erodes a child's confidence and sense of self-worth.
- Difficulty trusting others: Witnessing deceit and exploitation within the family dynamic makes it harder for children to form healthy relationships as adults.

Breaking the Cycle

Understanding the Risks

Acknowledging the profound risks of raising children with a DTGD is the first step toward breaking the cycle. It is important to recognize that the damage extends far beyond the immediate relationship, shaping values and behaviors for generations.

Taking Proactive Measures

If you're in a relationship with a DTGD or suspect manipulative tendencies, consider these steps:

- Seek counseling: Counseling is valuable for both you and your children, as it helps you navigate the emotional challenges of living with a DTGD.
- Establish legal safeguards: Ensure your estate planning and custody arrangements minimize the DTGD's influence.
- Foster healthy role models: Surround your children with trustworthy, empathetic adults who can provide positive examples of integrity and respect.

A Vicious Cycle Worth Breaking

DTGDs are not just bad parents—they are destructive forces that poison their children's emotional, psychological, and moral foundations. The impact of their entitlement, manipulation, and ethical void ripples across generations, creating a vicious cycle of trauma and toxicity.

Breaking this cycle begins with awareness. Recognize the risks, take proactive steps to mitigate the damage, and, if possible, shield future generations from DTGDs' corrosive influence. Parenting should be about building legacies of love, respect, and stability—not perpetuating chaos and dysfunction.

Tools: Spotting DTGDs and Knowing Your Personal Risk Profile

48

Spotting the Red Flags: Early Signs of a DTGD

Detecting Predatory Intent Early

Spotting the red flags early in a relationship is critical to defending yourself against DTGDs' manipulative strategies. Recognizing patterns of behavior, verbal cues, and subtle manipulations can save you from becoming their next victim.

This chapter provides readers with a comprehensive guide to identifying the early warning signs of DTGDs. Whether it's in the words they use, the stories they tell, or the behaviors they exhibit, these red flags serve as a protective radar to avoid entanglement.

How to Spot a Gold Digger: Attitudes, Hallmarks, Behaviors, Social Cues, and More

DTGDs often operate in calculated ways to secure financial benefits, often at the expense of their partners' well-being. The following is a list of how to identify them based on their more commonly exhibited attitudes, behaviors, and social cues.

Attitudes and Mindset

1. Entitlement Without Merit

- They believe they deserve financial privilege without contributing equally.
- Red flag: Complaints about not having luxuries despite little effort to earn them.

2. Obsession with Status

- They are hyper-focused on appearances, expensive brands, luxury experiences, and the prestige of their social circles.
- Red flag: More interested in showcasing wealth than genuine connection.

3. Exaggerated Self-Importance

- They view themselves as exceptional and entitled to special treatment, often inflating their personal achievements.
- Red flag: They claim they were "too good" for past jobs or relationships.

4. Transactional Thinking

- They view relationships as business deals where emotional investment should yield financial rewards.
- Red flag: They equate generosity with proof of love and commitment.

5. Victim Mentality

- They frame themselves as victims of unfair circumstances to justify financial dependence.

- Red flag: "I've just been unlucky" or "People always take advantage of me."

6. Dismissive of Hard Work

- They avoid personal ambition and prefer financial shortcuts through relationships.
- Red flag: They have vague business plans that never materialize.

Behaviors That Reveal a Gold Digger

7. Fast-Tracked Intimacy (Love Bombing)

- Over-the-top declarations of love, pushing for major commitments early (moving in, joint accounts, marriage).
- Red flag: They tell you "I've never felt this way before" within weeks.

8. Mirroring and Mimicry

- They study your interests and values, then reflect them back to seem like your perfect match.
- Red flag: Their sudden enthusiasm for your hobbies feels too convenient.

9. Shifting Financial Expectations

- They initially claim to be independent, but gradually shift financial responsibilities onto you.
- Red flag: "I just need help until I get back on my feet" turns into indefinite dependence.

10. Emotional Manipulation to Extract Money

- Using guilt, anger, or affection to pressure financial support.
- Red flag: "If you really loved me, you'd help me with this."

11. Winding Down Their "Work" While Enmeshing in Your Life

- Gradually reducing their professional commitments while integrating deeper into your home and financial life.

- Red flag: They initially claim to have career ambitions, but slowly phase out work, citing stress or relationship priorities.

12. Resistance to Prenups or Legal Protections

- They aggressively push back against any financial safeguard that limits their access to your wealth.
- Red flag: Accusing you of mistrust when discussing financial protection.

13. Conspicuous Spending Despite Limited Income

- Maintaining an expensive lifestyle without a legitimate source of income.
- Red flag: They always have designer goods, but no stable job.

Social Cues and External Red Flags

14. A Pattern of Wealthy Exes

- They consistently date or marry people of means.
- Red flag: They've never dated anyone outside their financial "target range."

15. A Social Circle of Other Gold Diggers

- Their friends also prioritize wealth in relationships.
- Red flag: Conversations revolve around materialism, vacations, and "getting the bag."

16. Unexplained Financial Dependence

- They live comfortably, without clear means of support.
- Red flag: They can't explain how they afford their lifestyle.

17. Curiosity About Your Financial Standing

- Asking pointed questions about your assets early in the relationship.
- Red flag: "So, do you own or rent?" "What kind of car do you drive?"

18. Downplaying Financial Independence

- They dismiss questions about their financial stability or career path.
- Red flag: "Money isn't important to me" (while heavily relying on yours).

19. Avoidance of Personal Responsibility

- They blame past failures on others or unfortunate circumstances.
- Red flag: Excuses for job loss, bad investments, or legal troubles.

20. Spotty Work History or Pseudo-Business Ventures

- Their employment record is inconsistent, often filled with vague "entrepreneurial" efforts.
- Red flag: They claim to run a business, but lack tangible income or structure.

21. Strained or Non-Existent Relationships with Close Family Members

- They have frequent conflicts with family members and limited contact with relatives.
- Red flag: They say things like "I had to cut off my whole family," without providing a clear reason. (When you have a problem with everyone in your life, maybe *you're* the problem.)

22. Few (If Any) Close Friends

- They have more acquaintances than deep, long-term friendships.
- Red flag: Their social circle consists mostly of party friends or superficial connections. Those who come closer inevitably see through them and leave.

23. Living with Family While Hunting for a Target

- They reside with family rent-free while positioning themselves to enter financially advantageous relationships.
- Red flag: They have no financial urgency to leave their parents' or relatives' homes, but expect you to provide stability.

24. Isolating You from Your Support Network

- They discourage or sabotage your relationships with friends and family to increase dependence on them.
- Red flag: Complaining about your family/friends, or picking fights to make you choose between them and your loved ones.

25. Intermittent Reinforcement Tactics

- They alternate between affection and withdrawal, creating emotional highs and lows that deepen attachment.
- Red flag: They shower you with attention, then disappear or become cold, making you crave their approval.

Protecting Yourself Against a Gold Digger

- Set financial boundaries early: Establish clear expectations for financial independence in the relationship.
- Watch for patterns, not just one-off actions: A single red flag may not mean much, but a pattern of behavior confirms the danger and likely sinister intent.
- Ensure legal protection: FFTs, prenuptial agreements, separate bank accounts, and financial transparency prevent entrenchment.
- Trust your instincts: If something feels off, investigate before committing further.

Personal Risk Profile Exercise 1

To accurately assess your long-term prospects of maintaining your happiness and economic autonomy, it's critical to assess whether you're dating a DTGD or The Real Deal. After reading this list of red flags, what does your gut tell you?

Action step: Count the number of hits on the list above, but don't write them down. Just make a note of them. If you notice five or more red flags from this list in your relationship, it's a sign to tread cautiously. Gather more intel, be vigilant, and protect your finances comprehensively. Failing to do so could result in financial and emotional devastation. Take decisive steps now to ensure your security before it's too late.

49

NON-INTERVIEW TESTS FOR DTGDS

Observing Without Confronting

Direct, transparent discussions are critical in healthy relationships, but when dealing with a potential DTGDs, direct confrontation can lead to manipulation, defensiveness, or a carefully curated façade. Instead, non-verbal tests provide subtle and effective ways to assess someone's character without raising suspicion or triggering defensive tactics.

This chapter outlines advanced strategies for assessing intentions in real-world scenarios, focusing on behaviors, values, and potential red flags. These approaches allow you to observe patterns over time and make informed decisions about your relationship.

Why Non-Verbal Tests Work

1. Actions Reveal More Than Words

- DTGDs' actions often provide clearer insights into their intentions than their words. Observing their behavior in specific situations offers invaluable clues about their authenticity and values.

2. Minimizing Manipulation

- By relying on observation rather than confrontation, you reduce the risk of emotional manipulation, such as guilt-tripping, love bombing, or gaslighting—all common DTGD tactics.

3. Gaining Organic Insights

- Non-verbal tests create natural scenarios that force DTGDs to respond authentically, exposing inconsistencies, entitlement, or selfish tendencies that they might otherwise conceal.

Non-Verbal Tests for Each Dark Triad Trait

Narcissism: Testing for Excessive Self-Importance and Lack of Empathy

1. The "Spotlight Shift" Test

- Strategy: In conversations, subtly shift the focus to someone else's achievements or emotions.
- Red flag: A narcissist will quickly steer the topic back to themselves, showing minimal interest in others.

2. The "Inconvenience" Test

- Strategy: Introduce a mild inconvenience, such as a delayed plan or last-minute change.
- Red flag: A narcissist will overreact, expressing frustration or making it about how it affects them personally.

3. The "Empathy Check" Test

- Strategy: Share a personal story about a struggle or hardship.
- Red flag: A narcissist will minimize your experience, redirect the conversation, or display little emotional engagement.

Machiavellianism: Testing for Manipulation and Deception

1. The "Ethical Dilemma" Test

- Strategy: Casually bring up a scenario involving ethics (e.g., "Would you ever cheat on your taxes if you knew you wouldn't get caught?").
- Red flag: A Machiavellian partner will rationalize unethical behavior, demonstrating a "win-at-all-costs" mentality.

2. The "Loyalty Test"

- Strategy: Observe how they talk about past relationships, friendships, or colleagues.
- Red flag: Frequent stories of betrayal or blame-shifting signal a pattern of self-serving behavior.

3. The "Calculated Kindness" Test

- Strategy: Watch how they treat people who have nothing to offer them (e.g., waitstaff, cashiers).
- Red flag: If they are charming to those in power but dismissive or rude to those they see as being below them, they likely use relationships for strategic gain.

Psychopathy: Testing for Callousness and Risk-Taking

1. The "Compassion" Test

- Strategy: Observe how they respond to distress in others, such as a crying child or an injured animal.

- Red flag: A lack of concern or amusement at suffering indicates a troubling absence of empathy.

2. The "Thrill-Seeking" Test

- Strategy: Bring up topics involving risk, such as reckless driving, gambling, or breaking rules.
- Red flag: If they frequently boast about taking unnecessary risks or disregard consequences, they may have psychopathic tendencies.

3. The "Reaction to Consequences" Test

- Strategy: Casually mention personal boundaries or social expectations (e.g., being faithful in a relationship).
- Red flag: They may brush off consequences or mock those who follow moral codes, revealing an indifference to social norms.

How to Use the Results of These Tests

Non-verbal tests are designed to gather information and observe patterns over time. Use these insights to make informed decisions about the relationship.

1. Look for Patterns, Not Isolated Incidents

- One bad day doesn't make someone a DTGD, but consistent behaviors across multiple tests are strong indicators of one's character.

2. Seek External Feedback

- Share your observations with trusted friends or family members for additional perspective. They can often spot red flags you've overlooked.

3. Trust Your Instincts

- If something feels off, don't ignore your intuition. These tests are tools to confirm or challenge your gut feelings.

Observing Beyond Words

Non-interview tests provide a discreet and effective way to assess a partner's character without creating conflict or suspicion. By observing behavior in real-world scenarios, you can identify red flags, confirm genuine intentions, and protect yourself from manipulation. Trustworthy partners will pass these tests with ease, while DTGDs will struggle to maintain their façade under scrutiny.

50

Income at Risk Self-Assessment

The True Cost of Divorce: A Financial Breakdown

Many people assume that, if their marriage ends, the financial fallout will be limited to dividing assets evenly. In reality, the financial impact can be far greater. Between income taxes, spousal support, and child support, you could be left with a tiny fraction of your post-divorce earnings. Worse still, exorbitant spousal and child support payments create a vicious cycle that make it virtually impossible to set aside money for retirement, leaving many high earners unable to retire at all.

This chapter presents a monthly income grid showing what happens when government taxation and court-ordered financial obligations reduce your take-home income. The goal is to provide a clear and sobering look at what remains after these deductions.

Income Breakdown Grid

The table below provides three income scenarios: $10,000/month, $25,000/month, and $50,000/month. Each scenario deducts:

1. Income tax: Estimated at 35% (varies by jurisdiction).
2. Spousal and child support: 50% of post-tax income (can reach up to 55% in some states).

Gross Monthly Income	After 35% Income Tax	After 50% Spousal/ Child Support	Remaining Take-Home
$10,000	$6,500	$3,250	$3,250*
$25,000	$16,250	$8,125	$8,125*
$50,000	$32,500	$16,250	$16,250*

*Expect a court-ordered requirement to maintain life insurance *paid out of your share*, with the DTGD as a beneficiary so their annuity is unaffected if you die.

DTGD Extraction vs. Investment Growth

The table below contrasts the impact of paying spousal and child support versus investing the same amount at a 6% annual return over time.

Scenario	In 10 Years You Will Have	In 20 Years You Will Have	In 30 Years You Will Have
$10,000/month salary DTGD Extraction Entitlements of $3,250/mo	$0	$0	$0
$10,000/month salary Investing DTGD's $3,250/mo Entitlements Instead	$532,608	$1,501,633	$3,264,674
$25,000/month salary DTGD Extraction Entitlements of $8,125/mo	$0	$0	$0
$25,000/month salary Investing DTGD's $8,125/mo Entitlements Instead	$1,331,520	$3,754,082	$8,161,685
$50,000/month salary DTGD Extraction Entitlements of $16,250/mo	$0	$0	$0
$50,000/month salary Investing DTGD's $16,250/mo Entitlements Instead	$2,663,039	$7,508,165	$16,323,369

Personal Risk Profile Exercise 2

To better understand your potential financial impact, locate the column that aligns closest to your anticipated retirement date and the row that represents your expected average income between now and then.

Action step: Circle the ballpark amount you would have if you invested those funds instead of losing them to DTGD extraction entitlements. This will give you a tangible perspective on what's truly at stake.

Key Takeaways

If the money goes to spousal and child support, there is no long-term financial benefit—zero return. If the same money were invested at a conservative 6% annual return, over 30 years you could accumulate:

- $3.26 million from a $10,000/month salary
- $8.16 million from a $25,000/month salary
- $16.32 million from a $50,000/month salary

The cost of paying out instead of investing can mean millions lost in potential retirement security.

Forewarned Is Forearmed

The financial cost of divorce is staggering, and many are blindsided by how little they have left over after taxes and court-ordered obligations. Understanding these numbers is critical to making informed decisions about relationships, financial planning, and long-term security.

If you're considering marriage, ensure that you have airtight financial protections in place (see Chapters 53 to 62). If you're already married, start thinking about proactive asset and income protection strategies before it's too late (see Resources).

51

Premarital Assets at Risk Self-Assessment

Understanding Post-Marital Appreciation on Premarital Assets

Premarital assets are often assumed to be protected in divorce, but, in many jurisdictions, the increase in value (appreciation) of those assets during the marriage is subject to division. While interpretations vary by state, the general principle holds that if a premarital asset appreciates due to market growth, business expansion, or investment gains during the marriage, the increase in value can be considered marital property—meaning an ex-spouse may be entitled to half of that growth.

This chapter examines how post-marital appreciation is calculated and what it means for individuals with significant premarital wealth. We present real-world financial scenarios illustrating how wealth compounds over time and the staggering amounts at stake in a divorce.

Post-Marital Appreciation Calculation

The table below shows three starting net worths—$5M, $25M, and $50M—and projects their growth at 6% annual appreciation over 10, 20, and 30 years. It also calculates the amount owed to a spouse in a divorce, assuming a 50% entitlement to post-marital appreciation.

Scenario	In 10 Years	In 20 Years	In 30 Years
Premarital Asset Value: $5M	$8,954,238	$16,035,677	$28,717,456
Owed to Ex-Spouse (50% of Growth)	$1,977,119	$5,517,838	$11,858,728
Premarital Asset Value: $25M	$44,771,192	$80,178,387	$143,587,279
Owed to Ex-Spouse (50% of Growth)	$9,885,596	$27,589,194	$59,293,640
Premarital Asset Value: $50M	$89,542,385	$160,356,774	$287,174,559
Owed to Ex-Spouse (50% of Growth)	$19,771,192	$55,178,387	$118,587,280

Personal Risk Profile Exercise 3

To better understand your potential financial impact, locate the column that aligns closest with your anticipated retirement date and the premarital asset value in the column on the left that is closest to your present-day net worth.

Action step: Circle the amount you would be required to transfer to a DTGD if you did not protect your premarital assets by transferring them into a trust prior to marriage or excluding them in a prenup (ideally *both*). This will expand your perspective on what's truly at stake in your lifetime.

Key Considerations

- Not all states treat appreciation the same: Some states differentiate between passive appreciation (due to market growth) and active appreciation (due to effort from either spouse). Courts may apply different formulas based on the circumstances.

- Active vs. passive growth matters: If the appreciation is linked to your active efforts, such as managing a business or improving a property, courts are more likely to consider it marital property.
- Protecting your growth: Prenuptial agreements and trust structures (like the FFT) can shield assets from being considered joint marital property, reducing your risk of significant financial loss.

Protecting Your Premarital Assets

If you want to keep your wealth intact, proactive financial and legal measures are essential.

1. Utilize asset trusts: Holding assets in a trust before marriage can help keep them separate.
2. Use a prenup: Clearly define how appreciation will be handled in case of divorce.
3. Avoid co-mingling funds: Mixing premarital and marital assets can erode legal protections.
4. Document passive vs. active growth: Keep detailed records of how your investments appreciate to counter claims of active marital contribution.

Know Your Risk

The financial impact of post-marital appreciation is enormous, yet many individuals overlook it. Understanding these calculations and taking preventative legal measures can protect generational wealth from unnecessary loss.

52

YOUR PERSONAL RISK PROFILE SELF-ASSESSMENT

Many people enter marriage with a sense of optimism, believing that their relationships will stand the test of time. However, statistical reality—particularly for affluent individuals—paint a different picture. While the baseline marriage failure rate is often quoted at 50%, this number is significantly higher for those with high net worth or substantial income.

Though hard data on affluent divorce rates are often shielded by confidentiality agreements, there can be no doubt that DTGDs cluster disproportionately around wealthy individuals, increasing the risk of financial exploitation. The more red flags your partner exhibits, the higher the likelihood of divorce. A refusal to sign a prenuptial agreement is often the clearest sign that your partner is positioning for future financial extraction.

This chapter will guide you through a Personal Risk Profile Self-Assessment, combining your Income Risk Self-Assessment Value and Asset Risk Self-Assessment Value to determine your total economic risk in marriage. We will then adjust your marriage failure probability based on critical financial and behavioral factors that strongly influence the likelihood of divorce. The final result is a sobering evaluation of your actual risk level.

Step 1: Combining Your Economic Risk Factors

To calculate your approximate lifetime economic risk exposure, add together:

Personal Income at Risk Self-Assessment Value (Exercise 2)
$________

Personal Premarital Asset Risk Self-Assessment Value (Exercise 3)
$________

Personal Total at Risk*: $____________

*Post-marital business ventures and intellectual property originating from your premarital skills, talents and credentials would further *increase* this value at risk for redistribution in a divorce. The higher your combined risk value, the more vulnerable you are to financial devastation in a divorce.

Step 2: Adjusting for Key Risk Multipliers

We begin with the baseline 50% marriage failure rate and then apply the following additions based on known high-risk factors.

High Net Worth or High Income

If you have a net worth over $1 million or your annual income exceeds $300,000, add 10% to your marriage failure rate.*

*These attributes make a person more likely to be targeted for economic exploitation.

Red Flags in Your Partner
If your spouse exhibited five or more red flags from the red flags chapter (Chapter 48), add 10%.

Prenuptial Agreement Refusal
If your partner refused to sign a prenup, add 20%.

Step 3: Your Final Marriage Failure Probability

After applying the risk additions, your final failure probability might look something like this:

Starting Marriage Failure Rate: 50%
You have a high income/net worth (+10%)
• 60% probability of divorce
Your SO exhibits five or more DTGD red flags (+10%)
• 70% probability pf divorce
Your SO refuses a prenup (+20%)
• 90% probability of divorce

If multiple risk factors apply to your situation, the odds of your marriage ending in divorce approach certainty.

The Silver Lining

If your SO is accepting of your premarital asset and income protection planning and agreeable to a prenup without overt or covert forms of resistance, their motivations are likely pure and your odds revert to the 50/50 baseline for the general population. Why is this? Because of self-selection. DTGDs will opt-out of any scenario as soon as they recognize they can't win, which is a huge benefit for you, as you can then focus your heart and energy on an authentic partner.

Here's the Kicker

Even if you make all the right choices and marry The Real Deal—someone with integrity, genuine affection, and no predatory financial motives—a 50% chance of divorce is still abysmal odds for encountering a life-altering financial disaster. Even without the malicious intent of a financial predator, the legal and financial structures of marriage don't change.

That means that, even if your spouse entered the relationship with honest intentions, the moment your marriage heads toward divorce, the same entitlements that apply to a DTGD will still be in play. By the time a couple reaches the breaking point, it's fair to assume there will have be a level of friction—anger, frustration, hurt—that may influence decision-making. A previously rational and fair-minded spouse can be encouraged by family, friends, or legal counsel to pursue an aggressive divorce strategy, particularly if emotions run high.

In other words, even Real Deal partners can approach divorce with a scorched-earth mindset if the circumstances lead them there. The crucial distinction is this:

- DTGDs actively enter marriage with financial extraction as their endgame.
- The Real Deal may not intend to take more than their fair share—but they will almost certainly insist on getting *at least* their fair share under the state's rules for wealth redistribution, including your future income.

This means that, whether you marry a DTGD or The Real Deal, your financial exposure remains *unacceptably high* if you don't have safeguards in place.

If you enter marriage without an FFT and without a prenup, then you are willfully exposing yourself to catastrophic financial risk. You wouldn't sign a business contract with no exit plan, so why would you sign a marriage contract without protecting yourself?

- An FFT isn't about paranoia. It's about strategic defense.
- A prenup isn't about expecting failure. It's about ensuring fairness.

Without these structures in place, you are gambling your financial future at the altar. And when the house always wins, why would you place a bet where the best-case scenario is breaking even, and the worst case is total devastation?

Key Takeaways

- The financial risk of marriage for affluent individuals is significantly higher than the general population.
- DTGDs disproportionately cluster around affluent targets, increasing risk beyond standard divorce rates.
- A refusal to sign a prenup should be considered a massive red flag, strongly indicating financial extraction as a motive.
- A marriage to The Real Deal still has a 50% chance of failure, which means a 50% chance of financial devastation without an FFT and prenup.
- Recognizing these risk factors before marriage allows you to make informed decisions and implement necessary legal protections.

A Sobering Reality

Marriage carries inherent risks, but for high-income and high-net-worth individuals, those risks multiply exponentially. The affluent must seriously consider whether entering into marriage without proper legal safeguards is worth the risk.

In the next chapters, we will explore advanced financial protection strategies, including legal structures that can help mitigate the financial devastation of divorce.

The Ultimate DTGD Defense and Deterrent

53

The Old Money Silver Bullet: Compulsory Prenups

An Unbreakable Fortress: How Dynastic Wealth Is Engineered, not Left to Chance

For generations, the ultra-wealthy have relied on ironclad legal frameworks to ensure that their fortunes remain untouched by divorce settlements, opportunistic lawsuits, and predatory financial claims. These strategies, once the exclusive domain of billion-dollar family offices, have now been refined and modernized for individuals who understand one essential truth: Wealth is never an accident, and it must be protected with precision to stand the test of time.

The Legacy of Dynastic Wealth Preservation

The wealthiest families in history did not preserve their fortunes by trusting in love, luck, or good intentions. They adhered to unbreakable financial doctrines, passing down not only their wealth, but also the exact playbook for keeping it intact across generations. This is the core of dynastic wealth preservation—not just making money, but ensuring that it never leaves the family.

Among the foundational principles of this legacy, one rule reigns supreme: Prenuptial agreements are effectively compulsory.

For many of the world's richest families, the family business serves as the ultimate mechanism of control. These structures are not just well thought out—they are meticulously engineered to prevent wealth from ever being redistributed through divorce settlements or reckless financial decisions. They are designed not for reaction after a threat emerges, but to make sure no threat ever gets past the gates in the first place.

The Shareholder Agreement Model: The Ultimate Financial Safeguard

The most bulletproof wealth protection strategy deployed by dynastic families is the shareholder agreement model. In this model, wealth is housed within a family business, where shares are exclusively held by blood descendants of the original founders. These shares, which yield massive dividends, are governed by a simple, ironclad rule.

If a shareholder decides to get married, they have two options:

- Sign a prenuptial agreement with preordained clauses ensuring that shares remain within the family. This legally guarantees that, in the event of divorce, the shares and their corresponding dividends stay within the bloodline.
- Refuse the prenup and lose the shares forever. The moment a family member marries without a prenuptial agreement, they automatically forfeit their shares and all future dividend payments—permanently.

Guess how often family members willingly surrender their shares?

Never.

The genius of this system is self-evident.

- It creates an indisputable financial incentive to sign a prenup.
- It eliminates personal negotiation and emotional manipulation.
- It preserves family harmony by applying the rule to everyone equally.
- It prevents outsiders from walking away with a portion of the family business.

The approach is both powerful and self-enforcing. It is not a personal attack—it is simply how the system works. If you want access to the family fortune, you play by the family's rules.

But what if you're not part of a multi-generational business empire? What if you're an individual who built wealth through intelligence, strategy, and discipline, and you can't afford to gamble your financial future on a court system that favors wealth redistribution over wealth protection? That's where The Bloodline Alliance's Family First Trust comes in.

The Family First Trust: A Masterclass in Legal Engineering

Unlike a shareholder agreement, which only protects business assets, the FFT is engineered to lock down *all* significant wealth—present and future—no matter its source. It is not a passive document, it is a self-executing, multi-layered financial defense system that leaves nothing to chance.

Here's what makes the FFT so effective and valuable:

- Automatic activation: The act of becoming engaged to be married triggers a self-executing lockdown of your present and future wealth.

- Beyond business assets: Unlike shareholder agreements, which only apply to company equity, the FFT protects everything—real estate, liquid investments, intellectual property, and any other form of wealth, including your future income. Nothing is left exposed.
- No negotiation, no manipulation: DTGDs thrive on exploiting gray areas—convincing their targets that prenups are "unromantic" or "unnecessary." The FFT eliminates these conversations entirely. It doesn't ask for compliance. It enforces it.
- A multi-generational safety net: This trust extends beyond individual wealth, serving as an education, entrepreneurship, and housing fund for the settlor's blood relatives (typically nieces and nephews). It legally mandates asset and income protection from third-party claims, including divorce. By requiring proactive defenses such as a qualifying prenuptial agreement or qualifying DAPT/FAPT, the trust ensures long-term security for beneficiaries while safeguarding family wealth.

The Psychological Edge: Controlling the Narrative Before DTGDs Can

The most dangerous phase in DTGDs' strategy is the lead-up to financial entrenchment. This is when they deploy their most sophisticated tactics—love bombing, mirroring their targets' values, and feigning self-sufficiency.

Their goal? To manipulate you into believing that financial protection is an act of betrayal. The FFT neutralizes this manipulation before it even begins. By making wealth protection a legal requirement, not a personal choice, it flips the script. The message is clear:

This isn't about you and me. This is about the system, and honoring the legally-binding commitments I made that predate marriage.

DTGDs can no longer frame prenups as a lack of trust because trust doesn't enter into the equation. There's no room for emotional coercion. The trust dictates the rules, and the rules are non-negotiable. If the DTGD aims to dodge a prenup. No problem. Your wealth will be locked down even tighter based on the signal that an economic predator appears to be laying the foundation for an economic assault.

Why the FFT Is an Exclusive Strategy

The legal architecture behind the FFT has been painstakingly refined by elite financial strategists, family law + asset protection attorneys, and family office advisors. It is a best-in-class structure designed for those who understand that wealth preservation is a strategic discipline, not a matter of luck.

This is why the FFT is positioned not just as a legal tool, but as a status symbol of financial intelligence. The ultra-wealthy do not guess their way into lasting wealth. They engineer it.

The Compulsory Prenup as the Cornerstone of True Wealth Preservation

At this stage in the book, you now understand that a compulsory prenuptial agreement isn't just a good idea—it is the foundation of any serious financial defense strategy.

But on its own, a prenup is not enough. It still requires negotiation. It can still be challenged in court. It is still just one layer of defense.

The FFT is the next evolution in proactive asset protection. It doesn't just require a prenup—it ensures that a prenup is executed *under the right conditions.* And it does so automatically, without negotiation, without emotional blackmail, and without exposing the settlor to unnecessary risk.

In the following chapters, we will break down exactly how the FFT works, how it integrates into a larger wealth protection strategy, and why it is the ultimate safeguard against financial predation.

54

The Family First Trust: The Gold Standard of Income & Asset Protection

The Ultimate DTGD Shield and Psychological Deterrent

The FFT is not merely a trust deed—it is a sophisticated, multi-layered protective structure designed to preemptively thwart exploitation by DTGDs. Its mere existence signals to DTGDs that their battle is over before it even begins—a clear message that your wealth is beyond their reach. Anchored by the FFT Deed, this system integrates auxiliary agreements that collectively secure premarital assets, protect post-marital income, and create no-win scenarios for would-be exploiters.

The FFT encompasses:

- The Trust Deed: The foundational document that outlines the trust's purpose, protections, and mandatory requirements.

- The Unregistered Lien Agreement: A mechanism to secure premarital assets and their post-marital appreciation.
- The Income Sharing Agreement (ISA): A safeguard against spousal support claims against post-divorce income (also shields against exploitative child support claims made by an ex-spouse seeking to use proceeds to fund a luxury lifestyle).
- The Intellectual Property Pre-Assignment Agreement: A pre-assignment agreement ensuring that all future intellectual property (IP) derived from premarital skills, talents, or credentials is pre-emptively protected from marital claims.
- TBA Pact and Covenant: A values-driven agreement ensuring alignment with family goals and legacy protection.
- The Trustee Services Agreement: An agreement outlining the roles and responsibilities of the corporate trustee of your FFT.

The FFT also synchronizes with future external documents drafted by your legal counsel to ensure your legal and financial protections mirror and complement one another on all fronts. The Trust Deed requires and defines baseline financial protections in:

- A qualifying prenuptial agreement (QPA). Or, if the settlor's spouse refuses a prenup, then:
- A qualifying DAPT or FAPT to secure premarital assets prior to marriage.
- A qualifying estate plan (QEP) to ensure continuity of the intentions and directives expressed in the QPA or DAPT/FAPT.

The Trust Deed: The Core of the System

At the heart of the FFT is its deed, which establishes the framework for asset protection, compliance requirements, and fallback mechanisms to address every conceivable angle of attack. The trust deed defines the rules and conditions under which all auxiliary agreements function, ensuring cohesive and comprehensive protection. It governs how assets are held, how control is delegated, how successors are appointed, and how beneficiaries are treated across all phases of life—and death. In short, it's the rulebook that your financial fortress will follow.

Crucially, the Family First Trust deed is engineered to align with global best practices in trust governance. It adheres to the internationally recognized guidelines of the Society of Trust and Estate Practitioners (STEP) and conforms to the Uniform Trust Code (UTC) standards where applicable, ensuring legitimacy, enforceability, and credibility across jurisdictions. This is not a structure selected for convenience or based on the jurisdiction where the purveyor happens to be licensed. It's a system designed with one priority in mind: maximum protection. The FFT is domiciled in Belize, arguably the most impenetrable jurisdiction on the planet when it comes to divorce-proofing your wealth. That choice of jurisdiction isn't incidental—it's strategic. Belize provides robust trustee privacy, no recognition of foreign judgments in matrimonial cases, and legal provisions that make it a nightmare for gold diggers and divorce attorneys alike.

For US residents, the same intentionality applies to the domestic side of the equation. When the time comes to implement a Domestic Asset Protection Trust (DAPT), your trustee will not recommend the jurisdiction that's merely convenient—we'll recommend the one that's proven to work. Jurisdiction is everything. And when you're playing a high-stakes game where your financial future is the prize, you don't want a trust that's built for convenience. You want one that's built to win.

Key Features of the Trust Deed

1. Mandatory Prenuptial Agreement or DAPT/FAPT
    - Requires the settlor to establish either a QPA or a qualifying DAPT or FAPT to ensure assets, future income, and future creative works remain protected from redistribution.

2. Triggering Events

The Trust Deed outlines specific events that automatically activate the trust's protections:

- Engagement event: The act of becoming engaged to be married is a triggering event. If the settlor has not already disclosed their FFT to their SO, they must do so within two weeks of becoming engaged.
- Cohabitation event: In any jurisdiction where spousal entitlements begin accruing against the settlor's property and income (spousal support) for simply living together (aka "common law marriage"), the move-in date is a triggering event.
- Elective triggering: Settlors who desire to remain single and self-identify as being at high risk of being targeted for economic exploitation outside of wedlock (i.e., reproductive coercion schemes, or "baby trapping") may elect to trigger their trusts by notifying the trustees at trust inception or any time thereafter. The TBA-certified trustees will provide referrals to qualified DAPT/FAPT practitioners. For US resident males who have not had vasectomies, TBA strongly recommends elective triggering so that a history of income flowing through their FFT-aligned DAPT predates any potential reproductive coercion pregnancy event. Attempts to shield income after conception will not be considered by the courts, regardless of whether the birth occurred as a result of reproductive coercion.

Disturbing but true: *In California, one "accidental" pregnancy entitles the perpetrator of reproductive coercion to 25% to 35% of your income for 18+ years.*

3. Preordained Timeline

Ensures proper execution of protective measures. For a marriage:

- Engagement notification to trustee must occur within two weeks.

- In the Trust Deed, the settlor agrees by covenant (a legally enforceable promise) to not set a wedding date for at least a year from their engagement event.
- Six-month cure period: The engagement event starts a countdown clock, with the first six months reserved for negotiating and finalizing a prenup—or, if the settlor's SO refuses a prenup, then to establish a personalized asset protection trust that will receive and protect premarital assets and rights to future income and future creations (intellectual property).
- US resident males who have not had vasectomies must set up asset protection trusts *regardless* of whether or not their SOs agree to prenups. However, the settlor-appointed trust protector may modify or waive this requirement.
- Six-month attachment and transfer period: The second six months are for the trustee to secure the settlor's premarital assets and future income in such a way that **the settlor continues to have full use and enjoyment** of them, but that they are shielded from third-party claims that could put the interests of the trust beneficiaries at risk. (The settlor is a beneficiary). By the end of the attachment and transfer period, 100% of the settlor's income will flow through the trust before being distributed back to the settlor (designed to be tax-neutral). If income distributions to the settlor were to become subject to redistribution through divorce proceedings in the future, the trustee is obliged to exercise their income-shielding powers.
- At the end of the attachment period, the wedding may proceed.

For cohabitation in any jurisdiction where the decision to cohabitate introduces spousal entitlements against the settlor's property and income:

- Cohabitation event notification to trustee must occur within 14 days of moving in.
- Six-month cure period: In the event the qualifying cohabitation agreement (QCA) was not already executed *prior* to the start of

cohabitation, the cohabitation event starts a countdown clock, with the first six months reserved for negotiating and finalizing a QCA—or, if the settlor's SO refuses a QCA, then for establishing a personalized asset protection trust that will receive and protect assets and rights to future income and future creations (IP) from potential common law status claims.

- US resident males who have not had vasectomies must set up asset protection trusts *regardless* of whether or not their SOs agree to a QCA. However, the settlor-appointed trust protector may modify or waive this requirement.
- Six-month attachment and transfer period: The second six months are for the trustee to secure the settlor's pre-common law status assets and future income in such a way that the **settlor continues to have full use and enjoyment** of them, but that they are shielded from third-party claims that could put the interests of the trust beneficiaries at risk. (The settlor is a beneficiary). By the end of the attachment and transfer period, 100% of the settlor's income flows through the trust before being distributed back to the settlor (designed to be tax neutral). If income distributions to the settlor were to become subject to redistribution through common law separation proceedings in the future, the trustee is obliged to exercise their income-shielding powers.

4. Protector Authority
Grants sweeping powers to amend, dissolve, or redomicile the trust to oversee compliance with its terms and adjust for evolving threats.

5. Trust Flexibility
The trusts' assets may be distributed thereby triggering its termination if an alternate structure emerges or the settlor's needs change, ensuring it remains future-proof and aligned with the settlor's goals.

The Psychological Significance of the FFT

The psychological deterrents embedded in the FFT are as critical as its legal and economic safeguards. DTGDs face an environment where their traditional tactics are proactively neutralized before they can be deployed.

- Perception of total futility: The layered protections signal that their time and efforts will be wasted.
- Fear of exposure: The trust's mechanisms guarantee that any attempt to circumvent or challenge it will backfire, revealing their true intentions.
- No emotional leverage: The preordained systems of compliance remove opportunities for stall tactics or coercive emotional manipulation.

A Blueprint for Protection

The FFT is not merely a legal tool—it is an ecosystem of protections designed to ensure that wealth remains secure, family legacies are preserved, and predators are thwarted at every turn. By integrating the trust deed with auxiliary agreements, like the Unregistered Lien Agreement, Income Sharing Agreement, Intellectual Property Pre-Assignment Agreement, TBA Pact and Covenant, and the Trustee Services Agreement—and external agreements like a QPA and/or a QDAPT/FAPT and a QEP—this system creates an unbreachable defense that reflects the settlor's values and priorities. With its mandatory requirements, clear timelines, and flexible protections, the FFT stands as the ultimate safeguard against exploitation.

If you're already convinced that the FFT is a necessity, feel free to skip ahead to Chapter 66 and secure your coverage.

If you want to understand in more depth how each layer of protection works together to safeguard your wealth, keep reading.

55

Double-Securing Premarital Assets: Unregistered Lien Agreement

The Unseen Guardian of Your Wealth

Your biggest financial risks aren't always visible. The most dangerous losses happen silently—premarital assets being reclassified as marital property, post-marital appreciation being claimed, and legal loopholes turning your personal wealth into a joint asset.

Most people assume that what they owned before marriage is automatically safe. That assumption has bankrupted countless high-net-worth individuals. Courts don't just look at what you owned before marriage—they look at what it became after you said, "I do."

This is where the Unregistered Lien Agreement comes in—a silent but impenetrable shield within the FFT. This confidential failsafe locks down your premarital assets and their appreciation, without anyone even knowing it exists.

When a financial predator tries to make a move, the liens activate, are legally registered, and secure your wealth—before anyone can lay a claim.

Why Most People Are Vulnerable—Even With a Prenup

A prenup is critical, but it's not bulletproof. Courts routinely challenge prenuptial agreements, especially regarding premarital assets that gain value during marriages.

- Your biggest risk isn't just losing half of what you have now—it's losing half of what it's worth years from now.
- If your $5 million property appreciates to $12 million after marriage, that $7 million growth could be considered "marital property" that's eligible for 50/50 division.
- Your prenup may be challenged, but an enforceable lien with a prior claim that predates the marriage is a different game entirely.

The Unregistered Lien Agreement ensures your assets and their appreciation stay out of reach.

The Unregistered Lien Agreement: What It Does and Why You Need It

Unlike public liens that can be discovered in a title search, the Unregistered Lien Agreement remains invisible—completely undetectable unless triggered by a financial threat.

How It Works

Phase 1: Silent Protection Mode (No Visibility, No Public Record)

- Your premarital assets remain entirely under your control, but with an invisible legal safeguard in place. Unlike conventional asset transfers, the Unregistered Lien Agreement (ULA) ensures that your wealth remains accessible without creating a public record that could attract scrutiny or enable a DTGD to build a dossier on your property holdings.
- While dormant, the liens remain unregistered and undiscoverable, allowing you to maintain full flexibility ownership over your assets without interference.

Phase 2: Activation upon a Triggering Event
Triggering events automatically convert silent protection into active defense, ensuring that your assets are shielded before any financial threats materialize.

- Engagement event: If a DAPT or FAPT is established, the trustee immediately registers the liens or causes them to be registered prior to the marriage event, ensuring that:
  - Your premarital assets and their appreciation cannot be classified as marital property.
  - Liens are interest-bearing, equity-capturing, or both, meaning post-marital appreciation remains protected within the trust and is not subject to redistribution in divorce proceedings.
- Cohabitation without a protective agreement: In jurisdictions where common-law marriage triggers spousal financial entitlements, the liens are registered following a cohabitation event (moving in together) and well in advance of common law spousal rights against your property and income coming into effect, adeptly blocking financial claims before they can arise.

Phase 3: Enforced When Needed
Once activated, the ULA transforms from an invisible safeguard into an unbreakable financial barrier, making it impossible for financial predators to access your wealth.

- Registered liens have legal priority: Once activated, the liens are officially recorded prior to marriage, ensuring that your trust—not your spouse or any claimant—has the superior legal claim over your assets.
- Stops asset redistribution cold: Liens neutralize divorce claims, creditor attacks, and legal challenges by preventing unauthorized financial reclassification or forced asset redistribution.
- Protects investment mobility: Rather than requiring an asset be transferred into the trust, liens secure the trust's interest while allowing you to retain full ownership, access, and investment flexibility.
- Seamless property exchanges: If you choose to sell or exchange real estate or other types of property and investments, the liens transfer to new properties, ensuring continuous protection without disrupting liquidity, asset mobility, or your personal enjoyment.

The ULA is an indispensable layer of protection, functioning as an invisible legal shield until the moment it's needed—at which point it becomes a powerful financial weapon against any attempts to attach to, seize, or redistribute your assets.

Why You Need This Protection—Now

- Shields premarital wealth: Your assets and their appreciation remain separate—no forced redistribution, no "joint property" loopholes.
- Locks out financial predators: Even without a prenup, these liens ensure that your wealth isn't up for redistribution.
- Prevents business and investment losses: Real estate, businesses, stocks, and investments remain yours alone, free from legal claims.
- Eliminates post-marital appreciation claims: Without this, growth in your premarital assets could be considered marital property. The liens stop that before it starts.

The Ultimate Deterrent for Gold Diggers

DTGDs are looking for every possible angle of attack to legally attach themselves to your assets and any future appreciation on those assets.

The Unregistered Lien Agreement eliminates these angles before they even start.

No negotiation. No arguments. Just total financial control.

If DTGDs discover they have zero chance of attaching to your premarital assets or their future growth, they'll realize this is an economic dead end.

And without a financial incentive, they won't even bother trying to entrench themselves.

A Silent Guardian and Powerful Defense

If you think your wealth is protected because you haven't given your spouse direct access, think again.

Without this protection, everything you've built—and everything you'll build in the future—could be at risk.

But with the Unregistered Lien Agreement, your financial legacy remains under lock and key—completely invisible until the moment it needs to defend you.

If you're ready to lock down your wealth, move on to Chapter 66 and secure your coverage.

Still want to see how all the pieces fit together? Keep reading—we'll break down how every layer of the FFT works in unison to create an impenetrable financial fortress.

56

Securing Future Earnings: Income Sharing Agreement

Your Biggest Financial Risk Isn't What You Have—It's What You'll Earn

Most people assume wealth protection is about assets—real estate, investments, businesses, etc. But what about the income you haven't earned yet?

Your future earnings are a goldmine for financial predators. If unprotected, your post-marriage income becomes the easiest target for divorce-driven financial extraction—whether through exploitative spousal support claims or child support payments that go far beyond what's needed to provide for your children.

The Income Sharing Agreement (ISA) is a failsafe mechanism that ensures your future income remains yours.

Understanding Income Sharing Agreements in Other Contexts

You may have heard of ISAs in other contexts—most notably, in student loans or professional athlete representation agreements. In these arrangements, a person commits a portion of their future income to a specific person or entity after a defined event occurs.

For example, early in their careers, professional athletes sometimes enter into representation agreements where portions of their future earnings are allocated to entities that helped finance their training and development. This structure anticipates astronomical future earnings and creates financial certainty in advance.

Similarly, the FFT's ISA is the perfect vehicle for capping future personal income amounts that will fall within the court's purview for calculating spousal and child support payments. By stipulating how much of your future income remains available for division, the ISA ensures that your wealth is not treated as an unlimited resource for an ex-spouse to exploit.

Securing Future Earnings: The ISA

We Presume You Want a Prenup—but That's not Enough

If you're reading this book, we presume you're already proactive enough about protecting your finances to want a prenup. But here's the problem—a prenup has zero influence over child support—and you don't even need to be married to become liable for child support.

- If a child is born from a casual intimate partner, you're financially on the hook for 18+ years—whether you agreed to parenthood or not.
- If you're married and a DTGD wants to circumvent your prenup, the easiest way to do so is to get pregnant. Child support is the one financial attack vector that completely overrides the protections of a prenup.

When you take a step back and look at the system, child support reveals itself as one of the most potent DTGD attack vectors—one you should be especially concerned about.

Here's how the game is played against you:

- Courts calculate child support as a percentage of your income, rather than based on actual expenses required to raise a child.
- For high earners, this can mean paying tens of thousands per month—even when your ex doesn't need the money, is capable of working to support themselves and is blocking your custody rights to increase their financial entitlements "for the children."
- Child support is non-negotiable, non-dischargeable, and enforced with the threat of jail time.

What happens if you reduce the amount of income upon which child support is calculated to a level that would only finance a modest standard of living?

- Suddenly, you're not a viable target for DTGDs.
- They want way more than that. A millionaire payor earning $500,000+ per year is a goldmine, but someone whose legal, tax, and liability planning is structured so the annual income that can be garnished is under $100,000 is not worth the effort.

This is why the ISA exists—to nullify the financial incentive for DTGDs before they ever target you. Your ISA is DTGD-repellant.

The ISA: A Multi-Layered Shield Against Reproductive Coercion and Spousal Support

Much of the ISA discussion focuses on its role as a deterrent and safeguard against reproductive coercion—and it is highly effective in that regard.

But what many people don't realize is that the ISA is also an exceptionally powerful defense against *spousal* support claims.

- While child support primarily targets high-earning men, spousal support (alimony) is a financial landmine for both affluent men *and* women.
- The ISA doesn't just limit exposure to reproductive coercion—it also ensures that your income isn't unjustly siphoned away in alimony payments to an able-bodied ex who is allergic to work.

Take the case of Kelly Clarkson as an example.

- After divorcing her ex-husband Brandon Blackstock, Clarkson was ordered to pay him nearly $200,000 per month in combined spousal and child support.
- Over two years, this amounted to approximately $4.6 million in payments—a staggering financial windfall for an ex-spouse.

This is exactly why the ISA exists.

- It protects high-earning men from DTGDs looking to weaponize child support and spousal support.
- It also protects high-earning *women* from opportunistic male spouses looking to weaponize spousal support.

The ISA is the ultimate financial firewall, neutralizing two of the most devastating financial attack vectors used in modern family courts.

How the ISA Works: A Preemptive Legal Claim on Your Future Income

Your ISA sits dormant inside your FFT, waiting for a triggering event to activate it.

The ISA is triggered by any of the following events:

1. Engagement event: Getting engaged to a partner.
2. Cohabitation event: Moving in together.
3. Elective triggering: Activating your ISA at your discretion.

Once triggered, the ISA secures your income before financial predators can lay claim to it.

The ISA: A Multi-Faceted Financial Defense System

The ISA is engineered to do what no other legal tool can—preemptively shield your earnings before a predator stakes a claim.

This ensures that:

- Your future income streams are contractually secured within the trust before child support or spousal claims can be made against it.
- Your trust protector and trustee control distributions, limiting what a court can consider as income when calculating child support.
- Your ex's only valid claim is limited to the actual income distributed to you by the trustee, keeping child and spousal support obligations within the $2,500–$4,000/month range.

This is the most powerful deterrent to reproductive coercion—but only if the predator is made aware.

It is important to note that the full mechanics of the ISA are proprietary and deliberately excluded from this book to ensure maximum security and effectiveness.

- The ISA is not one-dimensional—it is a robust, multi-layered shield designed to operate within multiple legal and financial frameworks to neutralize financial predators.

The ISA vs. Divorce Court: A Game-Changer

Factor	Without the ISA	Without the ISA
Spousal Support	Up to 50% of your income—potentially for life	Severely limited—only a modest standard of living
Child Support	Court assigns payments based on your income—not actual child needs	Ensures reasonable support for children—no ex-spouse windfall
Income Protection	At risk—courts can garnish wages indefinitely	Trust's prior claims shield income, ensuring trust beneficiaries take priority
Trust Beneficiary Protection	Courts can divert funds meant for family legacy	Trustee ensures education, entrepreneurship, and housing funds remain secure

Bottom Line

The ISA ensures you control your income—not your ex.

How the ISA Strengthens the FFT Framework

The ISA isn't just a contract—it's a financial fortress.

- Works in tandem with the trust's triggering events—ensuring income protection aligns with other asset safeguards.
- Pairs with the Unregistered Lien Agreement—creating a multi-layered wealth shield.
- Stops financial predators before they start (if DTGDs know your income is locked down, they'll move on to an easier target).

The Final Line of Defense: Securing Your Financial Future

DTGDs assume they'll walk away from marriage with a blank check for life.

The Income Sharing Agreement ensures they walk away with only what's fair.

No lavish payouts. No indentured servitude. No surprises.

If you're ready to secure your future income, move to Chapter 66 and activate the ISA today.

Still want to see how all the FFT layers work together? Keep reading—we'll break down the full financial shield that ensures your wealth stays yours.

57

Securing Your Creations: Intellectual Property Pre-Assignment Agreement

Protecting Future Intellectual Property Creations

Wealth protection isn't just about what you have now—it's about securing everything you'll build in the future. If you have unique skills, high-income potential, or creative expertise, your greatest financial threat isn't just losing existing assets in divorce—it's losing control over the wealth you haven't even generated yet.

The Intellectual Property Pre-Assignment Agreement (IPPAA) is a proactive strike against this threat—pre-assigning all intellectual property you haven't even created yet so that it is legally secured against any attempt by a DTGD to attach to it.

Wealth Creation Is Separate from Income—and They Want Both

A DTGD's strategy isn't just about attaching to your future income—it's about something much bigger:

- They want to attach to your ability to create wealth.
- They want to own half of the companies, intellectual property, and assets you haven't even conceived of yet.
- They want a permanent stake in the value of what you build—not just the money you take home from it.

Imagine that, through your talents, connections, and hard work, you create an incredibly successful company out of thin air during your marriage.

- Your partner makes no contribution to it, other than living with you and spending your money.
- When the divorce happens, your ex doesn't just want half of your $500,000-per-year salary—they also want half of the company that's now worth $100 million.
- That's a $50 million payday for the DTGD—just for having the foresight to target you for your potential to create wealth.
- If you didn't have the same foresight, the courts will award it to them—no questions asked.

Unless you preassign your IP in a way that places it well beyond the court's reach, everything you build is fair game for redistribution in divorce proceedings. And you may end up with a hostile ex causing chaos as a shareholder in *your* business.

Your IP Is a DTGD's Dream Target—Unless You Protect It

If you have a high-income skillset, unique expertise, creative talent, or a track record of success, you're not just a target for economic attachment to your income—you're also being sized up for the businesses, creations, and innovations you haven't even thought of yet.

Historical performance is the strongest predictor of future performance.

If you've already had a few wins, DTGDs know you're likely to have more—and they are waiting in the wings to ensure that, when those wins happen, they get half.

- They don't care that the wealth creation originates from you alone.
- They don't care that they contributed nothing.
- They don't care about fairness.

All they care about is getting in the door legally so that, when you succeed, they can cash out with half.

If you haven't already preassigned the attachment rights to your future creations, you are financially exposed—and DTGDs know it.

And that's exactly why the IPPAA exists.

How Courts Seize IP in Divorces

Most people assume intellectual property is protected—but it's not.

If you don't act before marriage, the courts will treat everything you create as marital property—meaning your ex gets half.

How the Scam Works Against You:

- If you write a book? They own half.
- If you invent something? They own half.
- If you start a company? They own half.
- If your song goes platinum? They get half the royalties.
- If you create a billion-dollar patent? They own half.

Don't think for a second that judges will side with you. If you didn't take steps to protect yourself prior to marriage, everything created during the marriage is deemed "marital property"—and your ex is entitled to half in most jurisdictions.

The IPPAA: Your Firewall Against IP Theft

The IPPAA is a legally binding contract that ensures all intellectual property you develop during a marriage remains yours.

It's a non-negotiable safeguard within TBA's FFT, creating an impenetrable legal barrier that prevents future financial entanglement before it happens.

The Psychological Deterrent Effect: Cutting Off DTGDs' Angles of Attack

DTGDs thrive on ambiguity—stalling prenup discussions, pretending to support your career, and then claiming ownership after the fact.

The IPPAA shuts this down completely.

- There's no loophole.
- There's no delayed legal battle.
- There's just a clear, enforceable barrier that protects your creations forever.

More Than a Prenup: A Dynamic Shield for Future Wealth

The IPPAA within the FFT ensures that your ideas, royalties, and business ventures remain yours and yours alone.

Here's What You Secure Immediately

- Full ownership of all IP developed after marriage
- Ironclad legal boundaries that eliminate future claims

- Protection of royalties, patents, copyrights, and businesses from spousal entanglement
- Preservation of family wealth for future generations

If you're ready to protect everything you'll ever build, turn to Chapter 66 and secure your coverage today.

Still want to understand how the full system works? Keep reading—we'll break down each layer of protection so you can see exactly how your wealth remains yours forever.

58

A Moral Duty to Protect Wealth for Future Generations: The Bloodline Alliance Pact and Covenant

The Pact and Covenant: A Moral and Legal Shield

The Pact and Covenant is a multi-layered legal and ethical safeguard within the FFT framework. It ensures that wealth preservation remains aligned with the well-being of the settlor's consanguineous family—children, siblings, and extended relatives—while exposing the predatory motives of DTGDs who attempt to undermine these interests.

The Core Covenants: Legally Binding Promises That Protect the Family's Wealth

While the Pact and Covenant contains multiple provisions, its most powerful and enforceable covenant is the settlor's legally binding commitment to a threefold protection strategy:

- No Marriage Without a Prenup—or, If the significant other (SO) Resists, a DAPT/FAPT Instead
  - The settlor is obligated to secure a prenuptial agreement to protect the interests of the FFT's beneficiaries (i.e., family members entitled to educational, housing, and entrepreneurial funding).
  - If the SO resists a prenup, the settlor is bound by covenant to immediately safeguard their assets through a DAPT or FAPT.
  - This ensures that, even if the settlor marries without a prenup, the DTGD is still locked out from displacing the trust beneficiaries' rights in order to extract wealth through divorce proceedings.

- No Pressuring the SO into a Prenup (to Prevent Later "Coercion" Claims)
  - The settlor is explicitly barred from doing anything their SO could even remotely characterize as "feeling pressured."
  - This is a critical defensive strategy. If a DTGD later argues in court that they were "pressured" into signing, they can attempt to invalidate the prenup based on claims of duress or coercion (a classic DTGD maneuver).
  - By committing to a neutral, pressure-free approach, the settlor eliminates a common legal loophole that a DTGD might later exploit.

- For US Residents: A Mandatory DAPT—Regardless of the Prenup's Status
  - Whether or not the SO agrees to a prenup, a US-based settlor is bound to create a DAPT as an additional layer of protection.
  - A DAPT places the settlor's wealth into an irrevocable trust,

  preventing future spousal claims and ensuring that family assets remain untouchable.
- The ideal scenario is a combination of both a DAPT and a prenup—but the settlor's covenant guarantees that at least their DAPT is non-negotiable.

This three-pronged legal strategy ensures that the settlor's family wealth is protected under all circumstances, regardless of whether the SO initially agrees to a prenup. The DTGD is left without a viable path to wealth extraction, no matter how they attempt to maneuver.

How the FFT Exposes a DTGD Before Marriage

The FFT's brilliance lies in how it forces any DTGD into a collision course with exposure—not through speculation or accusations, but through their own actions.

The Prenuptial Test: An Unavoidable Dilemma for a DTGD
One of the strongest deterrents within the FFT framework is the settlor's obligation to request a prenuptial agreement as part of the family wealth preservation strategy.

- A legitimate, well-intentioned partner will:
  - Understand and accept the need to protect pre-existing family commitments.
  - Respect the trust's purpose, knowing it was not created to exclude them personally, but to honor long-standing obligations to family members.
- A DTGD, however, sees only one thing: A roadblock standing between them and the settlor's wealth.

This is where the FFT forces DTGDs to reveal themselves.

- If they push back against the prenup, they knowingly attempt to override the rights of the settlor's family members—proving that their goal is financial access, not love or partnership.
- The settlor's relatives now have irrefutable proof that the DTGD's interests conflict with the trust's intended purpose.
- Even worse for the DTGD, they know that the family now knows what they're really after.

At this stage, the DTGD is caught in a reputational and psychological trap. They have been forced into an unwinnable decision:

- Sign the prenup and forfeit their opportunity to extract wealth, or
- Refuse and expose themselves to the settlor's entire family as a financial predator.

The FFT Still Wins, Even If a DTGD Marries Without a Prenup

Even if the DTGD successfully manipulates the settlor into skipping a prenup, the Pact and Covenant remains legally binding—and its secondary fail-safes activate:

- DAPT/FAPT protections trigger: Assets are moved out of reach, ensuring that no wealth can be accessed in the event of divorce.
- The settlor's legal compliance is documented: The settlor followed their covenant by requesting a prenup and/or securing a DAPT/FAPT.
- Reputational fallout for the DTGD: By resisting the prenup, the DTGD has exposed their gold-digger intentions, permanently altering how the settlor's family perceives them.

The Final Reckoning: The DTGD's Uphill Battle in Divorce Court

Since the DTGD was made explicitly aware—prior to marriage—that the settlor's assets were reserved for pre-existing family commitments, their legal team faces an impossible argument:

- Claiming entitlement to family assets that were irrevocably earmarked for an education, housing, and entrepreneurship fund for future generations.
- Attempting to override a legally binding trust that was established long before they arrived on the scene.
- Convincing a judge that they deserve to displace the settlor's family members from their rightful financial security.

No judge wants to set a precedent that allows a spouse to hijack generational wealth that was clearly designated for legitimate family needs.

- The DTGD's legal argument collapses under its own weight.
- With airtight legal structures in place, the FFT ensures that the settlor's wealth remains fully protected, while the DTGD walks away empty-handed.

Why the Pact and Covenant Is an Unmatched Defense Strategy

By enforcing these three core legal commitments, the Pact and Covenant doesn't just protect wealth—it actively repels predators.

- Pre-Marriage: The Prenuptial Test—Forces the DTGD to self-expose when resisting protective agreements.
- During Marriage: The Asset Shield—Ensures that, even without a prenup, a DAPT/FAPT prevents spousal wealth extraction.

- Divorce Proceedings: The Final Legal Trap—Dismantles the DTGD's legal position, making their claims indefensible in court.

Through its multi-layered design, the Pact and Covenant ensures that any DTGD who attempts to exploit the settlor is met with immediate legal, reputational, and financial defeat.

The result? A family-first fortress that no gold-digger wants to waste their time and resources attempting to overturn.

If you're already convinced that the FFT is a necessity, feel free to skip ahead to Chapter 66 and secure your coverage.

If you want to understand in more depth how each layer of protection works together to safeguard your wealth, keep reading.

59

Qualifying Prenuptial Agreement (QPA): Essential Requirements for FFT Compliance

A Blueprint for Financial Security and Protection

We all know what a prenuptial agreement is, but in the context of your FFT, a prenuptial agreement must meet specific criteria to qualify as a *qualifying* prenuptial agreement (QPA). Not every prenup makes the cut.

Your trust deed outlines the requirements a prenup must meet to qualify, but it does not dictate the decisions within the prenup. Instead, it establishes the mandatory topics that must be addressed for it to be recognized as a QPA.

Each category in a QPA must either be:

- Explicitly addressed, or
- Omitted by mutual agreement, with both parties acknowledging the exclusion in writing, or
- Excluded because the category is unenforceable in the jurisdiction where the parties will reside

A properly executed QPA is a legally fortified barrier against opportunistic financial claims, particularly those leveraged by DTGDs. It ensures that premarital and post-marital wealth remain under the control of its rightful owner, while maintaining clarity and fairness for both parties.

How DTGDs Undermine Prenups

A DTGD's goal is to ensure the prenup is thin, shaky, or both, creating loopholes they can exploit later.

- A "thin" prenup: Lacks essential protections and allows ambiguity that can be challenged in court.
- A "shaky" prenup: Contains weaknesses that make it vulnerable to invalidation.
- A "thin and shaky" prenup: The worst-case scenario for the settlor, offering an illusion of security while being legally ineffective.

This is why the FFT requires a QPA—an airtight, legally defensible prenup designed to block financial exploitation. If a prenup does not qualify, the settlor is required to protect their wealth through a DAPT/FAPT, closing all potential loopholes a DTGD might attempt to exploit.

The Anatomy of a QPA

A QPA must meet specific legal requirements to ensure it is enforceable and impenetrable.

- Independent legal advisors for both parties: Ensures informed consent and eliminates coercion claims.
- The six-month rule: Must be signed at least six months before the wedding to prevent claims of duress.
- Submission to the protector and trustee: A copy must be delivered to the FFT's protector and trustee to verify compliance.

What Happens If a Prenup Fails to Qualify?

If a prenup does not meet the FFT's standards, it is considered a financial liability. In this case, the settlor is legally required to establish a DAPT/FAPT to safeguard their assets. This means:

- The non-qualifying prenup remains valid for the topics that it addresses, but cannot be used as a backdoor for wealth extraction on the topics it doesn't cover.
- The DAPT/FAPT locks down all protected assets, eliminating future spousal claims.
- The settlor remains legally compliant, securing their wealth even if the prenup is weak.

Closing the Loopholes: Why a QPA or DAPT/FAPT Is Essential

By requiring either a QPA or a DAPT/FAPT, the FFT eliminates every avenue for financial exploitation.

- If the prenup qualifies, it serves as a primary defense against predatory claims.
- If the prenup is weak, the DAPT/FAPT ensures all assets remain untouchable.

For a DTGD, this is an impossible scenario—every potential loophole is closed, ensuring that wealth extraction is off the table. This is why they resist strong prenups and seek to manipulate thin or shaky agreements. However, with a QPA in place, backed by the asset protection mandates of the FFT, the settlor holds the ultimate safeguard against predatory intentions.

The Gold Standard of Prenuptial Agreements

A QPA is not just a document—it is an essential pillar of financial defense. For individuals utilizing the FFT, a QPA is their frontline shield against financial exploitation, ensuring that wealth remains secure, intact, and beyond the reach of opportunistic claims.

With meticulous structuring, mandatory legal oversight, and a commitment to clarity and fairness, a QPA creates an unbreachable boundary between personal wealth and marital entanglements.

If you're already convinced that the FFT is a necessity, feel free to skip ahead to Chapter 66 and secure your coverage.

If you want to understand in more depth how each layer of protection works together to safeguard your wealth, keep reading.

60

Qualifying DAPT and FAPT: Prenup Refusal Triggers Premarital Asset Protection Trusts

You're Walking into a Financial Minefield—Are You Ready?

The greatest risk to your economic survival isn't a stock market crash or a real estate bubble—it's divorce. Every year, billions of dollars are extracted from unsuspecting individuals in predatory financial claims, wiping out fortunes that took decades to build. If you think your assets are safe because they're tucked away in investments, trusts, or even crypto, think again. Without an airtight structure in place, everything you've worked for is up for grabs.

For individuals with substantial assets, a standard prenuptial agreement is not enough. You need a fortress, not a fence—and that fortress includes not only your FFT, but also the seamlessly integrated supporting agreements it requires when the time comes. These include a qualifying DAPT or FAPT, seamlessly integrated with your FFT.

The Non-Negotiable Asset Protection Rule

- If you're a non-US resident, your FFT deed mandates that if your partner refuses to negotiate a fair prenuptial agreement, you must secure your wealth in a qualifying FAPT.
- If you're a US resident, the USAF-FFT takes it a step further. Regardless of whether your partner agrees to a prenup, you must establish a qualifying DAPT.
- Both are recommended. And if your SO objects to a prenup? Run.

In the US, the financial incentives for predators are extreme. Reproductive coercion, marriage fraud, and divorce-fueled wealth extraction are thriving *industries.* A qualifying DAPT or FAPT is the only thing standing between you and financial ruin.

DAPTs: The Best Protection Available—but not a Cure-All

As of 2025, 19 states in the US recognize DAPTs. This allows you to move all your premarital assets into a DAPT domiciled in a state other than where you live. In theory, this is excellent news—you can legally shield assets by leveraging the strongest jurisdictions available.

But what if a DAPT asset is physically located in a state that does not recognize them? This is where many people make the fatal mistake of assuming their DAPT is bulletproof. It isn't. Your home, rental properties, or other real estate assets physically located in a non-DAPT state could be at risk.

A judge in a non-DAPT state may decide that, since the asset is physically located within their jurisdiction, they have the power to override the DAPT's protections and order liquidation or redistribution.

That's where your FFT's Unregistered Lien Agreement becomes the ultimate failsafe.

How the FFT Fortifies Your DAPT

The DAPT is still the single best protection you can establish—but you can further fortify it with your FFT.

1. Your ULA is your trump card.

- Before marriage, your unregistered liens convert into registered liens. This creates legally recognized, pre-existing financial claims that predate any future divorce proceedings.
- If a DTGD attempts to claim your assets, their case is immediately nullified by prior encumbrances.
- Even if a judge invalidates your DAPT, the FFT's existing assignable liens make the asset economically worthless to a financial predator because lien-holders have established legitimate prior claims that predate the marriage.

2. Your IP is already protected in your DAPT/FAPT.

- Through your IPPAA, any future creations (books, patents, business earnings, etc.) are already secured under your trust's protective umbrella.

This eliminates the ability for an ex-spouse to stake a claim on your future capacity to create wealth from your creative works and inventions.

3. Your income has already been assigned to your DAPT/FAPT.

- The ISA ensures that your post-divorce earnings remain within your control, safeguarded from legal attacks.

With these three layers in place, your assets are functionally untouchable—even in the worst-case scenario.

FAPTs: The Final Nail in the Coffin for Financial Predators

FAPTs go one step further, removing your wealth completely from US jurisdiction.

- Established in offshore jurisdictions like the Cook Islands, Nevis, or Belize, these trusts are untouchable by US courts.
- Even if a US court demands asset liquidation, foreign trustees are under no obligation to comply, nor will foreign courts cooperate with enforcement orders.

Why Your FFT Requires a "Qualifying" DAPT or FAPT

Not all trusts are built for battle. If your trust doesn't meet the FFT's qualification criteria, it will not provide the fullest protection available to you.

A qualifying DAPT or FAPT must:

- Be established in a jurisdiction with rock-solid asset protection laws.
- Be structured to ensure that, even if challenged, the economic benefit remains out of reach for predators.

Most off-the-shelf DAPTs fail these criteria. This is why TBA provides referrals to carefully vetted practitioners upon request.

The Bottom Line: You Either Protect It, or You Lose It

- Every year, billions are lost in divorce-fueled financial extraction schemes.

- The only way to ensure your wealth survives is a multi-layered, bulletproof defense.
- A qualifying DAPT or FAPT, seamlessly integrated with your FFT, is the only way to guarantee long-term protection.

If you think you're safe without it, just ask the thousands of DTGD victims who thought the same—until they lost everything. Do not become another statistic.

Your fortune is yours to keep—but only if you take the right steps today.

If you're already convinced that the FFT is a necessity, feel free to skip ahead to Chapter 66 and secure your coverage.

If you want to understand in more depth how each layer of protection works together to safeguard your wealth, keep reading.

61

Qualifying Estate Plan (QEP): A Critical Safeguard for the FFT

Estate Planning Is a Battlefield

Most people think of estate planning as a bureaucratic formality—a will to sign later in life, a few trust structures, maybe some tax planning. But if you think estate planning is just about who inherits your assets, you've already lost. The real battle isn't just about wealth transfer—it's about defense against financial predators who are already strategizing how to hijack your estate.

If your SO refuses to sign a QPA, that is a very strong signal that they may be planning to exploit estate distribution laws to displace your heirs and take control of your wealth after you die. That is why, under the FFT framework, you are required to establish an estate plan that mirrors your prenup (if you have one) or protects your estate through trust structuring (if your SO refuses a prenup).

Two Paths, One Goal: Keeping Economic Predators Out of Your Estate

- If your SO agrees to a prenup: You must establish a qualifying joint estate plan (QJEP) that mirrors the prenup's terms to prevent estate distribution loopholes.
- If your SO refuses a prenup:
    - Non-US residents must establish a FAPT to shield assets from spousal inheritance laws that may conflict with intent.
    - US residents must establish a DAPT (and may also have an optional FAPT) to block spousal estate claims that may conflict with intent.
    - In both cases where a prenup isn't in place, you must also have a qualifying individual estate plan (QIEP) that ensures compliance with spousal share rules in your jurisdiction while minimizing what can be extracted against your expressed wishes.

Estate Planning Is About Protecting Your Wishes, not Just Your Assets

If you're still married when you pass, your estate plan will presumably reflect a balanced desire to provide for your spouse while also ensuring your wishes for bequests to others remain protected. A well-crafted estate plan isn't just about dividing assets—it's about ensuring that your wishes are respected and your other intended heirs aren't displaced or overridden.

Two key threats must be neutralized:

1. Challenges to your estate plan: A surviving spouse, ex-spouse, or other opportunist may attempt to invalidate your estate plan to take a larger share than intended.
2. Legal process abuses: A separated spouse may deliberately stall divorce proceedings to retain spousal rights and claim assets they were never meant to receive.

Without protections in place, your estate plan can be overridden, contested, or delayed, resulting in your wealth being distributed against your wishes.

The DTGD Playbook: Hijacking Your Estate

DTGDs—especially Grave Robber DTGDs—are experts in estate exploitation. They know the spousal share rules in your jurisdiction better than you do and will weaponize intestacy laws, elective share provisions, and legal process delays to extract the maximum financial windfall from your estate. Their goal is simple: displace your rightful heirs, override your financial wishes, and capture as much of your wealth as possible.

How They Do It

- Refusing a prenup and waiting you out: A spouse who refuses a prenup but stays in the marriage for years is likely banking on outliving you to claim the full spousal share of your estate.
- Intestacy manipulation: If you die without a properly structured estate plan, your spouse may automatically inherit a massive percentage of your estate under intestacy laws.
- Elective share claims: Even if you disinherit them in your will, they may be legally entitled to claim a statutory portion of your estate.
- Delaying divorce to secure a death payout: A DTGD in a failing marriage has every incentive to stall divorce proceedings—because if they outlive you, they win.
- Estate plan contests: They will challenge your will, forcing your legitimate heirs into legal battles that drain estate resources.

The FFT Solution: Closing Every Loophole

The FFT doesn't just require an estate plan—it requires a *qualifying* estate plan. That means your QJEP or QIEP must integrate ironclad defensive strategies to neutralize every attack vector DTGDs use to hijack estates.

1. If You Have a Prenup: The QJEP

Your QJEP must mirror your QPA. If your prenup excludes your spouse from certain assets, your estate plan must also exclude them. A contradictory estate plan can lead to claims that they were unintentionally included—a loophole DTGDs can exploit.

Key Features of a QJEP

- Prenup alignment: Consistency between prenup terms and estate plan terms.
- Proactive will updates: Regularly updated to eliminate ambiguity that could be exploited posthumously.
- No intestacy exposure: Clear asset designations prevent courts from defaulting to intestacy laws.

2. If You Don't Have a Prenup: The QIEP + Trust Protection

If your SO refused a prenup, your estate plan must operate as a defensive firewall.

- Non-US Residents: Establish a FAPT so that no part of your estate remains within reach of spousal inheritance laws unless you specify otherwise.
- US Residents: Establish a DAPT to legally lock assets away from spousal claims beyond what you wish to leave your surviving spouse, and optionally use an FAPT for additional protection.
- Your QIEP must:
    - Address any remaining assets that weren't transferred into the trust.
    - Comply with spousal share rules while ensuring that your spouse receives only what you decide and no more.
    - Eliminate ambiguity that could allow a court to override your intentions.

3. The Not-So-Secret Benefit: Filtering Out Grifters Before Marriage

One of the biggest advantages of an FFT is that its required disclosure immediately exposes any SO with financial motives.

A DTGD who realizes they have no financial path to inheritance will almost always self-eject rather than waste years in a marriage that won't pay off. Your FFT serves as an early detection and ejection system, ensuring that only partners who are truly committed to you—rather than your estate—move forward.

Final Warning: Act Before It's Too Late

If you're not yet married, this is your chance to ensure your estate is protected before a DTGD secures legal entitlements. If you are already married and don't have a prenup, you may be able to protect your estate and intended beneficiaries with a FAPT (see Resources).

If you're already convinced that the FFT is a necessity, feel free to skip ahead to Chapter 66 and secure your coverage.

If you want to understand in more depth how each layer of protection works together to safeguard your wealth, keep reading.

62

Built to Evolve With the Law and Your Unique Scenario

Your Trustee and Strategic Defender

A Trustee certified by The Bloodline Alliance serves as the trustee of your FFT, ensuring your present and future wealth remains protected—not just for you, but for generations to come. To maintain the highest level of legal adaptability and protection, FFTs can only be established through TBA-certified corporate trustees who have passed a rigorous training and certification program. These licensees have exclusive access to the FFT amendments generated by TBA's legal intelligence division.

TBA certification ensures:

- Consistent implementation of trust protections across all jurisdictions where FFTs are available.

- Exclusive access to strategic updates that neutralize emerging threats.
- An ongoing connection to the legal intelligence division at The Bloodline Alliance, ensuring the trust remains at the forefront of wealth protection.
- Local-level threat reporting: These corporate trustees serve as an important feedback loop, identifying jurisdiction-specific challenges that can influence macro-level fortifications of the FFT.

This network of corporate trustees ensures that every FFT benefits from the most current, battle-tested legal protections.

Why Specialized Trustee Services Are Essential to Your Wealth Protection

Built for Long-Term Security: A Trust That Evolves with You

1. Proactive Monitoring and Legal Adaptation
Unlike traditional trustees who act only when required, TBA actively tracks changes that could impact your trust. When a new legal precedent or legislative shift poses a risk, we adapt the trust before your assets and income become vulnerable.

2. Empowering Your Legal and Financial Advisors
Your FFT is structured to be adaptable by your legal and financial team, allowing them to modify the trust in ways that best serve its purpose and protect you and your family. If customized structuring beyond what we provide is required, your advisors are fully empowered to implement those modifications and, if necessary, appoint a new trustee to oversee the revised trust.

3. A Living, Breathing Defense System
Life changes, laws evolve, and financial threats emerge. TBA ensures your trust remains a fortress, not a relic.

- Adjustments for life events: Your trust can be modified to include new beneficiaries, protect additional assets, or adapt to changing wealth structures.
- Preemptive action against DTGD strategies: We stay ahead of evolving financial exploitation tactics to ensure your trust is never vulnerable.
- Ongoing evaluation and reinforcement: Your trust is reviewed regularly to ensure it remains as strong tomorrow as it is today.

The Legal Fortification of the FFT: The Ultimate DTGD Deterrent

To the attorneys who contributed to the architecture and comprehensive legal strategy of the FFT, TBA posed the following question: If you were representing a DTGD attempting to dismantle the FFT, what would be your legal approach? More importantly, what would be your confidence level of success? The responses varied in approach, but the overarching takeaway was exactly what was envisioned in its architecture: The FFT's architecture holds firm, and its multilayered defenses perform exactly as designed.

The Reality of DTGD Attack Vectors

DTGDs don't rely on a single legal attack. They combine multiple overlapping tactics to overwhelm their victims and the legal system, hoping that at least one avenue will lead to a financial extraction. Whether it involves prenup invalidation, strategic pregnancies, asset co-mingling, or estate hijacking, their playbook is vast and ruthless. A prenup alone is woefully inadequate, because it only addresses one facet of their attack strategy. The FFT, however, was engineered to withstand these coordinated assaults.

Every lawyer consulted acknowledged a fundamental truth: The law is ever-changing, fluid, and subject to the unpredictable whims of judicial interpretation. The legal landscape is rife with inconsistency. What holds up in one courtroom may crumble in another. Yet, despite these uncertainties, the FFT's layered, interlocking safeguards ensure that even if one component is successfully challenged, the overarching protection remains intact.

Winning Battles, Losing the War

Many of the legal minds we consulted focused on one or two primary attack vectors that they believed could be leveraged to challenge specific elements of the trust. However, even those who felt they could "win a battle" on a particular legal argument (if they "got the right judge") admitted that they would ultimately lose the war due to the FFT's multitiered failsafe mechanisms. The trust was purpose-built to ensure that no single weakness could compromise the overall structure. A successful challenge on one front only leads to an unscalable wall on the other side.

One of the most insightful observations from our discussions was the recognition that the lawyers who architected the FFT are intimately familiar with both its hidden traps for DTGDs and its escape hatches for those it is designed to protect. Any attempt to dismantle the FFT would first have to navigate its structural redundancies, only to run into yet another layer of legal fortification. The FFT is not just legally sound—it is psychologically discouraging for any DTGD or their legal counsel attempting to challenge it. The family first format has been quietly protecting family wealth for generations because challenging it is an exercise in futility.

The Confidence to Act Now

By now, it should be clear that this isn't just a trust—it's an elite financial defense system. What does this mean for you? The FFT is your legacy's insurance policy against financial predators, bad faith actors, and evolving legal risks.

63

Full Disclosure: The Ultimate DTGD Deterrent

A Character-Revealing Moment of Truth

There comes a point in every serious relationship when the conversation inevitably shifts toward the future. Maybe it starts subtly—the DTGD testing the waters, making casual comments about long-term plans, shared goals, or where you both see yourselves in 5 or 10 years. Maybe it's more direct—a pointed conversation about exclusivity, moving in together, or even marriage. For someone with substantial assets and a clear financial strategy, this is the precise moment to take control of the conversation.

It's a critical opportunity to introduce an essential truth: You don't just prefer a prenuptial agreement—you have a family obligation to either have a prenup, or protect your present and future wealth in an asset protection trust.

This isn't about personal preference or an arbitrary decision. It's a non-negotiable requirement—one that exists not just to protect you, but to preserve a legacy that has been carefully structured to benefit future generations through the education, entrepreneurship, and housing fund you established for your nieces and nephews. If the person sitting across from you is the Real Deal, they'll take this in stride, understanding that financial responsibility is just as crucial as emotional commitment. But if they're a DTGD, this is where they start looking for an exit strategy—or scrambling to devise a counterattack.

When to Have "The Talk"

These conversations don't happen in a vacuum. They arise naturally as relationships evolve. You don't need to force the conversation. If you're dealing with DTGDs, they will get there on their own—because financial entanglement is always their endgame.

When they finally do, that's when you make the situation clear.

"I should share with you—I set up a trust fund for my nieces and nephews' education, entrepreneurship, and housing that also has a strict policy when it comes to marriage. A prenup isn't optional for me. It's a requirement. Of course, that's not something I can require of you, so I want you to know I would prefer to have a prenup. If you're against that, I'm obligated to move my present and future wealth into another type of structure that ensures the education, entrepreneurship, and housing fund cannot be compromised."

Pause. Let that sink in. A Real Deal partner will nod, ask reasonable questions, and maybe even express appreciation for your transparency. A DTGD, on the other hand, will immediately begin calculating their next move.

This is when you introduce the FFT.

The Non-Negotiable Disclosure

At some point in this conversation—perhaps after a few follow-up questions or a casual "That makes sense"—you'll need to share something else: Full disclosure of the trust isn't just a choice. It's a requirement.

"I actually have an obligation to disclose my trust to anyone I get engaged to. And the terms of the trust deed require me to wait at least a year between getting engaged and a wedding."

This statement serves three key purposes:

1. It introduces the trust as an immovable force. It's not up for debate. It exists, it's structured, and it's legally binding.
2. It signals there is zero opportunity to attempt an end run on the trust by rushing a wedding before the wealth protections required by your FFT are fully in place.
3. It allows you to naturally transition into sharing the trust documents. There's no need to explain every intricate detail—it's far easier to hand it over (or email it) and say, "Honestly, it's pretty complex. But you're welcome to read it over."

And here's where the magic happens. A Real Deal partner will read it, ask questions, and engage in a practical, constructive discussion. Despite the calm they attempt to display on the surface, a DTGD will be enraged at the realization they have wasted their time targeting you only to hit an impenetrable wall.

The DTGD's Nightmare: Full Transparency and Neutralized Economic Opportunity

For DTGDs, this moment neutralizes their entire psychological warfare playbook. It thwarts their planned tactics that rely on urgency, emotional manipulation, and finding loopholes before financial defenses are put in place. Ordinarily, the DTGD playbook involves:

- Pushing for a fast engagement.
- Resisting discussing prenups until the last minute so they can dodge it altogether or create a meticulously laid trap that invalidates it due to "feeling pressured" to sign too close to the wedding.

- Manufacturing emotional crises to delay legal conversations.

The one-year engagement requirement annihilates all of these strategies in one fell swoop. It eliminates the possibility of a rushed marriage before legal protections are finalized. It ensures there's enough time for independent legal advice, prenuptial agreement negotiations (or the formation of an asset protection trust if they refuse a prenup), and estate planning alignment with the "family first" principles of your FFT. It forces DTGDs to recompute their long game—a game where they no longer have an economic path to victory at your expense.

When they finally receive the FFT disclosure bundle (if they haven't already read this book—many DTGDs have studied it in horror), the reality of their situation fully sets in. Every tactic they might have used, every financial vulnerability they hoped to exploit—it's all been accounted for. In addition, DTGDs are acutely aware the FFT was purpose-built to expose economic predators by their own hand.

- For you, the prenuptial agreement is effectively compulsory. For the DTGD, it's optional, but the prenup suggestion presents an opportunity to negotiate a fair set of potential outcomes, including terms on post-marital asset acquisitions (typically, what each party contributes financially, they are entitled to exit with, including pro rata equity appreciation).
- Their refusal to participate in good faith negotiations on a prenup simply causes your wealth to be protected in alternate ways before they can attach to it.
- The trust structure prevents asset reallocation and any ability for a DTGD to capture post-marital appreciation on your premarital assets.
- Any businesses, patents, creative works, or other IP you create during the marriage that originate from your premarital skills, talents, or credentials have been *pre-assigned* to third parties prior to marriage and are therefore excluded from division under marital property laws.

- The post-divorce income protection measures are built-in to support a spousal support waiver in your prenuptial agreement. As a failsafe, the trust effectively neutralizes the basis for exploitative and abusive spousal support calculations, elegantly removing the financial incentive for a DTGD attempting to circumvent or invalidate the prenup.
- The post-divorce income protection measures are designed to transparently limit the income calculation for child support entitlements to a decidedly reasonable standard of living (neutralizing the incentive to have children as a vehicle for securing higher child support entitlements that fund a lavish lifestyle and pay someone else to handle the childcare). With the disclosure of your FFT's existence, none of this can come as a surprise to a DTGD who was sizing you up as a target for a child support annuity.
- Your estate planning is mandated to address exclusions of a former spouse that become effective immediately upon legal separation (not an official divorce, which often takes years to complete).

This is the moment where DTGDs realize they have no viable path forward.

The Ultimate Litmus Test: Their Reaction to Full Disclosure

How someone reacts to full financial disclosure says everything about their intentions.

A Real Deal partner might have questions. They might want clarification. But they won't panic. They won't accuse you of "not trusting them." They won't try to argue that these measures are "unnecessary" or "extreme." They'll simply take the information in stride, recognizing that you are a person who plans for the future, protects what you've built, and has taken a pragmatic approach to the 50/50 odds of marriage success.

DTGDs, on the other hand, will not take it well.

They'll start searching for weak spots. They'll push back with emotional appeals. "Don't you trust me?" "Why are you assuming we'll ever get divorced?" If you stay firm, they might escalate, turning to guilt trips or even threats of leaving. And if that happens, it's actually a good thing. They've just revealed their true motivations.

No prenup = get *nothing*. With prenup = get something *fair*.

It's important to understand—and this will become self-evident to your SO when they read your disclosure bundle—that your FFT has been designed to take virtually every single economic incentive off the table for an exploitation-focused partner. More importantly, it has also been designed to allow you and your SO to reintroduce (in your prenup) whatever economic outcomes the two of you decide together would be *fair* if the marriage didn't work out. If your SO refuses to participate in negotiating a fair set of possible outcomes in a prenup, then everything that is ripe for economic exploitation will be automatically locked down prior to marriage—no questions asked.

The incentive is clear and self-enforcing: Don't sign a prenup, and the SO gets zilch. Participate in good faith negotiating of a prenup, and the SO gets a fair set of possible outcomes. The only thing taken off the table entirely is the state's prenup. because it mandates a redistribution of wealth that is decidedly *un*fair where there is a significant wealth and/or income-earning disparity between two parties.

The Trust That Ends the Game Before It Begins

The FFT isn't just an asset protection tool—it's a masterclass in psychological deterrence. It doesn't just make a DTGD's job difficult—it makes it impossible. It removes ambiguity, eliminates leverage, and forces transparency before financial entanglement can occur.

It ensures that DTGDs walk away before they even get started.

And that's the point. Because when every financial loophole is closed before they can exploit it, there's no reason for them to stay. Your trust is more than protection for you—it's a moment of truth for pursuing a life together.

The next time a conversation naturally drifts toward the future and your SO starts testing the waters, be ready—not with a defense or an argument, but with the truth.

"I have a family obligation to protect what I have and what I *will* have for future generations."

"I also have to wait at least a year between engagement and a wedding."

"I'm required to disclose my trust in full. You're welcome to have a look whenever you like."

That's all it takes. In that moment, the game is over for a DTGD.

Next Steps

64

If You're Enraged, We've Done Our Job

If you've made it this far in the book, chances are you're feeling a mix of emotions—anger, fear, perhaps even outrage. That's intentional. Our goal was not just to inform you about DTGDs and their manipulative tactics, but to ignite a fire within you to take action. These emotions, while uncomfortable, are powerful. Anger and outrage are often the catalysts for meaningful change.

This chapter serves as a rallying cry. If you or your loved ones are obvious targets for DTGDs, now is the time to act. Don't let the scenarios described in these pages become your reality. Instead, channel your anger into proactive steps to defend yourself and your family from the economic, emotional, and intergenerational damage DTGDs can cause.

Why You Feel Angry—and Why That's a Good Thing

Anger is a natural reaction to learning about injustice, especially when it's targeted at individuals or families who have built wealth through hard work and sacrifice. Here's why your anger is valid and useful:

- It's a response to exploitation: DTGDs exploit trust, love, and generosity, turning virtues into vulnerabilities. Anger is a natural reaction to this betrayal.
- It highlights what's at stake: The thought of losing not only your wealth, but also your freedom, peace of mind, and legacy, can be infuriating. This anger underscores the urgency to protect what you've built.
- It motivates action: Anger, when channeled correctly, is one of the most effective motivators for change.

Your outrage is proof that you care deeply about safeguarding yourself, your loved ones, and your family's legacy. The key is to use that energy constructively.

The Cost of Inaction

DTGDs thrive on complacency. Every moment you delay taking proactive measures to protect yourself is an opportunity for DTGDs to infiltrate, manipulate, and exploit. The scenarios outlined in this book are not just hypothetical—they happen every day to unsuspecting individuals and families who thought they were invulnerable.

What's at Risk?

- Your wealth: Hard-earned assets, investments, and properties are at risk of being siphoned away.
- Your future income: Money you haven't even earned yet is at risk of being redistributed for decades—potentially your entire lifetime.
- Your future creations: Businesses and intellectual property you haven't even conceived of yet are at risk of being declared "family property" that's subject to 50/50 division in a divorce.

- Your emotional well-being: The stress, humiliation, and emotional toll of battling DTGDs can be devastating.
- Your family's legacy: Intergenerational wealth and assets can be destabilized, leaving future generations to deal with the fallout.
- Your time: Legal battles, prolonged disputes, and emotional recovery consume precious time that could be spent enjoying life or building a future with an authentic partner.

Turning Anger into Action

1. Acknowledge the Threat

The first step in protecting yourself is to accept the reality of the threat DTGDs pose. They are cunning, persistent, and often operate under the radar. Ignoring the possibility that you or your family could be targeted is exactly what they count on.

- Know the signs: Familiarize yourself with the red flags and tactics DTGDs use to identify and exploit targets.
- Have honest conversations: Discuss the risks with your loved ones to ensure everyone is aware and prepared.

2. Educate Yourself and Others

Knowledge is power. The more you understand DTGD tactics, the better equipped you'll be to defend against them.

- Learn from experience: Reflect on the scenarios described in this book and identify parallels in your own life or family dynamics.
- Share the knowledge: Educate your family members, especially younger generations, about the risks and how to spot manipulative behavior.

3. Commit to Proactive Measures

Anger is only useful if it leads to action. Channel your emotions into concrete steps to protect yourself and your family.

The Urgency of Acting Now

Waiting until a DTGD has already infiltrated your life or family is a recipe for disaster. Prevention is far easier and less costly—both financially and emotionally—than trying to mitigate damage after the fact. Here's why now is the time to act:

- DTGDs are always laying track: As you've learned, DTGDs are patient and methodical. They begin setting the stage for exploitation long before their intentions become obvious.
- Assets are harder to protect retroactively: Once DTGDs have legal or financial claims, protecting your wealth becomes significantly more complicated.
- Your peace of mind is worth it: Taking proactive steps now allows you to focus on enjoying your life and family without the constant worry of being targeted.
- The prenup conversation is easy when having one is compulsory: Leverage the time-tested strategy of the ultra-wealthy and join them in making your wealth impenetrable with an FFT.

You Have the Power to Protect Yourself

While DTGDs are adept at exploiting vulnerabilities, you are not powerless. The knowledge you've gained from this book, combined with proactive measures, puts you in a position of strength. Remember:

- You're not alone: Many have faced the same threats and successfully shielded themselves in advance or defended themselves retroactively. You can too.
- It's never too late to act: Whether you're just starting to build wealth, have already made your fortune, or are protecting a multigenerational legacy, there are steps you can take right now.

- You can be part of the solution: By safeguarding yourself and sharing your knowledge with others, you contribute to a larger movement of awareness and prevention.

Channel Your Outrage Into Action

The anger you are feeling is a call to action to protect yourself, your family, and your legacy from the devastating impact of DTGDs. Don't let that outrage fester into fear or self-doubt. Instead, use it as motivation to take control of your future.

This book has armed you with the knowledge to recognize the threat, the tools to defend against it, and the motivation to act. The next steps are yours to take. Protecting yourself and your loved ones starts today.

65

Your Economic Sovereignty: The Greatest Gift You Will Ever Own—Or Lose

The Power and Fragility of Economic Autonomy

Your financial autonomy is not just an asset—it is a foundation upon which every other aspect of your life is built. It dictates your freedom of choice, your ability to walk away from toxic situations, and the legacy you leave behind. Aside from your health, it is the single most valuable intangible asset you will ever own. And yet, for so many, it is surrendered without a second thought, handed over to the whims of a legal system that is not designed to protect you, but to redistribute your wealth and control your life in a decades-long vice grip.

The idea that love is enough to ensure fair treatment in divorce courts is not only naive but statistically disproven. You wouldn't leave your business unprotected. You wouldn't give a stranger the right to access your bank accounts. So why, when it comes to marriage, do so many high-net-worth individuals suddenly decide that the best course of action is to relinquish total control of their financial future?

To marry without a prenup is to willfully surrender your economic sovereignty. It is to place your future earnings, your businesses, your investments, and your legacy in the hands of a state that has every intention of exacting an "equitable redistribution"—not in protecting what you have built and will achieve in the years to come.

The Ultimate Wealth Preservation Strategy: The FFT

For decades, the ultra-wealthy have known something that the average affluent individual is only just beginning to understand. Wealth is not merely built—it is defended. Those who fail to defend their wealth lose it, not through reckless spending, but through predatory relationships, opportunistic divorces, and legal loopholes that favor economic redistribution over financial autonomy.

This is where the FFT comes in. You now have access to a dynastic-level wealth protection strategy that has safeguarded family fortunes for generations. This is not just about keeping what you have today—it is about ensuring that everything you earn, everything you build, and everything you pass on remains exactly where it belongs: within your bloodline.

The Math Is Simple: An Ounce of Prevention vs. a Lifetime of Regret

Setting up the FFT, a prenuptial agreement, and the necessary legal structures costs a fraction of what an average divorce will take from you.

TBA has gone to great lengths to make the FFT accessible with a setup cost of less than $1000 and annual maintenance fees of around $500 per year. Let's compare that to the alternative:

- Entry-level high-net-worth divorces divvy up anywhere from $500,000 to $5 million+.
- Spousal support obligations can be in the tens of thousands of dollars per month and extend for decades.
- Child support calculations in high-income cases can also be in the tens of thousands of dollars per month, and can be easily misappropriated to fund a lavish lifestyle for your ex.
- Legal fees, forensic accountants, asset evaluations, and court proceedings will eat away at your net worth faster than you can imagine.

And the worst part? By the time you realize you need the protection you are holding in your hand *right now*, it's far too late.

The cost of protection is minimal, while the cost of failing to do so is catastrophic.

The decision you make in this moment will not be inconsequential to your economic wellbeing.

Exercise: A Moment of Choice

This is your opportunity to take control of your financial future and legacy. Use this exercise to solidify your commitment to protection and empowerment:

Instructions:

1. Pause and Reflect

- Consider your Personal Risk Profile from the exercise at the end of Chapter 52.
- Now imagine your future self looking back on this moment. How would they feel if you took proactive steps to safeguard your wealth and legacy? How would they feel if, instead, you did nothing?

2. Make the Commitment

- Write your name and today's date below as a declaration of your intent to act.

3. Take Action

- Follow through with the next steps.

Declaration:

I, ________________________________, commit to protecting my financial future and safeguarding my legacy through proactive legal and financial planning.

a) Now: Take Action (initial: ________)

Turn the page and scan the QR code provided to receive a 20% reduction on your FFT setup costs.

In less than 10 minutes, and with just a few clicks or taps, you can begin the process of securing your future.

b) Before I go to bed tonight (initial: ________)

c) By midnight on Sunday (and I have set aside 10 minutes in my calendar). (initial: ________)

Date: ____________________________

You *Will* Remember This Moment

This is your moment to make a conscious decision—a decision your future self will thank you for—to neutralize the very real threats outlined in this book. You are likely to reflect back on the decision you make in this moment with eternal gratitude if you choose to protect yourself, or with eternal sorrow and regret if you don't. The Bloodline Alliance's reason for existence is to protect *you* and your future wealth and happiness. We sincerely hope you choose to no longer walk through the world in a state that entices economic predators to classify you as easy prey for their economic exploitation.

If you're reading this, you already understand that waiting until you are vulnerable is not a strategy—it's a guaranteed loss.

There has never been a more important time to protect yourself and your loved ones.

Your economic sovereignty is not just a privilege—it is your right.

Secure it. Defend it. Protect it.

Or risk losing it forever.

Turn the page to secure your place among the financial elite.

66

GET COVERAGE

Act Decisively—Act Now

If you've made it to this chapter, you've learned about the devastating impact DTGDs can have on individuals, families, and legacies. You've seen how their manipulative tactics exploit trust, love, and generosity to cause financial, emotional, and intergenerational harm. Now, we reach the critical moment of truth—*your* moment of truth.

This chapter is about action. Everything in this book has led to this point: empowering you to make one decisive choice that could alter the course of your life for the better. That choice is to invest in an FFT. It's the gold standard of proactive protection, a tool designed to shield your assets and secure your legacy against DTGD exploitation. If there's ever been a moment to act decisively, this is it.

Establish your FFT now. Enrollment takes 5 to 10 minutes for a personalized, legally structured collection of safeguards designed to preempt financial exploitation before it begins. As a reader of this book, you are eligible for:

Enroll Yourself Now

Establish your FFT now. Enrollment takes 5 to 10 minutes for a personalized, legally structured collection of safeguards designed to preempt financial exploitation before it begins. As a reader of this book, you are eligible for:

- 20% off your personalized Family First Trust (at checkout, enter promo code : BOOK20).
- Offer expires December 31, 2026.

Scan the QR code below or visit bloodlinealliance.com to initiate your protection today.

Remember this moment.
Your legacy is worth protecting.

Spread the Word

Give Others the Chance to Protect Themselves

Financial predators thrive in secrecy, counting on people to remain unaware until it's too late. Now that you understand the risks, you have the opportunity to help others recognize them before they fall into the same trap.

Share a Free Preview: Share access to chapters 1-15 at no cost, along with a promo code for:

- 20% off a personalized Family First Trust (promo code: BOOK20).
- Offer expires December 31, 2026.
- Their discount will be applied at checkout.

Scan the QR code below or visit thebloodlinealliance.com to share this resource.

A simple warning could be the difference between security and financial ruin. Ensure those you care about are informed.

The Greatest Gift

Before Transferring Wealth, Transfer Protection

Affluence does not just attract opportunities—it attracts opportunists. Before passing down wealth, it is imperative to consider how to shield it from external threats and unintended redistribution through divorce proceedings.

A well-structured financial defense ensures that family wealth remains intact, preserved for its intended beneficiaries rather than siphoned away through manipulative legal tactics.

Consider these options when structuring your legacy protections:

1. Gift an e-Book version of this book (USD$9.95): A fundamental first step in financial awareness. (Gift with attribution or anonymously.)

2. Gift a Family First Trust: A legal and financial safeguard ensuring that wealth remains protected. Each trust includes a complimentary digital edition of this book. (Gift with attribution or anonymously.)

3. The Family Plan: For those with multiple heirs and intergenerational assets to protect, a multi-trust approach ensures that protection is not just an individual effort, but a family standard. Each trust includes a complimentary digital edition of this book to reinforce financial awareness.

As a reader of this book, you are eligible for:

- 20% off the first Family First Trust (promo code: BOOK20)
- Offer expires December 31, 2026.
- Your discount will be applied at checkout.
- Recipients will be notified based on the contact details you provide.

Scan the QR code below or visit thebloodlinealliance.com to gift a protective structure to a loved one or loved ones.

You have spent a lifetime building and preserving your wealth. Now is the time to ensure it is safeguarded for generations to come.

TBA: The Undisputed Authority

For generations, those who understand the ruthless nature of financial predators have quietly relied on the structures we reveal in this book to safeguard their wealth. These tools have been time-tested, legally refined, and deliberately shielded from public knowledge—until now.

TBA has chosen to break our silence, offering this knowledge as a defense against those who continue to exploit the uninformed. We recognize that, by publishing this book, we may invite imitation. We expect opportunists to emerge—frauds who will attempt to emulate, adapt, dilute, and distort the wealth-protection strategies detailed here. As such, we offer this solemn warning: Do not be deceived by those who mimic what they do not understand.

We label them now, before they surface, as exactly what they are: fraudulent opportunists and charlatans operating with the same Dark Triad traits that define the very financial predators we expose and seek to protect you from. Their self-serving emulations and adaptations will not be improvements. They will be trapdoors, designed to part the unsuspecting from their wealth under the guise of offering protection.

Accept No Imitations

The FFT was designed to be the definitive legal shield against economic predators. In addition to the multilayered protections that are plainly obvious, the FFT has also been conceived with a host of non-obvious "landmines," "poison pills," and "escape hatches," each woven into its fabric with surgical precision to protect you and your loved ones if and when the time comes to battle a DTGD in legal proceedings. Entrusting your financial future to a counterfeit version is not only inadequate, it is an invitation to disaster.

TBA is the only legitimate authority on the FFT. Your wealth is too valuable to gamble with deception. We invite and encourage you to accept no imitations.

67

Pay It Forward

Taking Power Back from Our Oppressors

This book has taken you on a journey—a deep dive into the tactics of DTGDs, the devastating effects they can have on individuals and families, and the strategies to protect yourself and your legacy. As we reach the conclusion, it's time to consider the greater impact you can have. Sharing what you've learned and supporting loved ones in taking proactive measures can create a ripple effect, protecting future generations and making it harder for DTGDs to thrive.

Sharing This Knowledge Is an Act of Rebellion

This book is more than information—it's a collective uprising against a system designed to bleed us dry. DTGDs thrive on secrecy, manipulation, and deception, weaving themselves into the legal and social structures that allow them to extract wealth and dismantle families with impunity. But knowledge is power, and by sharing these truths, we shatter their illusion of control.

Make no mistake—spreading this book is an act of war against those who have preyed upon trust, ambition, and familial bonds for far too long. DTGDs do not want their tactics exposed. They fear the light of truth because it renders them powerless. They will attempt to shame, silence, and discredit those who share this knowledge. They will hide behind false victimhood, co-opting genuine struggles to shield themselves from scrutiny. They will frame themselves as misunderstood or oppressed, all while systematically draining the financial and emotional reserves of those who fall into their traps.

Sharing this book is a collective middle finger at DTGDs. It sends a clear message: We *see* you, and your time is up.

Building a Future Where DTGDs Can No Longer Thrive

Education, awareness, and proactive safeguards are the keys to building a future where DTGDs face insurmountable obstacles. By spreading this knowledge, you contribute to a world where fewer families will fall prey to their manipulative tactics.

The Role of Awareness

- Empowering families: When families understand the risks and signs of DTGD behavior, they are better equipped to defend themselves.
- Breaking the cycle: Educating younger generations about financial literacy and relationship dynamics reduces their vulnerability to exploitation.
- Encouraging vigilance: Awareness helps families recognize red flags before they become significant threats.

The Legacy of Proactive Action

By taking action today, you set a powerful example for your family and community. Your decision to invest in protective measures, such as the FFT, signals your family's financial acumen and that safeguarding wealth and legacy is a priority.

Join the Resistance: Pay It Forward

This is not just about protecting yourself—it's about building an army of informed individuals who will no longer be deceived. When you share this book, you are striking back against the DTGD system, dismantling it through collective exposure and ensuring that fewer people fall into their traps.

Practical Steps for Paying It Forward

1. Share the Knowledge

- Discuss and share copies of this book: Encourage family members, friends, and colleagues to read this book and learn from its insights.
    - Visit thebloodlinealliance.com or see Chapter 66 for QR codes to instantly share or gift:
    - Sign up for alerts for flash promotions of free and almost-free e-Book versions
- Gift softcover or hardcover books (a tangible physical reminder of the ever-present threat we face)
- Scan and share a promo code for 20% off the setup cost of an FFT: See Chapter 66 for a promo code you can instantly scan and share with friends and loved ones.
- Host conversations: Use family gatherings or meetings to discuss the importance of asset protection and recognizing DTGD tactics.
- Leverage social media: Share key takeaways or anecdotes to spread awareness in your broader network.

2. Educate Younger Generations

- Teach financial literacy: Equip younger family members with the tools to manage wealth responsibly and recognize exploitation.
- Set an example: Model behaviors that prioritize fairness, boundaries, and accountability in relationships.
- Encourage open dialogue: Create a safe space for younger generations to ask questions and seek guidance about financial and relationship challenges.

3. Sponsor Protective Measures

If you have the financial means, consider sponsoring an FFT for younger family members or loved ones. This silent yet powerful gift can:

- Shield their futures: Protect their assets and income from manipulation, including whatever you may pass down to them.
- Encourage vigilance: Signal the importance of proactive protection and financial responsibility.
- Strengthen family unity: Align the family around shared goals of security and legacy preservation.

Join the Movement to Protect Families

TBA: A Collective Mission

TBA is more than an organization—it's a movement. As a not-for-profit Swiss society, its mission is to educate, protect, and defend families from DTGD exploitation. By supporting the alliance, you contribute to:

- Raising awareness: Empowering families with knowledge and tools to recognize DTGD tactics.
- Advancing advocacy: Driving legal reform to close loopholes and strengthen protections.
- Evolving safeguards: Continuously refining the FFT to address emerging threats.

Your Role in a Larger Mission

By applying the lessons from this book and sharing its insights with others, you become part of a movement that makes it increasingly difficult for DTGDs to exploit individuals and families. Together, we can create a world where knowledge, vigilance, and proactive measures render their tactics ineffective.

Your legacy is worth protecting—and your voice can help protect countless others. Act decisively, act now, and join the fight to secure a safer, stronger future for families everywhere.

Resources

POST-MARITAL ASSET/INCOME PROTECTION

Is It Too Late to Protect Your Wealth Now That You're Married? Not Necessarily

Marriage, in its most romanticized form, is about the merging of two lives, two hearts, and two futures. But if you're reading this, chances are that the merging of lives and finances hasn't gone quite as planned. If you've come to the unsettling realization that your spouse is a DTGD, you are likely now wondering if it is too late to protect yourself.

The short answer is not necessarily. The long answer? It's complicated—but with precision, adherence to the law, and the right legal guidance, there are still steps you can take to safeguard your financial future. It is important to note, however, that mishandling this can leave you vulnerable—not just to financial devastation, but also to legal consequences, accusations of fraud, and reputational harm. This is high-stakes chess, not checkers. Every move must be deliberate and legally sound.

The Importance of Legal Guidance: Why Every Step Must Be Strategic

If there is one universal truth in asset protection, it's that you should never make a move without the advice of legal counsel. The moment you suspect you're in financial jeopardy, the temptation to act swiftly—moving assets, shifting accounts, and making hasty legal maneuvers—can be overwhelming. But optics matter. Courts do not look kindly on financial restructuring that appears reactionary, especially if a divorce is on the horizon. The actions you take must be precise, legally sound, and justified. This is why the first call you make should be to an asset protection attorney—not a family lawyer.

Unfortunately, even the best asset protection strategies won't work if they're implemented too late. Where a divorce may be on the horizon, there is a fine line between making ordinary investment decisions and committing fraudulent conveyance. That line is determined by timing, documentation, and intent. The moment divorce proceedings are formally initiated, your spouse's legal team will gain the right to scrutinize every financial move you've made in the months leading up to the separation. If you wait too long, your options diminish significantly.

In addition to asset protection, a skilled asset protection lawyer may also be able to provide guidance on legally defensible strategies for shielding portions of your post-divorce income from spousal support claims. Spousal support laws often favor the economically weaker spouse, but structuring your income in specific ways—before a divorce is on the horizon—can minimize excessive obligations while remaining compliant with the law. The key is strategy, not evasion. This is where an asset protection lawyer's expertise can be invaluable.

Additionally, your asset protection attorney can advise you on the ideal timing for engaging a family law lawyer. The sequencing of these consultations is critical. Moving too soon could alert your DTGD spouse to your financial positioning efforts, while waiting too long could limit your legal options. A well-timed engagement of both legal professionals ensures that you remain in control of the process.

The Financial Colonoscopy: What Divorce Discovery Means for You

One of the harshest realities of divorce is the financial discovery process. This isn't just your spouse asking for a breakdown of assets—it's a full-blown forensic analysis of your financial history. Expect the DTGD's lawyer to come armed with a magnifying glass and an agenda.

- Asset transfers: Any movement of money, real estate, or investments before a divorce filing will be scrutinized. If it looks like you were trying to "hide" assets, expect an immediate legal challenge.
- Bank records: Every transaction, withdrawal, and deposit will be analyzed. Large, unexplained transfers? Red flags.
- Business accounts: If you own a business, expect them to dig deep into revenues, expenses, and ownership structures.

Even if your actions were entirely legal, optics matter. Your DTGD's lawyer will frame every financial decision as suspicious—as evidence of an attempt to manipulate the system. This is why your financial defense must be rock solid before divorce is even on the table.

Understanding DAPTs and FAPTs: Post-Marital Asset Protection

When it comes to asset protection, DAPTs and FAPTs are among the most powerful tools available. But using them post-marriage requires surgical precision to avoid accusations of fraud.

DAPTs

A DAPT is a US-based trust designed to shield assets from creditors, including ex-spouses. These trusts offer:

- Legal protection against claims—as long as they were established before financial disputes arose.

- Easier compliance with local regulations than offshore trusts.
- Lower cost and administrative burden compared to international options.

The risk is that not all states recognize DAPTs. If a physical asset is located in a jurisdiction that does not recognize DAPT protections, it may still be vulnerable to legal claims. In such cases, an asset protection lawyer is your best resource for exploring alternative strategies—such as foreign trusts, business structuring, or other legal instruments—to safeguard your wealth.

FAPTs

FAPTs, which are established in jurisdictions like the Cook Islands, Nevis, or Belize, take asset protection to another level. They are insulated from US court rulings, making it far more difficult for an ex-spouse to access the assets inside them.

The benefits:

- Stronger legal protection than domestic trusts.
- Greater privacy and security.
- Virtually untouchable by US courts.

The risks:

- Higher costs and regulatory complexity.
- Increased scrutiny from judges who view offshore trusts with suspicion.

Regardless of which option you consider, timing is key. A trust created in anticipation of divorce will be examined under a microscope. A trust created before any marital conflict arises is far more defensible.

Belize and the Cook Islands are renowned for their robust asset protection trust (APT) laws, offering significant safeguards for assets, particularly in the context of divorce proceedings.

Belize:

- **Asset protection features:** Belize's trust legislation provides strong protection against various civil judgments, including those arising from divorce settlements. Assets placed in a Belize trust are generally shielded from claims by creditors, bankruptcy proceedings, and divorce-related asset divisions.
- **Foreign judgment non-recognition:** Belizean law stipulates that foreign judgments related to divorce, succession, or insolvency are not recognized concerning assets held in a Belize trust. This means that court orders from other jurisdictions aiming to claim assets within a Belize trust are typically ineffective.
- **Confidentiality and legal advantages:** Belize offers a legal environment that emphasizes confidentiality and asset protection, making it a favorable jurisdiction for establishing trusts designed to safeguard assets from potential claims during divorce proceedings.

Cook Islands:

- **Asset protection mechanisms:** Cook Islands trusts are designed to place assets beyond the reach of foreign court orders, including those from divorce proceedings. The jurisdiction's legal framework ensures that assets held within these trusts are protected from division during marital disputes.
- **Legal precedents:** The Cook Islands have a history of upholding the integrity of their APTs, making them a reliable option for individuals seeking to protect assets in the context of divorce.

Considerations:

- **Timing of trust establishment:** For both jurisdictions, it's crucial to establish the trust well in advance of any anticipated divorce proceedings. Courts may scrutinize trusts created during marital discord for evidence of potential fraudulent conveyance, which could undermine asset protection efforts.

- **Legal compliance:** While these jurisdictions offer robust asset protection, it's essential to ensure that the establishment and funding of such trusts comply with all applicable laws to avoid potential legal challenges.

Proactive Strategies Before Divorce Becomes Inevitable

If you've realized too late that you married a DTGD who is seeking to exploit your wealth, timing is critical. Taking action before divorce is on their radar allows you to continue acting as the captain of your economic ship. Once divorce proceedings begin, courts often freeze assets to prevent improper transfers, limiting your ability to safeguard your wealth.

Steps to Take

1. Consult national and international experts through referrals (see below): Don't limit your consultations to local advisors. Seek out professionals who specialize in high-net-worth asset protection and understand the nuances of DAPTs and FAPTs.
2. Disentangle finances: Get counsel from your DAPT/FAPT attorney on when to start separating your accounts and how to reduce financial entanglements while maintaining legality.
3. Act civilly and cordially: Keeping the DTGD unaware of your plans allows you to remain in control. The moment they suspect your intentions, they will accelerate their exploitation and seek legal counsel that will invariably result in an almost immediate court-ordered lockdown of your assets for the duration of the divorce proceedings.

Why Courts Scrutinize Post-Marital Protections

While pre-marital protections generally face little resistance, post-marital measures are often subject to intense scrutiny. The burden is on you to demonstrate that your actions are both legal and justified.

Key Considerations

- Transparency when asked: Ensure all actions are documented and will pass muster as being above board.
- No violation of court orders: Once divorce proceedings begin, adhere strictly to court orders regarding assets.
- Reputation management: Be prepared to counteract negative optics by demonstrating fairness and good faith.

The Golden Rule: There Are no "Deals" in Asset Protection

Protecting your wealth is not an area where you should ever consider cutting corners. Anything worth doing is worth doing right. Hire the best legal advisors and take the time to ensure every step is compliant with the law and structured to withstand scrutiny.

What This Means for You

- Avoid bargain solutions: Discounted services or inexperienced advisors can lead to costly mistakes.
- Focus on quality: Reputable advisors with proven expertise in asset protection are essential.
- Invest in peace of mind: Proper planning now can save you years of stress, financial loss, and legal battles.

Not all DAPT/FAPT practitioners are created equal. There is a broad spectrum of qualifications, expertise, and jurisdictional nuances. Choosing the wrong "expert" can leave you exposed rather than protected. A simple Google search will flood you with options, but the best practitioners don't need to advertise. Elite experts in high-conflict divorce asset protection operate discreetly and are sought out through trusted referrals, not flashy marketing.

The right expert for your situation isn't just someone who can set up a generic trust—it's someone who specializes in shielding assets (and, potentially, income) from economic exploitation-oriented spouses

(DTGDs), and who understands the unique risks of high-net-worth divorces.

Jurisdiction also matters—a lot. The best jurisdiction for your specific needs may not be the one a service provider you find on Google happens to be selling. This is why it is crucial to seek a referral from a corporate trustee certified by TBA. Our licensees will connect you with elite, proven experts who operate at the highest levels of asset protection strategy and confidentiality, ensuring that your wealth remains exactly where it belongs—out of reach of opportunistic litigation. For an expert referral tailored to your unique situation, schedule a confidential consultation and assessment by scanning the QR code below or visiting thebloodlinealliance.com and scheduling a consultation via the Advisory Services page.

Timing Is Everything

If your DTGD's mask has slipped and you finally understand their true intentions, the time to act is now. Protecting your wealth requires legal compliance, strategic planning, and impeccable timing.

If you can keep things civil and cordial, you may still have a chance to maintain control of your financial future. The moment divorce proceedings begin, expect courts to lock down assets—and for the DTGD to attempt to maximize their payout.

Protecting yourself is not about deception—it's about defense. Consult the best experts, follow their advice, and execute every step legally. When this is done correctly, you can safeguard your wealth, protect your assets, and ensure that your financial future remains in your hands—not theirs.

Advisory Services Rate: USD $560/hr

The Private Wealth Manager: The Ultimate Asset Protection Strategy

For Those With $5M+ at Risk

For high-net-worth individuals facing the potential redistribution of $5 million or more in a divorce, standard, local asset protection strategies are not enough. The legal landscape is shifting, forensic accountants are becoming more sophisticated, and the ability to track hidden wealth—especially crypto assets—is advancing at a rapid pace.

This is why, when serious money is at stake, you need a private wealth manager who specializes in structures designed to withstand the most rigorous scrutiny in family law proceedings.

If your net worth is below $5M, the economics of this level of asset protection don't make sense. It is best to take your lumps in a divorce and take proper steps to protect yourself next time around. But starting at $5M, the cost-benefit equation shifts. At $20M+, it is an absolute imperative—unless you're comfortable flushing millions down the drain unnecessarily.

Forensic accountants in divorce cases are extremely skilled at what they do. They will find everything, whether you've structured your wealth legally or not. When you invest in doing everything 100% legally, by the book, and with surgical precision, what they uncover is an impenetrable, legally defensible structure—one that has moved wealth through a multijurisdictional chain of custody that withstands legal scrutiny on all fronts.

The DTGD and her legal counsel may not like it, but there will be no arguing that anything improper was done.

The Private Wealth Manager's Formula: A Well-Kept Secret for Those in the Know

The world's most sophisticated private wealth managers don't just protect assets—they future-proof them. Their methodologies are not widely advertised, nor are they offered to just anyone.

Their expertise spans:

- Advanced crypto asset protection: Ensuring fiat-to-crypto investments are structured within legal trust frameworks that hold up under forensic scrutiny.
- Multijurisdictional wealth shielding: Strategically placing assets in trust-friendly jurisdictions where legal challenges are neutralized before they begin.
- Divorce-proofed asset structuring: Creating legal frameworks that ensure assets remain out of reach of DTGDs and predatory divorce settlements.
- Legal compliance without vulnerabilities: Ensuring asset protection plans withstand legal challenges while remaining fully compliant with regulatory requirements.

This formula is a well-guarded secret. It's not something that will ever be published, because it's only relevant to those who need it. If you fit the profile and want an introduction, visit thebloodlinealliance.com to set up an assessment.

For an expert referral tailored to your unique situation, schedule a confidential consultation and assessment by scanning the QR code below or visiting thebloodlinealliannc.com and scheduling a consultation via the Advisory Services page.

Qualified candidates will be referred to the world's foremost expert.

Crypto Entrepreneurs: Your Crypto Assets Are not Safe Without the Right Protections

Many crypto entrepreneurs assume that because their wealth exists in decentralized wallets, it is inherently safe from litigation. This is a dangerous misconception. Courts are evolving, forensic accountants are innovating, and the ability to track and seize digital wealth has never been greater.

How Forensic Accountants Will Track Your Crypto in a Divorce

If you fail to structure your crypto holdings correctly, forensic accountants can and will find them using:

- Blockchain analysis: Tracking on-chain transactions across Bitcoin, Ethereum, and other public ledgers to trace movement.
- Exchange subpoenas: Obtaining transaction histories from centralized exchanges like Coinbase, Binance, and Kraken.
- Digital forensics: Extracting wallet addresses, seed phrases, and transaction records

- Lifestyle audits: Identifying spending patterns that reveal undisclosed crypto wealth.
- Off-ramping traces: Following the flow of assets from crypto to fiat and identifying bank transfers that expose hidden holdings.

Simply put, crypto is not an invisibility cloak. If it is not properly structured within a legally defensible asset protection framework, it is just as vulnerable as cash sitting in a bank account.

The Best Asset Protection Is Preemptive

By working with a private wealth manager specializing in asset protection, high-net-worth individuals can ensure their wealth is protected before they ever face litigation.

- If you haven't made an official decision to pursue a divorce, a proactive defensive structure can legally shield both fiat and crypto assets from legal attacks.
- Legal compliance at every step ensures the plan is rock solid and unbreakable in litigation.

For those with significant wealth at stake, this level of asset protection is not optional—it's essential. Without legally airtight protection, forensic accountants and divorce courts will find and claim assets you thought were safe.

The Bottom Line

If you are walking into a marriage or divorce with $5M+ at risk, it's time to seek the expertise of a private wealth manager who specializes in bulletproof asset protection structures. Without the right protection, your wealth is vulnerable—crypto included. With the right strategy, it is untouchable.

The best asset protection strategies are reserved for those in the know. Now, you know.

THE ANONYMOUS GIFT: A FAMILY FIRST TRUST

Have You Been TAG'd? Want to TAG Someone?

Imagine receiving an anonymous gift—an airtight, prepaid protective measure ensuring your assets and income are shielded from anyone who might exploit your love, generosity, or vulnerability for personal gain. This is *The Anonymous Gift* (TAG) from The Bloodline Alliance, a gesture so profound that it speaks volumes. Someone in your life cares deeply about your well-being and wants to ensure you remain informed, protected, and in control of your financial future.

If you've been TAG'd, understand that someone who knows you well has seen something—perhaps just a small red flag, an uneasy pattern, or a concerning shift in your dynamics—that prompted them to act. They aren't making accusations about your partner, nor are they questioning your judgment. Instead, they want to make sure you have the tools to recognize potential threats early, before small concerns become irreversible financial and emotional disasters.

You may have received this book, a Family First Trust, or both. Either way, it was sent as a safeguard—not as an accusation, but as a form of empowerment.

Why The Anonymous Gift Matters

DTGDs and other exploitative individuals thrive on identifying vulnerabilities. They assess your personal and professional networks, carefully categorizing those around you as either allies or obstacles. Those who might see through their façade—family members, trusted friends, or long-time mentors—often become the targets of subtle character assassination. DTGDs will plant seeds of doubt, creating friction and distancing you from those who might encourage you to pause and reevaluate. Meanwhile, they work tirelessly to win over those who are less suspicious, ensuring they are viewed as perfect partners in everyone's eyes.

But a TAG changes the game.

If someone in your circle has concerns about your situation, but they don't want to risk unnecessary confrontation or overstep boundaries, a TAG is the perfect way to empower you without pressure. It provides information, tools, and legal protection—all without making direct accusations or creating unnecessary conflict. Frankly, you are better off establishing a Family First Trust anyway, regardless of whether you're dating a DTGD or The Real Deal. It's just common sense for the affluent so take being TAG'd as someone saying the preservation of your future happiness is worth their investment.

What This Gift Means for You

Receiving a TAG isn't an accusation. It's an invitation—to stay aware, to stay informed, and to ensure that you're truly in control of your own future. If you've received this gift, it's because:

- Someone respects your ability to make informed decisions. They aren't trying to interfere in your life, they just want to ensure you're equipped with the best defenses, should you ever need them.
- They recognize that small concerns, if ignored, can become serious threats. Many victims of financial predators look back

and wish they had noticed warning signs earlier.
- They value your happiness, security, and independence. This gift is a proactive measure to help safeguard what you've built, ensuring that your future is dictated by your choices, not by someone else's hidden agenda.

Discretion Is Your Best Defense

If you've received this book or a Family First Trust anonymously, consider keeping it to yourself for now and using it as a tool to reflect on your own romantic relationships. Pay attention to patterns, behaviors, and financial discussions as you observe the dynamics unfolding around you.

If your partner becomes aware of the book—or if you choose to share it—be prepared for it to spark an important conversation. A healthy partner will welcome discussions about financial transparency and protection. However, someone with manipulative tendencies may react defensively, attempting to dissuade you from engaging with the book's content or establishing the trust you have been gifted. That, in itself, should raise serious concerns.

Why Timing Matters: Protect First, Talk Later

Before you initiate a conversation about financial protections, it's essential to have them firmly in place. Discussing asset safeguards *before* setting up your FFT can inadvertently invite DTGDs to escalate coercive tactics in an attempt to prevent you from protecting yourself. If they react aggressively to financial planning discussions, that reaction alone is a significant red flag.

Don't Help DTGDs Identify Their Adversaries

If someone with exploitative intentions discovers you've been TAG'd, they will likely become obsessed with identifying the source. DTGDs thrive on knowing who to target, attack, and manipulate in order to regain control of the situation. They may pressure you to ask around, subtly urging you to find out who gifted you this protection.

Don't fall into this trap.

The best course of action is to leave it alone. You don't need to know who sent this book or gifted you a Family First Trust. All you need to know is that someone cared enough about your future to ensure you have the resources to protect yourself. By keeping the focus on *your own awareness and preparedness*, rather than attempting to uncover who sent it, you maintain the advantage.

Final Thoughts: The Gift of Awareness

A TAG isn't about assuming the worst—it's about being prepared for anything. It's about ensuring that your financial security is as strong as your emotional well-being, and that you are protected not just today, but for years to come.

If you've been TAG'd, embrace it as a sign that someone sees your worth and wants to make sure you have the tools to recognize early warning signs before they become irreversible mistakes. Knowledge is power, and this gift is meant to give you exactly that—the power to make your own informed decisions, free from manipulation and regret.

Is the FFT an Appropriate Engagement Gift?

There's never a wrong time to give the gift of protection against one of life's biggest financial unknowns. If the idea of presenting a trust fund as an engagement gift feels awkward, consider offering it as The Anonymous Gift. But please — don't withhold it from someone you care about simply because the timing feels unconventional. For at least half of all marriages, the consequences of going unprotected are life-altering. Gift recipients will follow the same simple steps as self-directed enrollment outlined in Chapter 1.

TAG Someone You Care About

1. Gift an e-Book version of this book (USD$9.95): A fundamental first step in financial awareness. (Gift anonymously.)

2. Gift a Family First Trust: A legal and financial safeguard ensuring that wealth remains protected. Each trust includes a complimentary digital edition of this book.

As a reader of this book, you are eligible for:

- 20% off a personalized Family First Trust (promo code: BOOK20)
- Select the **'Gift Anonymously'** option.
- Enter your discount code at checkout.
- Recipients will be notified based via the contact details you provide.

Scan the QR code below or visit thebloodlinealliance.com to gift a protective structure to a loved one.

Appendix: The Grave Robber Timeline: "The Widow(er) Takes All"

The Grave Robber variant of the DTGD timeline diverges from the classic DTGD timeline starting at phase 7.

INTESTATE WINDFALLS AND MANIPULATIVE ESTATE PLANNING

Grave Robbers and the Redistribution of Wealth

For the Grave Robber version of a DTGD, the endgame is not divorce—it's inheritance. Unlike their divorce-driven counterparts who scheme for settlements and spousal support, these predators play the long game. Their eyes are on the redistribution of wealth, and their strategy is designed to ensure they walk away with the lion's share of an estate, often at the expense of adult children, family legacies, and long-standing charitable intentions.

The Slowest, Most Calculated Heist

Grave Robbers understand that staying married until the very end is worth far more than walking away with a fraction of the fortune in a divorce. With patience and precision, they consolidate their financial entrenchment, ensuring that, by the time the will is executed, their victims' wealth has been successfully rerouted in their favor.

The victims—often older, affluent, and isolated by years of calculated emotional manipulation—rarely see it coming. Their heirs, charities, and business partners may suspect something is amiss, but by the time they sound the alarm, the ink is already dry on the revised estate plan.

Understanding the Baseline Entitlement

Marriage is a legal contract, and with it comes a host of statutory entitlements that DTGDs know better than their victims do.

If an estate plan is not updated—or worse, if no estate plan exists—intestate succession laws kick in. In many jurisdictions, that means the surviving spouse is legally entitled to half or more of the entire estate, regardless of the deceased's party's prior wishes.

Even when an estate plan is in place, DTGDs find ways to push the limits, ensuring their share is maximized. They influence updates to wills, gain access to key financial accounts, and subtly structure assets to prioritize their interests. Once granted full visibility into an estate plan, they identify weak points—areas where they can manipulate revisions, consolidate assets, or diminish the claims of competing heirs.

Their greatest advantage is the gradual incapacitation of their targets. Whether targets are weakened due to aging, illness, or cognitive decline, DTGDs are always ready to step in as "caretakers," assuming control over finances, medical decisions, and, ultimately, the final say over where the wealth flows.

The Financial Manipulations Begin

Long before the will is finalized, DTGDs get to work consolidating control over financial resources. Estate planning only determines what happens after death—but financial decisions made beforehand are much harder to scrutinize—and DTGDs know this all too well.

The marital home is one of their first battlegrounds. They push to pay off the mortgage, ensuring the property is debt-free and easily transferrable. If the home is still in the victim's name alone, they engineer reasons for joint ownership or survivorship rights, ensuring it defaults to them without probate interference.

High-value assets such as jewelry, cars, and rare collectibles are gradually transferred into their possession, often under the guise of "gifts" or "sentimental gestures." They push for luxury purchases, framed as indulgences to enhance their partner's final years—but in reality they are diverting wealth into assets they alone control.

Financial accounts, once separate, become joint accounts, ensuring that, when the time comes, they can drain funds without question. If applicable, life insurance beneficiaries are revised. Powers of attorney are quietly secured. Even charitable donations or family trusts—long intended to benefit others—are scrutinized and challenged, all to ensure the money stays with them.

By the time the final months arrive, they have consolidated as much as possible, leaving only the scraps for the heirs to fight over.

Isolation and Estate Hijacking

Perhaps the most chilling element of the Grave Robber's strategy is the systematic alienation of their victim from prior heirs and confidants.

Adult children are cast as selfish and neglectful, accused of only caring about their inheritances. Close friends and long-time advisors are painted as intrusive or meddling. Slowly but surely, the DTGD becomes the only trusted figure, ensuring that no external voices can warn their victim about what's truly happening.

Medical and cognitive decline only strengthen their grip. With power of attorney in hand, they make medical and financial decisions unquestioned, quietly shifting assets while framing themselves as the devoted spouse sacrificing everything for their partner's well-being.

By the time the will is executed, they have already won.

Recognizing the Red Flags

By the time most heirs and advisors realize what's happening, the damage is done. But there are warning signs that one can look out for—indicators that a DTGD is consolidating power.

A sudden increase in secrecy around financial discussions, a new spouse pushing for "simplification" of estate plans, or a previously independent elder suddenly pulling away from long-standing relationships are all indications of entrenchment.

A DTGD's insistence on joint accounts, property transfers, and controlling access to legal and financial advisors should send alarm bells ringing. Particularly if financial decisions are being framed as "gifts" rather than structured estate planning choices, it's time to take action.

Safeguarding Your Legacy

Breaking the grip of a Grave Robber requires proactive estate planning and unshakable financial boundaries.

Regularly updating estate plans with trusted legal counsel is crucial—especially before entering a marriage with a significant age gap. No-contest clauses can deter estate challenges. Trust-based estate planning can lock in allocations before manipulation takes hold. Independent oversight of financial decisions can ensure wealth is distributed as intended.

Most importantly, open and ongoing conversations with family members and financial advisors can prevent isolation tactics from taking hold. Transparency is the greatest weapon against a DTGD's secrecy.

A Long Game with High Stakes

For age-gap DTGDs, patience is a virtue. They don't need to rush—they just need to outlast their victims. Every move they make is calculated, every relationship they sever is intentional, and every financial shift is a step closer to securing a fortune at the expense of rightful heirs.

By understanding their tactics, setting ironclad legal protections, and fostering transparency in estate planning, you can prevent the slow, methodical hijacking of your legacy.

In the next chapter, we will explore the Grave Robber "Happy Couple Phase," where DTGDs perfect their image of loyalty and devotion—while quietly laying the groundwork for the redistribution of wealth.

Grave Robber Phase 7: The Grave Robber "Happy Couple" Phase

The Illusion of Everlasting Devotion

For age-gap DTGDs, the long game isn't about passion or partnership—it's about power, permanence, and positioning. Unlike their divorce-driven counterparts who scheme for quick financial windfalls, age-gap DTGDs invest deeply in building a narrative of unwavering devotion, ensuring they hold financial dominance long after their partners are gone.

This phase is a masterclass in controlled affection, carefully curated to remove doubt, deepen trust, and subtly entrench financial leverage. For some DTGDs, this phase is also the setup for the "Grand Slam" strategy—introducing children into the relationship as an additional financial backstop. Parenthood fast-tracks legal and financial entitlements, securing immediate child support and reinforcing inheritance claims for years to come.

Understanding the tactics at play during this stage is critical to disrupting their narrative before it's too late.

The Performance of a Lifetime

Age-gap DTGDs aren't just playing the role of loving partners—they are staging entire productions. Every gesture, every word, and every carefully timed act of devotion is crafted to reinforce their reliability and indispensability.

They lean into acts of service—cooking meals, managing schedules, and assuming roles that make them appear irreplaceable. They subtly erode independence while making it feel like a loving favor. It starts small—handling finances "just to help" and consolidating responsibilities "so you don't have to worry." Before long, they are not just spouses, but gatekeepers, overseeing finances, health decisions, and long-term planning with a calculated touch.

Conflict is avoided at all costs. Peace is their currency. Any disagreement is met with patient understanding, ensuring that the victims believe they are in the most stable and harmonious relationships of their lives. This calculated patience isn't about love—it's about ensuring that, when the time comes for major financial decisions, there is no hesitation, no second-guessing, and no outside intervention.

Subtle Moves with High-Stakes Impact

While maintaining the façade of devotion, DTGDs are actively embedding themselves deeper into their victims' finances. These actions are measured, calculated, and often disguised as acts of love.

They encourage financial co-mingling, not through force, but through gentle persuasion. *"Why keep things separate? We're a team."* They offer to manage bills, investments, and taxes, ensuring they have full access while the victims, convinced of their reliability, increasingly disengage.

They steer conversations toward "responsible planning," encouraging large purchases—bigger homes, upgraded vehicles, extravagant vacations—all under the guise of "enjoying life together." But these purchases aren't for the victims' benefit. They are strategically structured acquisitions designed to ensure that, when estates are settled,

DTGDs' claims are undeniable.

Once joint accounts, real estate holdings, and financial oversight are secured, the next phase is legal consolidation. They subtly influence estate planning discussions, ensuring they are included in wills, insurance policies, and retirement planning. If done correctly, these changes appear organic—a natural reflection of a long-term, devoted partnership.

The "Grand Slam" Strategy: Introducing Children

For DTGDs looking to maximize financial entrenchment, introducing children into the equation isn't about love or family—it's about fortifying their claims and ensuring long-term payouts.

They accelerate conversations about parenthood, using emotional persuasion to fast-track pregnancy. If their victims hesitate, they reframe concerns as selfishness. *"Why wouldn't you want to build a family with me?"*

For the most manipulative DTGDs, reproductive coercion is a very real option. Contraceptive tampering, strategic timing, and even false claims of infertility struggles are tools used to secure an unbreakable financial tether.

Once children are introduced, DTGDs' financial positioning is locked in. Even the strongest prenuptial agreements can't circumvent child support laws. They know that child support payments begin immediately and are far harder to renegotiate than spousal support.

Recognizing the Warning Signs Before It's Too Late

Because age-gap DTGDs are playing the long game, red flags don't come in the form of dramatic fights or sudden financial demands. Instead, they reveal themselves in the small but unrelenting erosion of independence, financial autonomy, and outside relationships.

If they insist on joint accounts and financial entanglements sooner than necessary, pay attention. If they subtly discourage professional financial oversight, take note. If they redirect estate planning discussions toward their benefit, recognize the pattern.

Perhaps most tellingly, if they begin isolating victims from their existing family, heirs, or advisors, the strategy is in full effect.

Protecting Against the Slow Takeover

The best way to counter the age-gap DTGD strategy is to fortify financial boundaries before manipulation takes root.

Maintaining separate financial accounts and avoiding premature co-mingling is key. Estate planning should remain in the hands of long-trusted attorneys, not influenced by a new spouse. Every major financial decision should involve outside counsel, ensuring that changes are made with clarity, not coercion.

For those in relationships with significant age gaps, ongoing conversations with trusted family members, heirs, and financial advisors can act as a safeguard against gradual isolation and estate hijacking.

Legal structures like trusts, no-contest clauses, and clear directives on inheritance priorities ensure that assets are distributed as intended, no matter how persuasive or patient DTGDs might be.

A Calculated Illusion of Security

Phase 7 is where the final, seamless foundation is laid. Age-gap DTGDs spend years creating the illusion of devotion, selflessness, and commitment, all while strategically positioning themselves for the ultimate financial takeover.

By the time their victims begin to notice small inconsistencies, strange financial shifts, or growing isolation from outside influences, DTGDs are already cemented in place.

Recognizing these tactics early and implementing strong financial and legal protections is the best defense against the longest con of all.

In the next chapter, we will explore "Phase 8: The Friendship Phase," where DTGDs shift their strategy away from physical intimacy and toward companionship and control, ensuring that their influence remains unchallenged as they inch closer to full financial dominance.

GRAVE ROBBER PHASE 8: THE FRIENDSHIP PHASE

The Long Game of Loyalty and Control

Time changes everything, and for age-gap DTGDs, that change is a crucial moment to pivot. As the years pass and the once-vibrant dynamics of the relationship shift, so does the DTGD strategy. Physical intimacy takes a backseat, and a new phase—the friendship phase—begins. This stage isn't about passion anymore—it's about securing long-term financial entrenchment under the guise of unwavering companionship.

DTGDs recognize that, as their partners age, priorities shift toward stability, routine, and companionship. The goal now is to ensure there are no gaps in financial security and that any remaining barriers to ultimate entitlement are eliminated. If their long-term plan includes a "Grand Slam"—introducing children into the relationship to further cement financial claims—this phase is their last opportunity to execute that strategy seamlessly.

For those on the receiving end of this shift, it's critical to recognize the signs before the transition is complete and to implement safeguards before DTGDs' control becomes absolute.

The Reinvention of the Relationship

When physical attraction or youthful energy no longer holds the same weight in their relationships, DTGDs reshape the narrative. They morph from passionate lovers into perfect life companions—always present, always supportive, and always indispensable.

They become the ultimate emotional confidants, positioning themselves as the only people who truly understand their partners' needs. This isn't just about love—it's about making themselves irreplaceable. They remind their partners—subtly, but frequently—of the sacrifices they've made, their unwavering commitment, and how "no one else" will ever care for them the way they do.

DTGDs excel at fostering dependence. They make their partners feel as if they cannot navigate life without them, slowly but surely steering every major decision—financial, medical, and personal. They create an environment where questioning their presence feels disloyal, where outside voices are unwelcome, and where their authority goes unquestioned.

Shoring Up Financial Control

With the emotional groundwork laid, DTGDs shift their focus toward fortifying financial entitlements. This phase isn't about demanding wealth outright—it's about strategically embedding themselves into every aspect of financial decision-making so that, eventually, their positions are unquestionable.

Estate planning discussions become commonplace, always framed in terms of "fairness" or "ensuring security" for the future. DTGDs suggest updates that shift inheritance shares in their favor, gradually eroding prior commitments to children, charities, or other heirs. They secure joint access to bank accounts, persuade their partners to consolidate assets, and covertly restructure ownership to ensure that control remains with them.

They normalize luxury spending, presenting extravagant purchases as necessary lifestyle enhancements. A new home? An upgraded car? Exclusive travel? All of it is framed as "enjoying the good years together."

But the subtext is clear—these are purchases that further tie wealth to the DTGDs, while simultaneously draining resources that could be passed down to others.

With enough patience, DTGDs can orchestrate scenarios where their financial stake is so deeply embedded that removing them would be more complicated than simply leaving things as they are.

Recognizing the Red Flags

The transition to the friendship phase doesn't happen overnight. It is a gradual, deliberate shift, marked by subtle changes in behavior and increasingly assertive financial positioning. If an individual starts to notice these warning signs, it is time to act:

- Sudden interest in financial discussions—especially estate planning, account access, and major purchases.
- Isolation from trusted family members and advisors, often framed as "simplifying things" or avoiding unnecessary stress.
- A shift from emotional support to financial influence, where affection is intertwined with control over assets and major decisions.
- Frequent reminders of their sacrifices and dedication, often coupled with subtle guilt-tripping to justify financial concessions.

Recognizing these patterns before they are deeply entrenched is the only way to prevent full-scale financial takeover.

Protecting Against the Friendship Phase Takeover

The best way to counter the Phase 8 Grave Robber strategy is to maintain clear, enforceable financial boundaries.

- Keep finances separate. Avoid co-mingling funds, even under the guise of convenience.

- Limit financial decision-making authority. Maintain control over accounts, investments, and estate planning.
- Engage outside advisors. Ensure that financial planning and estate discussions are overseen by trusted professionals who have no vested interest in the relationship.
- Document agreements. If financial changes are discussed, they should be formalized legally to prevent posthumous disputes.
- Strengthen family communication. Keeping heirs and trusted individuals informed makes it significantly harder for DTGDs to manipulate estate changes in secret.

A Calculated Pivot Toward Total Control

By the time DTGDs reach the friendship phase, they have already set deep roots. Their patience, their years of careful narrative building, and their ability to shift strategies seamlessly have ensured they are indispensable in their partners' eyes.

Their shift from passionate lover to devoted life companion is not about evolving love—it is about eliminating risk, solidifying financial dominance, and closing any loopholes that could weaken their hold.

Recognizing this shift for what it is—a calculated maneuver rather than a natural progression—is the first step in protecting against it.

In the next chapter, we will explore Phase 9: The Nursing and Hospice Phase, where DTGDs take their control to its peak, positioning themselves as both caregivers and executors of financial and medical decisions, ensuring total control over the final years and the ultimate redistribution of wealth.

Grave Robber Phase 9: The Nursing and Hospice Phase

The Caregiver Façade

As time and age take their inevitable toll, the dynamics between age-gap DTGDs and their victims shift dramatically. The overt seduction and grand gestures of earlier phases fade into the background, making way for a carefully cultivated role: that of the devoted caregiver. This is not an act of love or selflessness—it is a final, calculated maneuver to ensure full control over victims' assets and financial future.

At this stage, DTGDs assume total authority over their partners' daily lives, overseeing medical decisions, household management, and—most critically—financial affairs. While some may see this shift as a genuine act of devotion, the truth is far more sinister. DTGDs are not just managing care—they are consolidating power, making sure that by the time their partners take their last breaths, the wealth redistribution plan is already locked in.

For those who can recognize this strategy in action, this is the last real opportunity to intervene and protect a loved one's legacy before it's too late.

Creating a False Narrative of Devotion

By this phase, DTGDs have spent years grooming not only their victims, but also their public images. They have crafted personas of unwavering loyalty, positioning themselves as the one person who has sacrificed everything to care for their partners.

They broadcast their role as caregiver, making sure friends, family, and medical professionals all view them as loving spouses who have selflessly taken on the burden of care. They frame their efforts as tireless and unappreciated, subtly implying that any interference from heirs, advisors, or other concerned parties is an insult to their dedication.

At the same time, they reinforce dependence, making their partners feel that they are the only ones who truly understands their needs. By slowly alienating family members and advisors, they ensure that, when the time comes to make major decisions, no one is left to challenge them.

Strategic Control Over Access and Information

With the mask of caregiving firmly in place, DTGDs' next move is controlling access—not just to the victims, but also to critical financial and medical information.

They limit visits, restrict phone calls, and monitor interactions with family and friends, using health concerns as an excuse. *"They're too tired for visitors,"* they say. *"It's best to keep their stress levels down."* Over time, even the most well-meaning loved ones begin to back away, unaware that their absence is not a natural progression, but a carefully orchestrated isolation tactic.

They also serve as gatekeepers of financial decisions, ensuring that their partners' estate planning remains under their influence. If the victims haven't already adjusted their estate plans to benefit the DTGDs, now is the time to apply pressure. Subtle suggestions become urgent requests. Conversations about "making things easier" for the surviving spouses morph into discussions about adjusting inheritance allocations, modifying trusts, and granting full financial control.

In many cases, DTGDs are already listed as power of attorney, giving them the ability to make unilateral financial decisions under the guise of protecting their partners' best interests.

Financial Manipulations in the Final Stretch

Estate changes made during this phase are often subject to legal scrutiny, so DTGDs pivot to other financial manipulations that are harder to challenge. They know that the distribution of assets after victims pass will be reviewed, but that the financial choices made before death rarely receive the same level of oversight.

One key maneuver is significant spending under the guise of comfort and quality of life. DTGDs persuade their partners to make large purchases, such as luxury home renovations, high-end vehicles, and extravagant travel, all in the name of "making the most of the time they have left." DTGDs ensure that these purchases primarily benefit them, securing assets that will transfer directly into their hands rather than being included in estates.

Another common tactic is liquidating assets while victims are still alive, and then moving money into accounts they control. They push for the sale of properties, stocks, or other valuable holdings, presenting it as a means of "simplifying" their partners' financial affairs. In reality, these transactions strip heirs of their rightful inheritance before they even have a chance to contest it.

The Danger of Mental Incapacity

As victims' health declines, their ability to challenge these manipulations weakens. If DTGDs hold power of attorney, they can begin making unilateral financial and legal decisions. Even without this authority, they often exert undue influence, convincing their partners to sign paperwork they don't fully understand.

In extreme cases, DTGDs seek full guardianship, giving them unchecked control over every aspect of their partners' medical and financial future. This position allows them to dictate spending, override family objections, and ensure that their financial entrenchment is legally unbreakable.

By the time loved ones realize the extent of the damage, DTGDs have already drained significant portions of the estates, leaving heirs with little recourse beyond long, expensive, and often fruitless legal battles.

Recognizing the Final Red Flags

By this time, DTGDs have become experts at masking their intentions. However, there are still telltale signs that reveal their strategy:

- Increased secrecy around finances and estate planning.
- Discouraging family members from visiting or participating in care decisions.
- Unexplained financial activity, including rapid spending and asset transfers.
- A growing insistence that they are the only ones capable of handling affairs.
- Dismissal of financial or legal concerns as "stressful" or "unnecessary drama."

For those who recognize these patterns, the time to act is now.

Protecting a Loved One's Legacy

Defending against a DTGD's final takeover requires early intervention and strong financial oversight. If estate planning protections haven't been put in place before this phase, the window to act is closing fast.

Loved ones and trusted advisors should insist on:

- Independent financial oversight. Appointing co-trustees or outside professionals to review financial activity and prevent unauthorized transactions.

- Legal audits. Conducting reviews of recent estate plan modifications to detect undue influence.
- Frequent visits and check-ins. Maintaining consistent access to the victim to counteract isolation tactics.
- Restricting unilateral decision-making. Ensuring that financial and medical decisions require multiple sign-offs rather than resting solely in the DTGD's hands.

The Last Move Before the Payoff

This is DTGDs' final stage of control, and they are more dangerous than ever. With their partners in declining health, their grip tightens. Every decision, interaction, and carefully spun narrative is crafted with one endgame in mind: securing their ultimate payday.

Recognizing these strategies and stepping in with legal, financial, and social interventions is the only way to prevent one of the most calculated financial heists in existence.

In the next chapter, we will explore "Phase 10: The Victim's Passing and the DTGD's Official Payday." We will uncover how these predators execute their final move—and what can still be done to protect a stolen legacy before it's too late.

Grave Robber Phase 10: The Victim's Passing and the DTGD's Official Payday

Crossing the Finish Line

For Grave Robber DTGDs, the victims' passing is not the tragic end of their relationships—it is the finish line of a race they have been running for years. This is the moment when their patience, careful manipulations, and strategic positioning finally pay off. The estate is now in play, and, if they have done their job correctly, their financial haul is secured, often at the direct expense of the victims' intended heirs.

Everything leading up to this phase—the emotional entanglement, the estate planning adjustments, and the isolation of family members—was about ensuring that, by the time probate begins, DTGDs are in the strongest possible position. The grieving widow or widower act is fully deployed, garnering sympathy, deflecting scrutiny, and keeping challengers at bay long enough to ensure maximum financial extraction.

For the victims' family and heirs, however, the battle is just beginning.

The DTGD's Position After the Victim's Passing

The moment the victim is gone, the DTGD shifts from manipulation to asserting absolute control. They are no longer playing the role of the devoted partner—they are now the primary claimant, the executor's nightmare, and the force that stands between the rightful heirs and the wealth their loved one intended for them.

They rely on statutory entitlements, knowing that intestate laws often favor surviving spouses. If the estate plan was left unprotected or updated in their favor, they ensure their automatic share is as significant as possible. In many jurisdictions, this means at least half of the estate—sometimes more if no protections were put in place.

And then there are the probate loopholes. Life insurance policies, joint accounts, and properties with survivorship rights bypass probate entirely, funneling assets directly to DTGDs without the need for legal battles. These assets are virtually untouchable, leaving heirs scrambling for whatever remains.

If they have successfully influenced estate revisions in previous years, their claim is even stronger. They have positioned themselves as the primary beneficiaries, cutting out children, charities, and other heirs in favor of their own interests. When questioned, they spin narratives of devotion and sacrifice, framing their windfalls as nothing more than the natural result of being the victims' most loyal companions.

The Probate Battlefield

For the rightful heirs, the process of contesting DTGDs' claims is exhausting, expensive, and emotionally draining. DTGDs use every tool at their disposal to ensure that challengers are discouraged before they even begin.

They are masters of delay, stretching out probate proceedings for as long as possible. They file objections, request extensions, and use every bureaucratic tool to drain the resources of anyone who dares to contest their inheritance. They know that time is on their side—the longer probate drags on, the more exhausted the heirs become.

They play the grieving spouse to perfection, ensuring that any accusations of manipulation or undue influence are met with outrage and indignation. They paint heirs as greedy, ungrateful, or even estranged, ensuring that their own victim narrative remains intact.

They exploit legal costs, knowing that most heirs do not have unlimited resources to fight protracted battles. Estate disputes are expensive, and many rightful heirs walk away from the fight simply because they cannot afford to keep going.

Maximizing the Haul

Even after probate begins, DTGDs are not finished. They look for ways to squeeze more money out of estates, finding every available angle to maximize their final take.

If children are involved, they push for child support arrears, even if the victim was fully supporting the family during their lifetime. The estate becomes the final ATM, and DTGDs ensure they withdraw every possible cent before moving on.

Recognizing the Red Flags Post-Mortem

Even after victims are gone, DTGDs' patterns of behavior remain visible. Recognizing these signs is critical to ensuring that heirs and family members are prepared to fight back.

A sudden urgency for quick estate disbursements is a major red flag. DTGDs pressure executors and heirs to finalize distributions immediately, hoping to prevent close scrutiny of financial transactions or last-minute estate revisions.

They work to alienate heirs, cutting off family members from discussions and presenting themselves as the sole legitimate beneficiaries. They frame all legal challenges as attacks on their grief, ensuring that anyone questioning their claims appears insensitive or opportunistic.

They withhold financial records, making it difficult to track where assets have gone in the final years of their victims' life. If major liquidations or transfers took place before death, heirs may find themselves fighting an uphill battle to reclaim what was taken.

The DTGD's Hollow Victory

For DTGDs, this phase represents the final stage of their con. With assets secured and challengers beaten down by legal fees and exhaustion, they walk away with their ultimate payday. But for the victims' rightful heirs, the fight is often far from over.

Many families find themselves fractured and struggling to reclaim what was rightfully intended for them. The emotional toll is heavy, and the financial damage often irreversible. And yet, DTGDs—now enriched (unless legally unchallenged)—move on without remorse, ready to repeat the cycle with their next unsuspecting targets. Understanding their strategy before they reach this phase is the only true defense.

In the next chapter, we explore "Phase 11: Legal Battles Over the Victim's Estate," where heirs take their fight to court to reclaim what has been stolen—and what strategies can ensure that justice prevails.

Grave Robber Phase 11: Legal Battles Over the Victim's Estate

Salt in the Wound

Losing a loved one is devastating, but for the family of a victim who fell prey to a Grave Robber DTGD, the grief is compounded by the brutal reality of what comes next: a legal battle over the estate. This is the final, calculated phase of the DTGD's long con—the moment when all their manipulations, whispered influence, and carefully planted seeds bear fruit.

For adult children and intended heirs, it's not just about money—it's about justice and reclaiming what their parent intended for them. Yet, they now find themselves locked in a draining war against a master manipulator, someone who has spent years crafting their role as the grieving spouse and rightful heir. This fight isn't just about assets—it's about truth, family, and legacy.

The DTGD's Position in Probate: Claiming the Throne

The moment victims pass, DTGDs pivot from doting spouses to aggressive claimants. They wield their legal position as surviving spouses like a sword, ensuring they maintain absolute control over assets, property, and any financial decisions.

If victims failed to secure airtight estate plans, DTGDs default into positions of power, often inheriting significant portions of estates through statutory entitlements. Many jurisdictions ensure that spousal shares supersede other claims, granting them an automatic portion—if not the entirety—of certain assets, including the marital home.

Even in cases where estate plans exist, DTGDs leverage every loophole, exploiting vague or ambiguous provisions in wills and trusts. If they successfully influenced estate revisions before their spouses' passing, their financial position is even stronger.

For them, the plan was set in motion long ago. Now, they just have to execute it.

Probate as a Battleground

For rightful heirs, probate isn't just a bureaucratic process—it's a war zone, one where they must fight to prove undue influence, manipulation, and the true intentions of their deceased parent. And standing against them are DTGDs who have spent years preparing for this exact moment.

DTGDs exploit every advantage the system offers. They position themselves as innocent, grieving spouses, painting heirs as ungrateful, greedy, or estranged. They lean on public sympathy, ensuring that any attempt to contest their claims looks like an attack on a mourning widow or widower.

They also weaponize delay tactics. The longer probate drags on, the more financially and emotionally drained the heirs become. Legal fees mount. Time wears on. The goal is to make it so exhausting that the heirs walk away.

The DTGD's Playbook: Strategies to Secure the Estate

DTGDs don't just rely on legal entitlements—they go on the offensive, ensuring that their financial haul extends far beyond what the law automatically grants them.

They file claims for unpaid spousal support or medical caregiving expenses, portraying themselves as selfless partners who sacrificed everything. Even if they lived in luxury throughout the marriage, they suddenly become *suffering caregivers*, deserving of additional compensation.

If children were part of the relationship, DTGDs move to extract as much as possible "for the children"—securing lump-sum payments, educational trust funds, or outright control over assets in the name of financial security for the kids. The other heirs, already struggling to navigate probate, now find themselves accused of wanting to take from their own siblings.

DTGDs also push for rapid liquidation of estate assets, arguing that selling off properties, investments, and heirlooms is necessary to "simplify" matters. What this really means is converting assets into liquid cash—cash they can quickly claim and control.

When legal challenges arise, they fight back ruthlessly. They question the legitimacy of heirs' claims, highlight minor family disputes to suggest estrangement, and fabricate "evidence" of the victims' true wishes—letters, conversations, or conveniently placed documentation that paints them as the intended beneficiaries.

The Emotional Fallout for Heirs

For the victims' adult children, this isn't just a legal dispute—it's personal. DTGDs have already taken their final years with their parents, often isolating them, poisoning relationships, and ensuring that the victims passed with distorted perceptions of who truly cared for them.

Now, those same children find themselves fighting for scraps—not because their parents didn't want them to inherit, but because they failed to anticipate just how deeply DTGDs would infiltrate their financial affairs.

Grief is overshadowed by legal stress. Family relationships fracture under the weight of accusations and betrayals. Even in cases where the heirs win, they rarely walk away feeling victorious. They walk away exhausted, disillusioned, and forever changed.

How Heirs Can Protect Themselves and the Estate

The only way to defeat DTGDs in probate is to be as relentless as they are—but with truth and legal precision on your side. Challenging a manipulated estate plan is possible, but it requires strategy, evidence, and persistence.

Heirs must act swiftly to challenge undue influence, gathering proof that their parents' decisions were manipulated. This means forensic audits, documentation of isolation behavior, and legal testimony from those who witnessed DTGDs' control.

Financial oversight is key. Following the money—examining transfers, sudden account changes, or revised beneficiary designations—can expose manipulations that might not be immediately visible.

Legal firepower also matters. Probate litigation attorneys with experience in undue influence cases are critical. These aren't standard estate disputes—they are psychological and financial battles, requiring experts who understand how to counteract DTGDs' tactics.

Family unity is a powerful weapon. DTGDs thrive on division, exploiting rifts between heirs to weaken their collective strength. When heirs present a unified front, they make it significantly harder for DTGDs to manipulate the narrative.

A Final War Over Legacy

Phase 11 is where DTGDs make their final moves—where they secure the ultimate payoff from a lifetime of calculated manipulation. But it is also where heirs have their last chance to fight for truth, justice, and the legacy their parents actually intended.

For those left behind, this isn't just about reclaiming financial assets. It's about honoring their loved ones' real wishes, protecting what remains of the family, and ensuring that no other predator can rewrite history.

www.ingramcontent.com/pod-product-compliance
Lightning Source LLC
LaVergne TN
LVHW050907210926
848482LV00012B/366

* 9 7 8 1 0 6 9 4 2 5 3 0 0 *